Soviet history has seldom been of such importance – both to historians and to a broader public in the Soviet Union – as it now is. In this timely volume, scholars from both sides of the Atlantic, using a breadth of source material including Soviet archives and the local press, present the most recent thinking and up-to-date research available. The focus of this collection is on cultural history and industrial relations during the interwar period. These two topics are at the forefront of current historical debate and this volume will therefore be essential reading for all professional students of Soviet history.

New directions in Soviet history opens with a provocative review of Gorbachev and Soviet history by Pierre Broué. This is followed by papers on the changing nature of mass culture in the 1920s and 1930s. Jeffrey Brooks explores how public identities were constructed in the party press, Denise Youngblood looks at the role of the cinema and James van Geldern examines tensions within the arts between the centre and the periphery. In the following section, Chris Ward, John Hatch, Catherine Merridale, John Russell and Robert Thurston discuss the distribution of authority in the workplace and, in particular, the politics of shopfloor culture between the wars. Finally, Evan Mawdsley assesses the changing nature of the Soviet political elite from the 1930s to the present day.

New directions in Soviet history

Selected papers from the Fourth World Congress
for Soviet and East European Studies
Harrogate, July 1990

Edited for the
INTERNATIONAL COMMITTEE
FOR SOVIET AND EAST EUROPEAN STUDIES

General Editor
Stephen White
University of Glasgow

New directions in Soviet history

Edited by

Stephen White

Professor of Politics, University of Glasgow

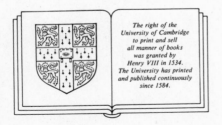

The right of the
University of Cambridge
to print and sell
all manner of books
was granted by
Henry VIII in 1534.
The University has printed
and published continuously
since 1584.

Cambridge University Press
Cambridge   New York   Port Chester
Melbourne   Sydney

Published by the Press Syndicate of the University of Cambridge
The Pitt Building, Trumpington Street, Cambridge CB2 1RP
40th West 20th Street, New York, NY 10011-4211, USA
10 Stamford Road, Oakleigh, Melbourne 3166, Australia

First published 1992

Printed in Great Britain at the University Press, Cambridge

A catalogue record
for this book is
available from the
British Library

Library of Congress cataloguing in publication data

World Congress for Soviet and East European Studies (4th: 1990:
    Harrogate, England)
        New directions in Soviet history: selected papers from the Fourth
    World Congress for Soviet and East European Studies, Harrogate, July
    1990/ edited by Stephen White.
            p.   cm.
        Includes index.
        ISBN 0-521-41376-1
        1. Soviet Union – History – 1917 – Congresses.   I. White, Stephen,
    1945–   . II. Title.
DK266.A2W67 1992
947.084 – dc20   91-4784 CIP

ISBN 0 521 41376 1 hardback

WV

Contents

Notes on contributors

JEFFREY BROOKS is Professor of History at Johns Hopkins University, Baltimore, Maryland, USA. The author of *When Russia learned to read: literacy and popular literature 1861–1917* (1985), he has published articles on various aspects of Russian and Soviet society and culture and is presently preparing a study of Soviet public discourse in the Stalin era.

PIERRE BROUÉ is President and Director of the Institut Leon Trotsky at the University of Grenoble, France. The editor of the French edition of Trotsky's works, his recent books include *1940: l'assassinat de Trotsky* and a full scale biography of Trotsky, both of which were published in 1988.

JOHN HATCH is Assistant Professor of Soviet History at the University of California at Los Angeles, USA. His articles have appeared in *Slavic Review*, *Soviet Studies*, *Russian History* and elsewhere, and he is presently completing a study entitled *Labor and politics in NEP Russia: workers, trade unions and the Communist Party in Moscow 1921–1928*.

EVAN MAWDSLEY is Senior Lecturer in Modern History at the University of Glasgow, Scotland. His publications include *The Russian Revolution and the Baltic Fleet* (1978), *The Russian civil war* (1987) and the *Blue guide to Moscow and Leningrad* (2nd edn, 1991), and he is currently working on a history of the Soviet political elite.

CATHERINE MERRIDALE is Research Fellow at King's College, Cambridge, England. The author of *Moscow politics and the rise of Stalin* (1990) and joint editor of *Perestroika: the historical perspective* (1991), she is presently writing a biography of the Bolshevik leader Lev Kamenev.

JOHN RUSSELL is Lecturer in Russian in the Department of Modern

Languages at the University of Bradford, England. He has published several studies under the auspices of the Minority Rights Group and is presently working on the impact of the ethnic factor on change in the contemporary USSR.

ROBERT THURSTON is Associate Professor in the Department of History at Miami University, Oxford, Ohio, USA. He is the author of *Liberal city, conservative state: Moscow and Russia's urban crisis, 1906–1914* (1987) and is presently preparing a book-length study of the impact of the Great Terror on Soviet society, 1935–1941.

JAMES VAN GELDERN is Assistant Professor of Russian at Macalester College, St Paul, Minnesota, USA. He is the author of two forthcoming monographs: *Festivals of the revolution: art and theater in the formation of Soviet culture*, and *Mass culture in Soviet society 1917–1953: A reader* (with Richard Stites).

CHRIS WARD is University Assistant Lecturer in Slavonic Studies and a Fellow of Robinson College, University of Cambridge, England. He is the author of *Russia's cotton workers and the New Economic Policy* (1990) and coeditor of *Perestroika: the historical perspective* (1991), and is currently working on a general study of Stalin's Russia.

STEPHEN WHITE is Professor of Politics and a Member of the Institute of Soviet and East European Studies, University of Glasgow, Scotland. His books include *The origins of détente* (1986), *The Bolshevik poster* (1988) and *Gorbachev in power* (2nd edn, 1991), and he is presently working on publishing on early Soviet Russia and on the contemporary political elite.

DENISE J. YOUNGBLOOD is Assistant Professor of History at the University of Vermont, Burlington, in the USA. A specialist in early Soviet cultural politics and the Russian film industry, she is the author of *Soviet cinema in the silent era, 1918–1935* (1985) and of the forthcoming study *Movies for the masses: popular cinema and Soviet society in the 1920s*.

Preface

The Fourth World Congress for Soviet and East European Studies met in Harrogate, Yorkshire, in July 1990. It was attended by nearly 2,000 delegates; it heard about a thousand papers; and it brought together, for the first time at gatherings of this kind, nearly 300 Soviet and East European participants as well as their scholarly counterparts from other nations. It was an unusual gathering in all kinds of ways. It was the first congress of this kind to take place in the United Kingdom; and it was the first to be able to reflect at any length upon glasnost, perestroika and the East European revolution (when the last ICSEES Congress took place, in Washington in 1985, Gorbachev had only just been elected and Honecker, Ceauşescu and their associates were still in power). Even the weather was unusual for an English summer: hot and sunny. The most distinctive feature of all, however, was the opportunity the Congress provided for a broad and relatively open exchange of views upon the nature of change in the USSR and its formerly client states in which scholars from these countries as well as outside them could engage on equal terms.

It was appropriate in many ways that history, and Soviet history in particular, should have generated the largest single number of panels and papers at the Congress. There are more historians than members of any other scholarly discipline within the Western Sovietological community; and history had for some time been the scholarly discipline in which an East–West dialogue had – arguably – advanced the furthest. The study of history had a still greater significance, in that it was one of the ways in which the Gorbachev leadership had first established its reformist credentials. Interviewed by the French press in February 1986, Gorbachev had insisted that Stalinism was a 'notion made up by opponents of communism and used on a large scale to smear the Soviet Union and socialism as a whole'. By February 1987, however, Gorbachev was already insisting that there must be 'no forgotten names [or] blank spots' in Soviet history or literature, and by the time of his address on the 70th anniversary of the revolution later in the year he was ready to concede that there had been 'real crimes' in the 1930s in which 'many thousands' had been subjected to wholesale repression. However inadequate an acknowledgement of the scale of Stalinist terror, this none the less made possible a reconsideration of the Soviet past which by the early 1990s had begun to address the October revolution itself and not simply the 'deformations' to which it was supposed to have given rise.

Historians, to begin with, were not among the leaders of this reassessment. Writers of thinly disguised fiction like Anatolii Rybakov, and playwrights of strongly reformist disposition like Mikhail Shatrov, were the first to explore the lessons of the past before a large public audience. Cinema, through works such as Tengiz Abuladze's 'Repentance', made a separate contribution. Societies like 'Memorial' began to collect oral testimony and to identify the sites in which the victims of the purges had been buried. Figures of the past whose writings had for some time been inaccessible, such as Bukharin and Trotsky, began to figure in the popular and specialist press; many of them, in addition, were rehabilitated by the special Politburo commission which began work in late 1987. A mass of documentation became available, from the 1937 Soviet census to the Nazi–Soviet Pact with its secret protocols. And historians, latterly at least, began to play a prominent part, as older radicals returned to favour and still others (like Roy Medvedev and Dmitrii Volkogonov) were elected to the new-style working Soviets.

All of the history papers at Harrogate reflected these new circumstances; in some cases too (although much less often for the modern period than one might have wished) Soviet historians were themselves present and able to contribute directly to the process of reevaluation in which both they and their Western colleagues have been engaged. The chapters in this volume are based upon the best of the papers in Soviet history that were presented at the Congress; two others, edited by Lindsey Hughes and R. D. McKean respectively, cover the Muscovite and late Imperial periods. All the papers that appear in this volume have been revised for the purposes of the present publication, and where necessary they have been expanded and brought up to date. I have also included a paper by an author (Jeffrey Brooks) who appeared on the programme but was unable to attend the Congress in person. So far as conventions are concerned, the spellings are British throughout but the transliteration system is based upon that of the Library of Congress, with the usual modifications in respect of persons or places that are already familiar in a different form. This may seem a reasonable arrangement for a volume about half of whose contributors are American, but the other half of whom are based on the European side of the Atlantic. Spellings, where necessary, have been modernized.

The volume opens with a provocative review of Gorbachev and Soviet history by Pierre Broué of the University of Grenoble, best known perhaps for his biography of Trotsky. Broué takes as his point of departure Gorbachev's speech on the 70th anniversary of the revolution in 1987 and then moves forward to 1990, pointing out at every turn the complex interplay between past and present. There were three main ways, he suggests, in which Soviet historiography could develop after Gorbachev's speech. The first was Stalinist orthodoxy, a position that became increasingly difficult to sustain as destalinization advanced and the evidence of repression accumulated. The second was 'counter-communism', a scholarly tradition that posited a direct continuity between Bolshevism and Stalinism and laid its primary emphasis upon the demogagy and (where necessary) coercive policies of the Soviet leadership. A third, more critical group of historians attempted – in both West and East – to rediscover some of the complexity of the period, including the interplay between leaders and led and between the party itself and the wider society. It is not unreasonable to suggest that Broué's paper itself and the others that are included in this volume belong, whatever their internal differences, to this third and broadly 'revisionist' position.

In terms of subject, the remaining papers in the volume are grouped around three key themes: the changing nature of mass culture in the 1920s and 1930s, the politics of shopfloor relations during the same period, and (a final paper) the changing composition of the political elite from the 1930s to the present day. Jeffrey Brooks's contribution, taking forward the work reported in his *When Russia Learned to Read* (1985), deals with public identities and the ways in which they were constructed in the party press in the 1920s. Denise Youngblood looks at another section of the mass media and the one that Lenin believed the 'most important of all the arts', cinema. Her particular concern, in this paper, is the tension between 'entertainment and enlightenment' and between their respective exponents, Ilya Trainin and Anatolii Lunacharsky. James van Geldern, in the third contribution to this part of the book, includes cinema among the other arts as he explores the tension between 'centre and periphery', between the culture and enlightenment that was identified at this time with the city and the dark and primitive hinterland. Moscow, the capital, was a place of heroic achievement in which the whole nation could take pride; the outer regions, with their dark forces and elemental nature, were depicted as an area to be conquered and then exploited.

The second and rather larger group of papers has a different but related focus: the distribution of authority in the workplace. Chris Ward's paper deals in this connection with the Soviet cotton industry of the late 1920s, John Hatch's with industrial efficiency campaigns in 1926, and Catherine Merridale's with the party in Moscow during the period immediately afterwards in which the first Five Year Plan was launched. John Russell considers the rise and fall of Stakhanovism in the 1930s, and Robert Thurston examines the extent to which the political authoritarianism of the 1930s was consistent with a degree of autonomy in the regulation of grievances on the shop floor. Several of these are openly 'revisionist' papers, and yet revisionism, in this sense, offers no exculpation for Stalinism. Rather, as Merridale suggests, it argues the need for historians to 'ask more searching questions about the relationship between post-revolutionary Soviet society and political change', once it is accepted that totalitarian control from the centre provides only a part of the explanation that is required. Equally, as Thurston points out, workers could remain silent on foreign policy in the late 1930s but still express views and influence outcomes on matters that they found of more immediate concern, from rates of pay to housing and their treatment by management. An adequate historiography of the period must attempt to do justice to both of these dimensions.

The third section of the volume consists of a single paper, by Evan Mawdsley, whose subject is the changing nature of the Soviet political elite from the 1930s up to the present. The elite is defined in the paper as the full membership of the CPSU Central Committee, with particular reference to its own elite (those who were not token workers or peasants). Quantitative studies of this kind have become increasingly feasible as a wider range of biographical sources becomes available and as computing techniques advance; and they have been actively pursued in the USSR itself, particularly at the Historical Archives Institute in Moscow, as well as by a number of scholars in the West. Considered in this way, the political elite experienced a period of relative stability – even a 'golden age' – from 1939 up to the 28th Congress, when the nature of Central Committee membership changed considerably. No one generation, however, dominated the Central Committee over the whole period; age distribution, life experience and party standing varied considerably within each cohort and from cohort to cohort, and the homogeneity of the elite (Mawdsley argues) should at no point be taken for granted.

What, finally, are the 'new directions' suggested by these studies, which are representative of the best of the work that is presently being conducted in Soviet history? One conclusion offered by these studies is certainly that there has been none of the 'revival of narrative' that Lawrence Stone claims to have identified in contemporary historiography more generally. The concern of the papers in this volume, rather, is with argument and explanation; and also with detailed and focused investigation rather than broad trends and patterns. The studies included in this volume draw more extensively than a comparable volume could have done five years ago upon Soviet archives, and not only those that are located in Moscow. There is a stronger emphasis upon local circumstances, resting upon a greater use (in some cases) of the regional, district and even factory press. There is a willingness to employ quantification, where this is appropriate. And there is an impatience with general labels – such as 'Stalinism' – that may conceal much more than they reveal.

Like the work of Sovietologists in other fields, the papers in this volume may also reflect a greater closeness to their parent discipline as the study of the Soviet area becomes less different and exotic. Many of the contributions that have been included in this collection, for instance, reflect the reorientation towards a history 'from below' that has been associated with the work of E. P. Thompson and the labour and social historians of other countries. The papers on shopfloor relations in industry make explicit use of the perspectives of writers like Michael Burawoy in his *Politics of Production*, a work based largely upon the Western experience. Jeffrey Brooks, in his paper, draws directly upon Erik Erikson, Erving Goffman and other social psychologists; Chris Ward relates the Moscow cotton industry of the 1920s to the mills of nineteenth-century Oldham.

It may not be too much, in fact, to suggest that this wider and more comparative perspective will turn out to be at least as important as the East–West exchanges for which Harrogate provided such an excellent opportunity. Paradoxically, the better we know Soviet history – through access to sources and to the scholars concerned with them – the more we need the wider context for the testing of ideas and propositions that is made available by the comparative method. Were Soviet literary tastes in the 1920s, for instance, in any way unusual? What can we learn about the social origins of Stalinism by drawing on the work of Ian Kershaw and other students of the 'Hitler-myth'? What conclusions should we draw from the fact that (as Robert Thurston points out) American unions were struggling for their physical existence at a time when their Soviet counterparts had substantial, albeit very localized influence? Has the Soviet political elite been unusual – compared, for instance, with its East European counterparts – in its tendency to draw disproportionately upon villagers rather than urbanites? It is a measure of the quality of the papers in this volume that they invite a dialogue not simply among Eastern and Western students of Soviet history but also with a still wider community of scholars whose concern is the universe of human experience.

STEPHEN WHITE
University of Glasgow

Part I

The Politics of Soviet History

1 Gorbachev and history

Pierre Broué

Everybody agrees that the writing of history falls heavily under the influence of the predominant political power, which is never indifferent to it. But the problem is particularly acute for the Soviet Union. Friends and foes alike have tended to agree that the history of the party is the backbone of Soviet history in general and that it ought at every moment to be revised and according to the needs of the time; that is, according to every turn in politics.

Is this still the case with history in the time of Gorbachev? Is it possible to say that, as it was before, the changes in Soviet history result today from the will of the General Secretary and from his decision? Discussion on these matters is still in its early stages. It is quite sure that Gorbachev wanted some changes, but not at all clear that he wanted such drastic changes as those that have occurred. It is sure that he wanted some measure of debate, but not at all clear that he wished to open so wide a debate.

According to one section of Western opinion, anyway, nothing new has happened in Eastern Europe. For members of the Western school called by Stephen Cohen 'counter-communists', we are witnessing a reform from above and the debate has been staged from the very beginning by the political power.

Others state on the contrary that Gorbachev's conception of the making of history is something radically new, that he really wanted free discussion and competition between antagonistic schools of thought and that, in that field at least, he won his war against the Stalinist past.

Gorbachev's 'Historical' Speech

The orientation as well as the limits of the changes in Soviet historiography were set by Gorbachev in his 2 November 1987 report, delivered on the occasion of the 70th anniversary of the October Revolution.[1]

In his report, Gorbachev explained at length the reasons which give Soviet history so tremendous an importance, the last but not the least of which is the necessity of drawing lessons from past experience and by this means advancing the cause of perestroika.

Concerning the oppositions, the report was rather limited and unconvincing, asserting that the Left Opposition – he seems to have stopped in his investigation in the year 1925 – was a 'hostile' trend and that Stalin struggled against them in defence of Leninism. He praised industrialization and collectivization, stating that 'Bukharin and his supporters underestimated in practice the importance of the factor of time in the construction of socialism in the 1930s'. For Gorbachev, there was no alternative to Stalin in the thirties. According to him, mass repression at that time affected 'many thousands of party members and non-party people' – quite an underestimation.

However – and here he went farther than Khrushchev – he mentioned 'the administrative-command system', 'an atmosphere of intolerance, enmity and suspicion, the cult of the individual', 'arbitrariness and repressions'. He insisted upon the necessity of throwing a complete light on the repressions, not only for the memory of the victims, but also to help the present tasks of perestroika, 'democratization, legality, glasnost and the elimination of bureaucracy'. Then he defended the Hitler–Stalin Pact of 1939, which, according to him, saved not only socialism but the very existence of the Soviet Union.

On 8 January 1988 Gorbachev returned to the history problem, asserting:

The understanding of our history which we achieved in preparing for the 70th anniversary of October is not something frozen and given once and for all. It will be deepened and developed in the course of further research.[2]

And more precisely, on 18 February 1988:

There are not and cannot be any constraints on truly scientific investigation. Questions of theory cannot and must not be resolved by any kind of decree. We need the free competition of minds.[3]

When Gorbachev took up position on the question of a free competition of ideas in history, three ways lay open before Soviet historians.

The first was Stalinist orthodoxy, more or less damaged by destalinization and the opening up of some gaps in that orthodoxy. Was Trotsky, for instance, a non-person or the Devil? What about the military chiefs' criticism of Stalin, already formulated in Khrushchev's time? What about the Old Bolsheviks sentenced to death during the Moscow Trials and never rehabilitated at that time? All had been seriously shaken, except one certainty: Stalin might not have been always right, but the party itself was. It took the historical decisions, it settled every matter correctly: so, the bulk of Gorbachev's report could be accepted in its entirety by every Stalinist apparatchik.

The second way was what Cohen calls 'counter-communism', the Cold War ideology and Sovietology. For its supporters, the political history of Soviet Union was a political history like no other. For them, according to Cohen's summary, the Bolsheviks had won in October 1917 because of their 'Machiavellian leaders, centralized organization, disciplined membership and manipulation of the masses'. The party won the Civil War through 'demagogy, ruthlessness, and organization'. NEP (the New Economic Policy) was only 'a cunning programmatic manoeuvre by the increasingly totalitarian party'. Stalinist policies of the 1930s and after, including forcible collectivization and mass terror, were explained as the inevitable culmination of the party's original 'blueprint'.

Such a general conception, 'studying the past for the sake of the present', led to bare 'moral judgments' detached from their historical context, and sought at any price an 'unfolding logic' and 'historical unbroken continuity' between Bolshevism and Stalinism.[4] These schematic ideas still constitute the framework of 'Soviet history' as seen by the Western media and a majority of politicians in the Western world. They have nothing in common with a real history, conscious of contradictions and inequality of developments; and are, in fact, a Cold War ideology.

And finally a third conception began to take shape, a critical one, born in the West from the reaction against counter-communism. Some who at first held this third view of history discovered the dialectical movement of 1917 between the masses and the Bolshevik leadership, looked for changes in the party, the struggle between members and apparatus, social influences to explain political conflict, and so forth. In some aspects and fields of interests, it came very close to the Marxist school related to Trotsky and several European historians who tried to find a social key explaining the 'degeneration' of the Bolshevik party by the birth of a bureaucratic stratum, usurping the power for themselves.

Such were in 1987–1988 the three paths opening before Soviet historians at the crossroads of perestroika. It is indisputable that, taking into account the material means of Western publishers and the freedom of circulation of books, journals and papers of this character, the second had the best chance of taking the lead.

The Pattern of Change

Everything seemed to begin according to the usual pattern: in the first ranks, the writers, playwrights, novelists and film-makers, then in a second stage the historians themselves, beginning with those who had suffered from censorship in the Brezhnev times and whose files are full of the long forbidden results of their past investigations.

The kick-off was given by Rybakov's novel, *Children of the Arbat*, the play by Mikhail Shatrov, *Onward . . . Onward . . . Onward*, and by Abuladze's film *Repentance*. Shatrov's play, published in January 1987, using archival documents, giving the floor to Trotsky and other victims of Stalin, showing the opposition between Lenin and Stalin, provoked real anger among the apparatchiki and conservative-minded people and created an atmosphere of protest, amid which was published, in *Sovetskaia Rossiia* on 13 March 1988, Andreeva's famous letter, the conservatives' political manifesto as well as a declaration of war against 'new history', that is non-Stalinist interpretations.

The party leadership's riposte, a full-page article in *Pravda* on 5 April 1988, opened wide the door to a real debate in the field of history. The simultaneous rehabilitation of the accused of the 1936–7 Moscow trials, including people like Zinoviev, Kamenev, I.N. Smirnov, Piatakov and Radek, added fuel to the controversy. And finally in the summer, the true historians, beginning with the peasant history specialist V.P. Danilov, followed by Polikarpov and others, entered the arena. The debate was really beginning.

At the time, no new conditions had as yet been created for investigation and nobody could guess who would win the contest and even whether the new historians would be able to hold the floor for several months. From that time on, one had entered in the field of uncertainty, immersed in a debate which was not expected by the leaders but which obliged them, because of the passionate interest of a large part of the nascent public opinion, to accept it.

In order to attempt a description of the rewriting of contemporary history in the USSR we will closely follow the line of the actual development, which began with the rehabilitation of the main actors and leaders – some measure of personalization being probably unavoidable after the deification and demonization which had taken place for almost two thirds of the century.

Lenin

Followers and sympathizers of the 'counter-communist' ideology have often regretted in the media during recent years that Lenin should have remained immune at the time of the new writing of revolutionary history. But now this subject also has been broached.

In the spring of 1988, Lenin was for the first time reassessed and severely set on by Vasilii Seliunin. Ferociously criticizing the repressive decrees against so-called speculators, Seliunin sought to demonstrate that it was not hunger which led to requisitions but rather the requisitions whose consequences were hunger and famine. He reminded his readers that Lenin was an irreconcilable enemy of the market and repeated that the free market meant the triumph of capitalism. According to him, the *kulaks* had already been destroyed as a class during the period of War Communism, that is long before the end of NEP. For him, Lenin shared his bad record with Trotsky, whom he called the theoretician of 'barracks socialism', who wanted to turn the whole country into a system of gigantic concentration camps – which, as we know, was done years later by Stalin, his police and party apparatus.[5]

Finally Seliunin considered War Communism and the Stalinist system as continuing the harmful road of state compulsion initiated by Lenin. Still more categoric was the nationalist Kozhinov, for whom the main cause of repressive mass actions was the nature of revolution as such. Like the French Revolution, the October Revolution opened the door to lawlessness and ruthless mass violence, engendered not by the Russian tradition but by the revolutionary one, embodied by Lenin.[6]

Seliunin found many followers. The most famous was at the end of 1988 and the beginning of 1989, the series of articles by Alexander Tsipko entitled 'The sources of Stalinism'.[7] The most violent came from the émigré journal *Posev* and was signed by Vladimir Solukhin,[8] who argued that Russia had been conquered by Lenin's group and submitted to 'a more cruel occupation regime than the history of humanity had known in any century'.[9]

More recently, the historian Tamara Krasotskaia has accused Lenin of responsibility for the expulsion from Russia of about two hundred members of the intelligentsia, among them the philosopher Nikolai Berdiaev.[10] The 'Leninist party', but also the person of Lenin, have been savagely attacked by the historian Iurii Afanasyev.[11] Whether it turns out to be true or not, what better instance of the present trend could there be than the rumour according to which Dmitrii Volkogonov is finishing his Trotsky biography with some sort of acknowledgement that Trotsky committed only one mistake, to be true to Lenin and to the October Revolution?

Bukharin

Also coming from hell, Bukharin, as we know, was for a time made the patron saint of perestroika, an honour which fell upon him because of his reputation as defender of a renewed and more profound NEP, an ancestor of the 'market economy', and as a result of a clever political campaign led by political clubs inspired by Vasilii Pisigin which were to become the 'Bukharin Clubs'.

During the months which followed his official rehabilitation, then his reinstatement in the party, several historians and politicians wrote as if there had been a 'Bukharin alternative' against Stalin. Even *Pravda* asserted that such an alternative had been 'the defence of the socialist concept against Stalinist distortions'.[12]

Such an interpretation, contrary to Gorbachev's assertions in his November report, was fought among others by Stalin's biographer, Volkogonov, who could easily lay stress on the Bukharin–Stalin alliance against Trotsky. The explanation offered by Volkogonov – Bukharin's repentance (*Literaturnaia gazeta*, 9 December 1987) – cannot be accepted, even in view of Bukharin's posthumous letter to the future party leaders.

Nobody has as yet seriously discussed the explanation given by Trotsky. Bukharin's policy was developed in the framework of NEP. After the abandonment of NEP by Stalin, the only 'Bukharin alternative' could have been an alliance with the class enemies of Bolshevism, *kulaks* and Nepmen, and so there could be no 'alternative' for Bukharin in the USSR of the thirties.

A volume of Bukharin's *Selected Works* was published by Politizdat in 1988. It included two important texts already republished at the time: 'Lenin's Testament' and 'Notes of an Economist'. There were also published *Problemy teorii i praktiki sotsializma* (1989) and *Put' k sotsializmu* (Novosibirsk, 1990). The memories of Anna Larina, his widow (*Nezabyvaemoe*, 1990), show a Bukharin far removed from legend. In 1990 his fans in Pisigin's Bukharin Club published his writings on youth, *K novomu pokoleniiu*.

Trotsky

Trotsky had the great honour of having been the one before whom the Stalinists never disarmed. *Sovetskaia Rossiia*, on 27 September 1987, still published a paper by V.M. Ivanov with the traditional slanders, under the title 'New face for a little Judas'. Attacks against him have continued since then, denying his role as commander of the Red Army and accusing him of major crimes such as execution without trial and the arrest of innocent people – in a word, he has been characterized as a hangman, and moreover a Jew, for these attacks carry with them the unavoidable reek of anti-semitism.

It is not surprising, then, that during the first stages of perestroika,

Trotsky was presented in USSR as well as in the West as the one who had thought up and even baptized the concentration camps, the 'Gulag', working relentlessly for the establishment of 'barracks socialism'!

The works of Volkogonov and even N. A. Vasetsky, who has also written on Trotsky, are of another brand. Their conceptions mark a real retreat from the slanders of the Stalinist period, and Trotsky gets back his prominent role both in the 1905 Revolution and at the head of the Red Army and so on. One may read, for instance, Volkogonov's 'Trotsky at the front'.[13] But for the following period they maintain, at least to some degree, the 'party line' – that is, the Stalinist slanders and distortions. Vasetsky recognized that Trotsky was murdered by a Stalinist agent, but at a time when everybody already knew it. The surprising assertion of a journalist according to which Trotsky and Mercader were both Stalin's victims has to be explained by psychoanalysis and by the journalist's own father's functions in Stalin's murder apparatus.

From the Soviet Union came the best criticism of the Volkogonov-Vasetsky school by A. V. Pantsov under the Trotsky-like title of 'The New School of Falsification'.[14] However, the year 1989 saw interesting publications of Trotsky works: *New Course*,[15] *The Letter to Istpart*,[16] *Our Differences*,[17] extracts from *Revolution Betrayed*[18] and *Permanent Revolution*,[19] *Revolutionary Portraits*,[20] *Stalin*,[21] *Literature and Revolution* and *Exile Diary*.[22] V. P. Danilov published, first, unknown extracts of Trotsky's speech before the Central Committee in October 1923,[23] then the text in its entirety.[24] The first articles and studies appeared under the pen of V. I. Startsev, V. P. Danilov, V. I. Billik, A. V. Pantsov, A. M. Poshchekoldin, and others.[25]

Vasetsky edited a volume of Trotsky's selected works.[26] The Novosibirsk magazine *EKO* has published three chapters of my own biography of Trotsky and a review of it by V. P. Danilov.[27] Now the book *The Stalin School of Falsification* itself has been published in a reprint edition. And we are expecting the appearance of *Revolution Betrayed* and *History of the Russian Revolution*. Three articles were published in 1990 by young writers, all of them apparently sympathetic towards Trotsky's ideas: V. Z. Rogovin, a sociologist, A. V. Pantsov and A. Iu. Vatlin, both of them historians.[28]

The 50th anniversary of Trotsky's murder was commented upon in the USSR. *Izvestiia*[29] published an unknown letter from Natalia Trotsky to President Cárdenas. Ramón Mercader's brother, Luis, attempted to present the murderer as a victim.[30] Karen Matchaturov explained once more that Trotsky and Stalin were both 'worse' than the other leaders,[31] but Genrikh Ioffe[32] admitted that Trotsky at least had been true to the revolutionary idea. Tsipko, a former CC apparatchik, attacked savagely, trying to imagine what Trotsky in power would have done (*Daugava*, no. 7, 1990).

With the financial sponsorship of American stars like Paul Newman and Dustin Hoffman, Vanessa Redgrave organized a 'Symposium 90' in Britain, a conference with Soviet historians,[33] carefully concealed from Western scholars. However, some lectures have been published.

The end of March 1990 saw a Trotsky symposium in Wuppertal, held with the participation of almost twenty Soviet scholars. Another, much more interesting, organized by Terry Brotherstone, was held at Aberdeen University in Scotland, then another one in Mexico City, the Trotsky Symposium in São Paulo University in September, organized by Osvaldo Coggiola, and finally a Tokyo symposium organized by Yashinobu Shiokawa. These are sure indications of a widespread interest in a Trotsky who is neither a demon nor a non-person but an historical figure of authentically gigantic importance.

Stalin

Gorbachev's friends sowed the rumour that Mikhail Sergeevich was already General Secretary of the CPSU when he was able to see for himself documents demonstrating the personal responsibility of Stalin for the slaughter of thousands of victims of the Great Purge, long lists of names signed by him, approving their execution and so forth.

New revelations show that Stalin violently beat some of his collaborators, including Beria,[34] that he had Kaganovich, Kalinin and Molotov's wife arrested, as well as one of the brothers of Kaganovich, driving a third to suicide, and that his personal secretary A. N. Poskrebyshev fell on his knees before him imploring for his wife a mercy which was refused![35] Everybody knows now that, as *Pravda* wrote, Stalin 'did not simply know' the acts of illegality, 'he organized them, directed them. Today this is a fact, already proved'.[36] Many examples have been given.

Other information, based upon the personal notes of Stalin, throw some light upon his personality, his cruelty, his ability to dissimulate, his passion for intrigue and his love of torturing and killing not only his enemies but those completely unknown to him.

Here, too, Volkogonov made an attempt to save Stalinism by partly sacrificing Stalin. In his book *Triumph and Tragedy* (1989) he attempts to show that 'one man's triumph has often resulted in tragedy for a whole people'. He speaks of 'Stalin's undisputable contribution to the struggle for socialism' and at the same time of 'an unjustified repression against many thousands of innocent people'. For him, in Stalin as in other big leaders, 'the human being was killed by the power'! 'Stalin regarded society as a human zoo.'[37]

New publications mention the famous diagnosis of Doctor Bekhterev, according to which Stalin suffered from paranoia. But one may ask oneself whether such an opinion, when expressed today, could not be the last means of saving Stalinism by sacrificing Stalin himself.

Many a discussion took place on the question of the genesis of Stalin and Stalinism. How could all that become possible? Alec Nove[38] summarized perfectly the discussion waged by Roy Medvedev and others, particularly the outspoken views of Mikhail Gefter. To conclude, one could cite an opinion expressed by O. Latsis:

Usurping not only the rights of the party but also the rights of workers and peasants, Stalin had to extend his measures of suppression beyond the party leaders. He would not arrest all the workers and peasants, though the system of Gulag did represent a large-scale experiment in creating a special kind of 'working class', but objectively everyone represented a danger for Stalin, as he acted against the basic interests of both workers and peasants.[39]

Many other people have been reexamined and their biographies had to be rewritten, for the worse or the better. In the first category we have to mention Molotov, Voroshilov, Budenny, Zhdanov, Kaganovich (who is still alive), Suslov and Vyshinsky. Others have been rehabilitated: let us mention Zinoviev and Kamenev, Christian Rakovsky, N. I. Muralov and the people whose children took the floor, Ikramov, Smilga, Krestinsky, V. A. Antonov-Ovseenko, Rykov, Piatnitsky, Radek, Putna, Preobrazhensky, Shliapnikov, Lominadze, Serebriakov, Lomov and many others.

The problem of the bureaucracy

The debate upon the origins and the meaning of Stalinism requires some explanation concerning its class roots. What forces did Stalin represent that enabled him to 'act against the basic interests of the workers and the peasants'?

One of the first scholars who tried to answer that question is Dzarasov, for whom the bureaucracy arose after Lenin's death as a social group alien to socialism, 'a rule of officials incompatible with democracy'. The main basis of the Stalinist system is the bureaucracy and the bureaucrats whose interests it defends.[40]

What is its class nature? Dzarasov does not answer. In a round-table discussion,[41] Anatolii Butenko, who surprisingly asserts – completely forgetting the very existence of Trotsky – that 'no one endeavoured to

12   *Pierre Broué*

analyse [our] society from the point of view of the growth and strengthening of the bureaucracy', sees in the 'huge stratum of state and party
bureaucracy, torn away from the people and not under its control' a
'huge danger for socialism'.

V. V. Zhuravlev severely criticizes the 'abstraction' of Butenko's
answer to the question of the 'class nature' of the bureaucracy and
asserts that, 'despite all its efforts to achieve power for itself', the
bureaucracy 'does not cease to be the instrument of a definite class', an
opinion that R. W. Davies thinks not remote from Trotsky's own
analysis[42] (an assessment I should have wished to discuss further had
space permitted). Butenko answered Zhuravlev in the columns of
Voprosy istorii KPSS (1988, no. 7).

One of the most interesting works on this theme appeared in
Argumenty i fakty under the title 'Factories to the workers, privileges to
the bureaucrats'.[43] This study by A. M. Poshchekoldin is the first to
investigate the origins of the crystallization of the bureaucratic
apparatus under the guidance of the Secretariat and of the *Gensek*
(General Secretary) himself. In line with Trotsky's instruments of
analysis, V. A. Kozlov and E. G. Plimak followed the trail of investigat-
ing the 'Soviet Thermidor'.[44]

The general line of development

In his chapter on 'Russia before the Bolshevik revolution' in *Soviet
History in the Gorbachev Revolution* (1989), R. W. Davies revealed very
clearly the mixing up of various interests one may see through the
differences which only reflect present concerns projected into the past.[45]
In his commentary on the serfs' emancipation in 1864, for instance,
Vaksberg compares it with the freeing of wholesale trade which today is
one of the demands of the supporters of the market economy.[46] Gavriil
Popov, a democrat and now mayor of Moscow, underlines the limits of
the impact of that emancipation, stating that it was insignificant because
the people concerned – the serfs themselves – did not take any part in
it.[47] The same author, with Nikolai Shmelev, regrets the failure of what
he calls the 'Stolypin alternative'.[48]

In the same way, at the time of the celebration of its millennium in
1988 we heard the expression of a wide range of differences concerning
the historical role of the Orthodox Russian Church. Academician
Dmitrii Likhachev, however contradicted by Aleksandr Iakovlev,[49]
celebrated the Old Believers and the Church's contribution to Russian
traditional culture.[50]

There has been an important debate concerning the Russian past and its 'Asiatic' aspects. We know that Stalin saw in the persons of Peter the Great and Ivan the Terrible modernizers by means of terror, and that a link has often been established between the three of them. Rybakov even spoke of 'Asiatic despotism' and of its Russian application. He was contradicted by Kozhinov who believed that revolution is the root of all evil, particularly despotism, Asiatic or otherwise.[51] The same difference exists about the question of industrial development in Russia. For Kliamkin, the credit for industrialization belongs to the autocracy which, by the way, created the only force capable of destroying it: the working class.[52] Seliunin, of course, credits the birth and the free running of the market for economic progress and development, in spite of state intervention and the hinderance of such ancient traditions as the *mir*.[53]

We must respect everybody's opinion, but we think that we must cite here Professor Davies on Seliunin, saying that 'he comes very close to offering a historical justification for the establishment of a capitalist system in the Soviet Union'[54] – a remark which casts a useful light on the methodological problems of our theme. The underlying opinion in many judgements about October is not that the Bolsheviks were wrong in taking power but rather that they were wrong to take it alone. For many writers, October is denied the quality of 'revolution' and becomes an ordinary 'coup', in opposition to February which was carried out by the masses.

A recent article by Genrikh Ioffe is in fact an apologia for Martov, making the latter's break with the Bolsheviks the fatal misfortune of the Russian Revolution.[55] Present-day historians seem to be more unsure about the Left Socialist Revolutionaries, who could have been in their opinion better 'democrats' than the Bolsheviks but were wrong either in their alliance with them or in taking the initiative in breaking with and then resorting to arms against them. There is no great abundance of literature on the Civil War and only a strong interest in the Whites as victims. Details have been published about the murder of the Tsar's family, generally considered an act of senseless cruelty.[56]

We owe the first serious study of the Brest-Litovsk peace negotiations without slanders or distortions of Trotsky's position to A. V. Pantsov,[57] and we owe two others to N. A. Vasetsky and V. V. Zhuravlev.[58] We may also note that V. Golovanov has been one of the first to give back to Makhno, described as a bandit during the Stalin era, his true physiognomy as an anarchist fighter, even mentioning the 'trap' contained in the Bolshevik proposals which appeared to offer him a limited territorial autonomy.[59]

Magazine articles often underline the ruthlessness of the requisitions in the country during the War Communism: peasants were called kulaks and stripped of everything, food and seeds included. Although it is frequently mentioned, the Kronstadt uprising is seldom studied, with the exception of a good clarifying summary by Roy Medvedev.[60] By contrast, a particular interest in the Cossack chief F. K. Mironov, shot in 1921, has drawn some attention to what is now called a 'decossackiza-tion' and to the responsibility of Budenny for their repression.[61]

The questions most discussed about the post-Civil War years relate to the party's internal regime. S. S. Dzarasov[62] emphasizes that at the 10th Congress Lenin argued against Riazanov in favour of proportional elections to the Central Committee based upon the competition of different platforms.[63] Burganov thinks that the banning of factions at the same congress had very negative consequences and became one of the Stalin's main weapons against the party itself.[64]

There is now some discussion about Lenin's orientation in the last period of his life. We have already mentioned the attacks against him and his attitude towards the intelligentsia. Starostin and Shatrov think that he was trying to liberalize the regime and was seeking some arrangement with the Mensheviks.[65] A study by V. I. Startsev on 'Lenin and Trotsky 1922–1923' opens a new road to Soviet investigators in this connection.[66]

One of the most interesting documents as yet published in USSR is the interview by Zhuravlev and Nenokarov in *Pravda* about the Geor-gian case of 1922.[67] Based upon archival material, particularly Rykov's correspondence at the time of his trip to Tbilisi, it gives a clear confirma-tion of the quality of Trotsky's memory and of his honesty as a historian. The last letters of Trotsky to Lenin have also been recently published.[68] Elena Kotelenets lectured in Tokyo on 'Trotsky and the nationalities question' and A. Kan in Aberdeen on 'Trotsky and small nations'.[69]

The crisis at the time of the debate upon the 'New Course' has been thoroughly studied by A. M. Poshchekoldin in his 'Prologue of a Tra-gedy', which has still to be completed with the publication of new and unknown documents.[70] The Russian reader is now able to read the text of the 'Letter of the 46' on the question of party democracy.[71] It is now recognized that the results of the votes in the party contest in Moscow were falsified by Stalin's men. A testimony of a former aide-de-camp of V. A. Antonov-Ovseenko, recorded by Anton Antonov-Ovseenko, asserts that several military collaborators of Trotsky including Muralov and Antonov-Ovseenko himself thought that a minor military coup could have swept away Stalin's clique without any problem, but that Trotsky refused any action of that kind.[72] Danilov – it was in itself a minor scandal – published extracts of a speech by Trotsky in the Central

Committee in October 1923, a clear illustration that the fight was for the control of the party, between the party itself and its own apparatus embodied by Stalin.[73]

Concerning 1924, the same Antonov mentions letters from Stalin to Lakoba in an effort to keep Trotsky far from Moscow at the time of Lenin's burial.[74] We have learned that, contrary to what everybody believed, Trotsky voted in the Politburo for the publication of Lenin's Testament but found himself in a minority,[75] which explains his silence at the Central Committee session that discussed the issue.

One of the most heated discussions is the one about NEP, the rate of economic growth at that time and its results. Yevgenii Ambartsumov, Latsis, Tikhonov and Seliunin[76] all describe it as a tremendous success and try to demonstrate that NEP of the past is the model for today. They generally deny the existence of what was called 'the kulak danger' at the time. But G. Khanin does not see any success in NEP[77] and we have had to wait until 1990 for more serious studies by M. M. Gorinov[78] and N. S. Simonov.[79]

V. P. Danilov, who was muzzled for years, is indignant about the 'discovery' of such a miraculous rate of growth, and protests against the attempt to discredit the cooperative idea;[80] he also believes in the existence of the 'kulak danger' and its pressure upon the Soviet authorities.

Many authors think that NEP in general was the road towards a politics opposed to Stalin's and call it the 'Bukharin alternative'. Danilov for his part sees three alternatives, Bukharin's, Stalin's and Gosplan's.[81] Kliamkin, while recognizing that Trotsky's Left criticism took place within the framework of NEP, is with Danilov one of the rare historians who admit that Trotsky was not an adversary of NEP nor a supporter of forcible collectivization.[82] Around these problems, the main articles of the polemics between Bukharin and Preobrazhensky have been published and commented on without distortions.[83]

The same disagreements arise concerning the end of the NEP. For some authors it was something like a deliberate decision by Stalin, the choice of a society. Others mention the grain delivery strike, which obliged Stalin to change course under the pressure of events.

It is only in novels that one can find the shadows and black sides in current descriptions of the NEP: the profits of the speculators, the violations of freedom of expression, the penetration of the party by careerists and businessmen. NEP was often the kingdom of corruption and demoralization. The camps as a system were organized from 1923 on, at the end of two years of NEP.

From the period of collectivization, it seems that no author has even

read Trotsky's articles or Rakovsky's writings, but everybody now rec-
ognizes the crisis, the flow of peasants to the towns, the opening of
camps for so-called kulaks, the violence against the peasants and their
desperate resistance, finally 'the organized famine', according to
Afanasyev,[84] which accompanied the forcible collectivization unleashed
by the 'Father of the Peoples'. Kliamkin is almost alone in arguing that
collectivization was necessary, although regrettable, and that it was
enthusiastically supported initially by poor peasants.[85] It is a real
debate. Danilov attempts to give a number of victims for the great
famine deliberately provoked by Stalin's policy in 1932–1933.[86] One of
the questions is to know whether Stalin really wanted to destroy the
middle peasants or if their extermination was only the result of excessive
zeal on the part of bureaucrats on the spot.[87]

The Rakovsky letter to Valentinov dated August 1928, well known to
Western specialists for some time but completely unknown in Soviet
Russia, has now been published,[88] as well as large extracts of the Left
Opposition 1930 declaration,[89] the first one by Danilov and the second
by Sirotkin. Nothing, except tiny details, has been as yet published
about the 'Opposition bloc' of 1932, discovered in the Trotsky archives.
On the other hand, we have plenty of information about the 'Riutin
group', about which previously we had only indirect testimony.[90]

One article at least, sharply criticized,[91] uses the material – sixty-four
volumes – of the Investigation Commission set up by Khrushchev on
Kirov's assassination: nothing in it is really new, except for the Soviet
public. The Rehabilitation Commission of the party gave some details,
part of which have been published. We know that Sosnovsky and
Beloborodov were in the hands of the police which tried to use them
against some of their comrades-in-arms but died without being able to
be brought before the court.[92] Through Chalikova, we learn that some
of the defendants refused to confess and died without yielding: among
them, Old Bolsheviks such as Preobrazhensky, Smilga, Shliapnikov and
Uglanov.[93] The Department of History of Saratov University is preparing a volume with the original minutes of the First Moscow Trial and
asked me to write a paper on 'Trotsky and the First Moscow Trial'.
Cherniavsky, Rakovsky's biographer, has published a paper on
'Rakovsky on Trial'.[94]

The addition of details allows the hope of a rewriting of the period of
the Purge Trials. We know that preparation for the First Trial with
sixteen defendants began in March and that seventy-eight persons were
at first involved.[95] The student D. G. Iurasov has established a card
index of more than 120,000 victims. We know that the trial of the Red
Army leaders was already prepared in 1936. We have details on the 1940

trials and the death sentences against Kol'tsov and Meyerhold.[96] We have the precise date of Rakovsky's death, shot in Orel prison with the old Socialist Revolutionary Spiridonova and members of families of Old Bolsheviks already shot, in September 1941.[97] There was a real resistance and the NKVD suffered about 20,000 victims in its own ranks, some of them charged with having 'sabotaged' the preparation of trials,[98] for which seventy-four military procurators were also shot.[99]

The circumstances under which the USSR entered World War II have been made clearer by the details given of the Red Army purge, on which Kulish writes that 'it was not possible to compensate by a material overequipment the terrific human losses provoked by the Stalinist terror'.[100] There were more than 400,000 cadres shot in the Red Army, among them the majority of the General Staff and commanding officers.[101] Tukhachevsky and Iakir were accused of sabotaging the defence by attempting to replace horses by tanks.[102] One of the aviation commanders was shot because he had said that Soviet aviators had to pilot 'flying coffins' too often.[103]

It was probably a shock for Soviet public opinion to learn the existence of the secret protocols of the Nazi–Soviet Pact of 1939, revealed for the first time in that country by Volkogonov.[104] Their discovery makes impossible the apology of a 'defensive pact' and the position of Gorbachev himself in his November 1987 speech. They also give strong support to the claim for independence of the Baltic countries, which fell among the first victims of an aggressive pact. Valentin Berezhkov, former first secretary at the Soviet Embassy in Berlin and then Stalin's interpreter, has given impressive details of Stalin's cynicism in his lecture at the Thionville symposium in November 1990.[105] In relation to the Pact, we must note that Iakushevsky revealed to the Soviet reader that Stalin handed over to Hitler German communists imprisoned by him in Soviet Russia.[106]

Boris Sokolov tells us nothing very new about the Russo-Finnish War of 1939–40, except that the generation of the 1919 revolutionaries volunteered in the Mannerheim army against Stalin's aggression. There is a debate about the human losses. The Soviet historian concludes with a judgement borrowed from an American historian: 'A crime, but also a mistake'.[107]

One of the great conquests of glasnost in the field of history is the recognition of the historical truth concerning the slaughter of Polish officers in the Katyn forest and probably elsewhere. It seems here that the official Russian-Polish commission met tremendous obstacles in its investigation from KGB officials, but the breach was finally made by the Soviet historian Natalia Lebedeva with the help of Polish colleagues.[108]

There is now no mystery about the more than 4,000 officers who were killed by the NKVD and buried in Katyn forest. Others seem to have been slaughtered in Khar'kov. But we know much less about the fate of the more than 30,000 other Polish officers murdered by the same 'mass murder machine'.

The history of World War II has changed considerably since the permission given for the publication of Simonov's interview with Marshal Zhukov.[109] Now we know that Stalin fought Shaposhnikov and Vasilievsky's proposal of reinforcement of the centre of the front, accusing them of 'preparing a retreat'. He probably really believed Hitler when the latter certified that German troops were transferred into Poland in order to protect them from British air bombings.[110] We know that Stalin looked for scapegoats and for a long time it was believed that General Pavlov had been one of them. In fact this man, who had been General Pablo, commander of the tank forces in Spain, was shot under the pretext of the initial defeats on the western front because he had signed a protest against Blucher and Rokossovsky's arrest.[111] We already knew that Meretskov had been arrested with about twenty other military chiefs and that they had been freed after some months. We did not know that they had all, with the exception of Meretskov, been arrested again, and summarily shot.[112] Immediately after them, two other heroes of the Spanish Civil War, G.M. Stern (Grigorovich) and Ia.M. Smuchkievich (Douglas), were shot with others.[113]

We know about the collapse of entire parts of the front, their commanders being terrified because they received no instructions from Stalin. Boris Sokolov is one of the first to raise the question of military losses: he estimates them at 11 million, including two and a half million dead after being wounded, to whom must be added 3,300,000 prisoners of war who died from starvation in German camps.[114] Now the methods of command are questioned: how is it possible that the battle of Berlin cost more than 100,000 victims in the Red Army? Veterans begin to speak: about frontal attacks under cannon fire, horsemen thrown against tanks, people shot because they were the first to protect themselves against fire by lying on the ground, or sentenced to death while involved in fighting.[115] The fate of the prisoners of war had been widely publicized: many of them were sentenced to prison, camps and even death.[116] But L.Z. Mekhlis, who forbade the digging of trenches in Kerch – he said that they were bad for the morale of the troops – was only recalled to Moscow.[117]

Anatolii Frenkin has written the first article about Vlasov and his men which does *not* belong to the category of demonology.[118] About the post-war period there have been more testimonies and memoirs than scientific studies. The 'Leningrad Case' seems to have had a political background: the main victim, A. A. Kuznetzov, was probably considered by Stalin as a potential rival and was more a political adversary than an innocent victim.[119] M. Ia. Gefter as well as Stephen Cohen think a new periodization is necessary for Soviet history, placing two periods of 'Moscow spring' before Kirov's murder and before the Leningrad affair.

We have been able to read new testimonies about the repression, by Gnedin,[120] Lev Razgon[121] and Sergei Mikoian,[122] and about investigations in the prisons and life and death in the camps. Mass graves of unexpected size have been found: more than 250,000 corpses, for instance, near Minsk.[123] We have been informed about the coup against Beria: he was arrested in the meeting room of the Presidium by Zhukov in person, and was shot in December 1953.[124] More recently, Semichastny has told how, as the head of the NKVD, he supported the plot of Brezhnev and others who succeeded in ousting Khrushchev.[125]

Concerning the last years of Trotsky's murderer, Ramón Mercader, we have learned through his brother Luis that he was cordially received in Cuba by Fidel Castro, whom he often visited, and became an adviser of the Cuban Ministry of the Interior.[126]

Conclusion

The Stalinist regime did its best with the extraordinary means at its disposal to destroy the memory of the people, the persons and the ideals of the October Revolution. It was helped in this by the counter-communist historiographical school. The collapse of the Stalinist construction does not for all that mean the discovery of a historical truth long distorted and hidden. On the contrary it gives a free hand to the old 'counter-communist' ideology, whose positive assets are its knowledge of facts and the huge means of diffusion at its disposal.

The rewriting of the Soviet history is still in the making. But it is a fight and, in every respect, a political fight. Or, more precisely, a part of the political fight waged on Soviet territory. The battle around history is a part of the general political fight for democracy. But the conclusion of the fight, that is the triumph in USSR of a capitalist democracy, of a socialist democracy or of a neo-Stalinist or military dictatorship, will in the last resort determine for decades the conclusion of the historiographical debate. Let us be modest!

Notes

There is a considerable secondary literature on the subjects that are dealt with in this chapter. See, in particular, R. W. Davies, *Soviet History in the Gorbachev Revolution* (London and Bloomington, 1989); Davies, 'History and perestroika', in E. A. Rees, ed., *The 28th Congress of the Communist Party of the Soviet Union* (London, 1991), which supplements the earlier discussion; Kertsin Herbst, 'Zur Trockij-Rezeption in der UdSSR seit 1986', communication to the Wuppertal Symposium, April 1990; Alec Nove, *Glasnost in Action* (London, 1989); Judith Shapiro, 'The perestroika of Soviet history', *Slovo*, vol. 2, no. 1 (May 1989), pp. 5–13; Shapiro, 'The prophet returned?', *Revolutionary History*, vol. 2, no. 2 (summer 1989), pp. 54–6; Jutta Scherrer, 'History reclaimed', in A. Brumberg, ed., *Chronicle of a Revolution* (New York, 1990); Isaac J. Tarasulo, *Gorbachev and Glasnost* (Wilmington, Del., 1989); Marilyn Vogt-Downey, 'Trotsky's voice heard again in the USSR', *Bulletin in Defence of Marxism*, no. 69, 1989, pp. 3–17; and Ian D. Thatcher, 'Recent Soviet writings on Leon Trotsky', *Coexistence*, vol. 27, no. 3 (September 1990), pp. 141–68.

1. *Pravda*, 3 November 1987.
2. *Pravda*, 13 January 1988.
3. *Pravda*, 19 February 1988.
4. S. Cohen, *Rethinking the Soviet Experience* (New York, 1985), pp. 40–6.
5. *Novyi mir*, 1988, no. 5.
6. *Nash sovremennik*, 1988, no. 4.
7. A. Tsipko, 'Istoki stalinizma', *Nauka i zhizn'*, 1988, nos. 11 and 12, and 1989, nos. 1 and 2.
8. *Rodina*, 1989, no. 10.
9. See Davies, 'History and perestroika'.
10. *Les nouvelles de Moscou*, 1990, no. 20.
11. Davies, 'History and perestroika', cites *Sovetskaia Moldaviia* and G. L. Smirnov citing Afanas'ev, *Pravda*, 1 February 1990.
12. *Pravda*, 9 October 1988.
13. *Literaturnaia gazeta*, 30 May 1990, and 13 June 1990.
14. A. V. Pantsov, 'La nouvelle école de falsification', *Cahiers Leon Trotsky*, no. 45 (1990).
15. *Molodoi kommunist*, 1989, no. 8.
16. *Voprosy istorii*, 1989, no. 6.
17. *Nedelia*, 1989, no. 39.
18. *Politicheskii sobesednik*, 1989, no. 12.
19. *Nauchnyi kommunizm*, 1989, no. 8.
20. *Slovo*, 1989, no. 11.
21. *Argumenty i fakty*, 1989, no. 34.
22. *Voprosy literatury*, 1989, no. 8, and *Teatr*, 1989, no. 8.
23. *EKO*, 1990, no. 1.
24. *Voprosy istorii*, 1990, no. 5.

25. See the discussion below, pp. 14–16.
26. *K istorii russkoi revoliutsii* (Moscow, 1990).
27. *EKO*, 1989, nos. 9–11, and 1990, no. 1.
28. Rogovin, *Argumenty i fakty*, 1990, no. 38; Pantsov, *Voprosy istorii*, 1990, no. 5; Vatlin, *Soiuz*, 1990, no. 44.
29. *Izvestiia*, 21 August 1990.
30. *Trud*, 14 and 15 August 1990.
31. *Literaturnaia gazeta*, 22 August 1990.
32. *Trud*, 19 August 1990.
33. *The Observer* (London), 6 May 1990.
34. *Komsomol'skaia pravda*, 2 April 1988.
35. *Trud*, 29 June 1988.
36. *Pravda*, 29 June 1988.
37. *Literaturnaia gazeta*, 9 December 1987.
38. Nove, *Glasnost' in Action*, pp. 24–7.
39. *Znamia*, 1988, no. 6.
40. *Moskovskaia pravda*, 21 January 1988.
41. *Voprosy istorii*, 1988, no. 2.
42. Davies, *Soviet History*, p. 96.
43. *Argumenty i fakty*, 1990, no. 27; the French translation in *Cahiers Leon Trotsky*, no. 45 (1990) is more complete.
44. *Znamia*, 1990, no. 7.
45. Ibid., pp. 11–26.
46. *Literaturnaia gazeta*, 8 June 1988.
47. *Znamia*, 1987, nos. 3 and 4.
48. Cited by Davies in 'History and *perestroika*'.
49. *Vestnik Akademii nauk*, 1987, no. 6.
50. *Literaturnaia gazeta*, 9 September 1987.
51. *Nash sovremennik*, 1988, no. 4.
52. *Novyi mir*, 1987, no. 11.
53. *Novyi mir*, 1988, no. 5.
54. Davies, *Soviet History*, p. 24.
55. *Les nouvelles de Moscou*, 1990, no. 50.
56. 'Velikii Oktyabr' i epilog tsarizma', in *Novyi mir*, 1988, no. 7; similarly G. Riadov in *Rodina*, 1989, nos. 4 and 5.
57. *Voprosy istorii*, 1990, no. 2.
58. Vasetsky, *Cahiers Leon Trotsky*, no. 44 (1990), and V.V. Zhuravlev, *Voprosy istorii KPSS*, 1990, nos. 6 and 7.
59. *Literaturnaia gazeta*, 8 February 1989.
60. *Iunost'*, 1988, no. 11.
61. *Sovetskaia Rossiia*, 10 July 1988.
62. Soltan, and not Sergei as suggested by Davies, *Soviet History*, p. 41.
63. *Moskovskaia pravda*, 3 June 1988.
64. *Druzhba narodov*, 1988, no. 6.
65. *Iunost'*, 1988, no. 5.
66. 'Lenin and Trotsky 1922–1923', *Marxist Monthly*, 1990, no. 3.
67. *Pravda*, 12 August 1988.
68. *Izvestiia TsK KPSS*, 1989, no. 11.

22

69. We hope to publish a French translation in *Cahiers Leon Trotsky*, no. 47 (1991).
70. *Molodoi kommunist*, 1989, no. 8.
71. *Izvestiia TsK KPSS*, 1990, no. 6.
72. Antonov-Ovseenko, Wuppertal Symposium (1990).
73. *EKO*, 1990, no. 1 (extracts), and *Voprosy istorii*, 1990, no. 5.
74. Antonov-Ovseenko, Wuppertal Symposium.
75. *Les nouvelles de Moscou*, 1990, no. 16.
76. See respectively *Moskovskie novosti*, 2 November 1986; *Kommunist*, 1987, no. 18, and *Novyi mir*, 1988, no. 6; *Voprosy istorii*, 1988, no. 3; and *Novyi mir*, 1988, no. 30.
77. *Rodina*, 1989, no. 7, and *EKO*, 1989, no. 10.
78. *Znanie*, History series, 1989, no. 2.
79. *Voprosy istorii KPSS*, 1990, no. 3.
80. *Voprosy istorii*, 1988, no. 3.
81. *Gorizont*, 1988, no. 5.
82. *Novyi mir*, 1988, no. 5.
83. *Voprosy ekonomiki*, 1988, no. 9, and N. Petrakov in *Ekonomika i matematicheskie metody*, 1988, no. 6.
84. *Literaturnaia Rossiia*, 17 June 1988.
85. *Novyi mir*, 1987, no. 11.
86. *Voprosy istorii*, 1988, no. 2.
87. Shmelev, *Oktiabr'*, 1988, no. 1.
88. Ibid., 1989, no. 12.
89. *Nedelia*, 1989, no. 21.
90. Vaksberg in *Literaturnaia gazeta*, 29 June 1988; *Iunost'*, 1988, no. 11; Shishkin in *Voprosy istorii*, 1989, no. 7.
91. Ol'ga G. Shatunovskaia was a member of the investigation commission and did not conclude that Stalin was guilty (*Argumenty i fakty*, 1990, no. 22). The criticism is in Tsel'ms, *Literaturnaia gazeta*, 27 June 1990.
92. *Izvestiia TsK KPSS*, 1989, no. 5.
93. *Neva*, 1988, no. 10.
94. *Novaia i noveishaia istoriia*, 1990, no. 4.
95. *Izvestiia TsK KPSS*, 1989, no. 5.
96. *Literaturnaia gazeta*, 4 May 1988.
97. Ibid.
98. *Moskovskie novosti*, 8 May 1988.
99. *Komsomol'skaia pravda*, 21 August 1988.
100. *Les nouvelles de Moscou*, 1989, no. 50.
101. *Ogonek*, 1987, no. 26.
102. *Pravda*, 29 April 1989.
103. *Znamia*, 1988, no. 5.
104. Nove, *Glasnost' in Action*, p. 47.
105. 'Stalin and Hitler', Scientific Franco-Soviet Symposium of the CORIDEH, Thionville, 21 November 1990.
106. *Voprosy istorii KPSS*, 1988, no. 9.
107. *Les nouvelles de Moscou*, 1989, no. 50.
108. *Mezhdunarodnaia zhizn'*, 1990, no. 5, and *International Affairs* (Moscow), June 1990, for the report.

109. Davies, *Soviet History*, p. 103.
110. There is agreement on this between Zhukov and Volkogonov.
111. *Voprosy istorii*, 1988, no. 7.
112. *Literaturnaia gazeta*, 21 April 1988.
113. *Les nouvelles de Moscou*, 1988, no. 24.
114. *Voprosy istorii*, 1988, no. 9.
115. *Literaturnaia gazeta*, 22 June 1988.
116. Maksimova in *Izvestiia*, 21 August 1987.
117. *Znamia*, 1988, no. 5.
118. *Literaturnaia gazeta*, 13 September 1989.
119. *Komsomol'skaia pravda*, 15 January 1988.
120. *Novyi mir*, 1988, no. 7.
121. *Ogonek*, 1988, no. 13.
122. *Komsomol'skaia pravda*, 21 February 1988.
123. *Moskovskie novosti*, 21 August 1988; *Daugava*, 1988, no. 9.
124. *Literaturnaia gazeta*, 24 February 1988.
125. *Sputnik*, 1990, no. 4.
126. *Trud*, 14 and 15 August 1990, and *Progreso* (Mexico), 10 September 1990.

Part II

Social Change and Cultural Policy

2 Revolutionary lives: public identities in *Pravda* during the 1920s

Jeffrey Brooks

The representation of individual and collective identities figured prominently in the public discourse of the late imperial and early Soviet periods. The common institutions for conveying and affirming notions of the self – the family, the churches, the schools, the army, the work places, the public institutions, and private organizations – were in disarray or ineffective during some or all of this period. Even the schools, so important in many other industrial societies, were constrained to operate under these conditions. Their institutional continuity was disrupted by war and revolution, and the children attended for such a short period in any case that the effects were necessarily limited.[1]

The media served as a means for the cultural construction of these new lives, sometimes disseminating values that were close to those of its audience and other times values that were exceedingly remote. The French anthropologist Marcel Mauss argued in a seminal essay in 1938 that the notion of the person has meaning both in terms of individual and spiritual life, on the one hand, and, on the other, in terms of the significant and organized contexts or collectivities embedded in law and other aspects of social life.[2]

Eric Erikson began an inquiry at roughly the same time that led to the illumination of a cluster of collectivities grouped around and inspired by the notion of an identity outside the self.[3] Mauss traced the evolution of the self from its weakest historical beginnings to the highly specific and dense contemporary idea of individualism. Erikson developed the concept of identity from a psychological perspective, exploring how youth can form ego identity or group identity, as distinguished from personal identity, in our modern era during which change is so rapid. From this perspective he suggested the existence of an identity crisis specific to the modern condition.

Mauss found identity both personal and social. The notion of identity comes to the fore when we ask: Who am I? Who is he or she? Who are they? People define themselves through structures of meaning in language and action, which some social psychologists call 'the selfing process' through which identities are typified. The notion of a single dominant identity has given way to the idea of various selves, what T.S. Eliot called 'a face to meet the faces that we meet' and Erving Goffman captured with the notion of the 'performed self'.[4] Changing alternative identities are in this sense a recognized feature of modern life. As Peter Berger expressed it, 'One identifies oneself, as one is identified by others, by being located in a common world'.[5]

Identity is also a technical term in social psychology that refers to a structural aspect of institutions such as religion, occupation, family, schools, etc. Identity is therefore linked in a broad sense with notions of normalcy and deviance. A group of social psychologists recently summarizing the literature on identity, suggested that on a micro-level, identity means 'multiple categorizations of the individual by both self and others that vary by situation, influence behavior, and constitute life's meanings', whereas on the macro-level identity is a 'positional definition of actors within institutions and society'.[6] This essay is necessarily concerned primarily with the representation of identities on the macro-level – in the press – and only secondarily with the meaning of identity in the lives of individuals.

How were these public new roles defined and what did they mean in terms of the identities described in the press? The Soviet press in the 1920s was not a simple instrument of control, despite party direction. It was an institution in which people from very different social backgrounds participated and expressed themselves, albeit within well-defined limits. Although the rules for Soviet public expression could be very stringent, the editors of Soviet newspapers, including the editors of *Pravda*, failed to create a monolithic discourse, just as the managers of Soviet literature failed to create a form of fiction susceptible only to a single reading.[7] The newspapers, indeed, evince greater diversity than literature, in the sense that a single issue was the work of dozens of separate authors.

The result, even in the central newspapers, was the creation of several rather distinct spheres of discourse in which different groups of authors wrote different types of articles for different purposes to suit different intended and actual readers.[8] The large divisions along these lines in the newspapers encompassed three relatively distinct spheres of discourse: (1) an interactive sphere, comprised of letters and local reports by worker and peasant correspondents and other semi-official and unofficial correspondents; (2) an informational sphere, composed of articles by the professional staff and others which were directed at the widest possible audience of passive readers; and (3) an inspirational sphere, which flourished particularly in holiday issues, contained materials remote from the daily news, and was organized according to widely understood directives. Although *Pravda* was and is a special newspaper, the *Pravda* of the 1920s was widely read outside the party, and was intended for conscious and advanced workers as well as for managers and party people.[9]

The representation of lives in *Pravda* during the 1920s was expressed largely in four types or genres of reportage, each of which contained a mix of discourses, but nevertheless had its own rules for the presentation of information. The genres include: (1) biographies submitted for contests (29% of the total); (2) descriptions of exemplary individuals (17%); (3) articles about individuals who were celebrating anniversaries of some sort (5.5%); and (4) obituaries (45%). Lives described in the interactive sphere, which included columns such as 'Workers' Life', comprised 35 per cent of the total. All other articles were coded for the purpose of this paper as informational.[10]

Two contests figure in *Pravda* during these years: the first, which finished in early 1923, was to name the best red factory directors; the second, conducted later in that year, concerned the best schoolteachers. The contests contain largely two types of information: (1) the published reports that were submitted as entries by local party committees, worker and peasant correspondents, and employees at the various enterprises, and (2) the results of the contests. These were announced in several page spreads for which the editors condensed and supplemented the earlier reports to emphasize the exemplary lives and performances of the winners, and, in the case of a couple of factory directors, the losers. Although the published entries were edited and selected, they nevertheless contained more of the thinking of those who submitted the entries than did the final results, in which the editors' voices sounded more loudly. As a result, they are coded as informational, that is as more narrowly representing the thinking of the professional journalists at the Moscow office of the newspaper.

Exemplary individuals were usually described in letters and reports from worker and peasant correspondents, unofficial writers, and people who were not professional journalists, and therefore most of such reports belong to the active sphere of the newspaper. A small proportion of such descriptions were written by central or professional journalists, and those are considered informational. The presence of reports on exemplary lives, which varied significantly over the 1920s and 1930s, is one indication of the input into the newspapers from the local *aktiv*, that is the local people who were actively involved in Soviet affairs and in the building of the Soviet institutions.

The obituaries and anniversary articles are in some respects a special case. The obituary was the closest thing to a formal literary genre of the three, but during this period it was nevertheless a very loose one. Soviet obituaries of the 1920s, unlike those of today or contemporary American newspaper obituaries, did not appear in a single format and were not produced through a standardized process. Obituaries during the 1920s were written by party leaders, by local party authorities, by professional colleagues, and even occasionally by family members, as well as by professional journalists at the central editorial office. Despite these variations, however, the obituary was the only description of individual life that appeared regularly during the whole period.

The anniversary articles share many of the characteristics of the obituaries, but they became common only in the late 1920s. The content and language of the obituaries and the anniversary articles reflected to a certain degree the character of the different authors. Yet the authors of the obituaries, with very few exceptions, were people who were much more prominent than the worker and peasant correspondents. For this reason, and because the obituaries themselves are items of general news, rather than part of an active exchange of information with participating correspondents, these reports belong to the informational sphere of discourse.

The range of authors of the accounts of individual lives in *Pravda* includes the Bolshevik leaders themselves, journalists working at the Moscow office, travelling professional journalists, semi-official and unofficial correspondents ranging from the worker and peasant correspondents to ordinary letter writers, and in the case of the obituaries, groups of comrades as well as organizations and institutions. The reports and articles by the Bolshevik elite, the professional journalists, and organizations and institutions belong to the official institutional definitions of identity that the new Soviet leaders were eagerly promoting among the population. The local reports and letters sent from unofficial correspondents and the semi-official worker and peasant correspondents do not represent alternative notions of identity, but rather the attempt by those much lower down the social scale to construct officially sanctioned identities within the framework of their own experience, language and capabilities. The editors reinforced these efforts by printing contributions they found acceptable and ignoring or modifying those they did not.

Lives were presented by these different authors in the different genres for rather different purposes. Worker or peasant correspondents, the semi-professional peripatetic contributors to Soviet newspapers, described exemplary individuals or submitted entries into contests for a variety of reasons, including efforts to further their own position, to promote local notables, and to satisfy local pride or public spirit. Bolshevik leaders and journalists used obituaries not only to mark the end of significant lives, but also to promote their agendas. The deaths of leaders such as M. V. Frunze in 1925, as well as those of lesser figures, were used, at least in part, for very specific political purposes. For example, when the Soviet ambassador to Poland, P. L. Voikov, was assassinated in 1927, the Bolsheviks responded with a flurry of obituaries as well as public tributes. Exemplary lives and anniversaries were also used in this fashion, as for example, the 50th birthday of Kalinin in 1925. Despite these divergent functions, however, the lives described in *Pravda* had much in common.

Not surprisingly, the people represented in *Pravda* were special.[11] Slightly more than half (54%) belonged to the party, and nearly half of these were either local leaders or party chiefs. Most were men (84%), and many lived in the city of Moscow. Age was given in only half the cases, but of these 47 per cent were fifty-one or older, reflecting the importance of the obituaries, as well as the representation of established people. Education and social origins were given too infrequently to judge, but by profession or calling, these people fall roughly into two distinct types: those near the top of the social scale and the others well below them. Most belonged to the first category; they were responsible people.

The managers of industry (8%), bureaucrats of the central administration (10%), party leaders (6%), and military officers (4%) comprised well over a third of the total. Educators (9%), who figured prominently in the contest to name the best schoolteacher, slightly outnumbered teachers. Revolutionary comrades, often old Bolsheviks, made up another important group (9%), as did cultural figures (4%) and foreign communists (7%). People lower on the social scale, such as schoolteachers (8.5%), workers (7%), peasants (2%), and inventors (4%), many of whom were autodidacts, figured less importantly.

If we treat these reports not as biographical information about actual people, but as the presentation of life in the new public culture; that is, as a means for defining and illuminating public roles, a number of features stand out and set these lives apart from the prerevolutionary popular culture. The central idea of almost all the lives presented was that of service; that is, the individuals' contributions to something larger than themselves. In this sense, the balance between the individual and society, which had swung in favour of the individual in the late prerevolutionary popular culture, shifted back toward society.

Self-denial was one of the most common qualities stressed in the lives described in *Pravda*, appearing in 37 per cent of the 494 cases. Self-sacrifice figured in pre-revolutionary popular culture, but primarily in terms of war. Bandit heroes could win a pardon and/or other benefits by fighting for tsar and country. Yet although these were presented as great causes, the promised benefits were usually personal – benefits to the individual and his or her family. Only in the officially promoted publications of the Orthodox Church and the tsarist government, particularly publications for the army, were there frequent representations of self-sacrifice without immediate material rewards for the individual involved.[12]

The Bolsheviks went further in promoting the ideal of self-sacrifice as a denial of personal needs and interests, as well as a rejection of home and family, than the supporters of the old regime. The Bolshevik elite came from a revolutionary tradition that stressed sacrifice, and they expressed this ideal in the newspapers. Yet the ideal was not exactly appropriate to the new Russia of the 1920s; nor did it necessarily make sense to the *aktiv*, those who contributed to the active sphere of the newspaper as worker and peasant correspondents.

The result was a double image. The leaders and the professional journalists close to them presented their ideals, but the unofficial correspondents, whose contributions were important in the central newspapers, were unable to adopt them fully, even when they tried. Unofficial worker and peasant correspondents and others far from the centres of power could hardly replicate the enthusiasm and devotion of the old guard. The dissemination of ideals also failed in a second way. As the relationship within the institutions of society became more paternalistic and authoritarian, the exchange of information became less frank, and the reports from worker and peasant correspondents and unofficial letter writers increasingly became letters to the boss. Thus, on the one hand elite ideals were willingly absorbed and changed, and on the other, there appeared a pattern of mimicry.

The efforts of the worker and peasant correspondents to follow official signals were also complicated by the fact that official values were transformed during the 1920s, as the composition and thinking of the Bolshevik elite shifted. The Bolshevik leaders' idea of sacrifice lost some of its meaning even among themselves because of the changing conditions under which they lived. As a result, even though old revolutionary ideals were disseminated, and people of common origins tried to adopt them, they could only do so incompletely. The notion of revolutionary sacrifice was thus imperfectly translated into the new conditions of Russia in the 1920s.

Old Bolsheviks recalled the ideals of the revolutionary movement when they wrote the obituaries of their revolutionary comrades, even though these people were now living very different lives. M.P. Ivanitskaia, an official at the Central Executive Committee, who insisted on living in a tiny cold room in a communal apartment despite her declining health, was praised for her dogged devotion to the revolutionary ideals. 'During the course of the winter', wrote the author of her obituary, 'I tried to convince M.P. to get herself a reasonable room, since the room she occupied was cold and full of smoke, but I received the answer: "the majority of workers live in such conditions; why do I need to occupy a good room, and not one of them?" ' (17 July 1921). The office manager at the Ministry of Education, Lepeshinskaia, is another example. She was praised for working late into the night and only going home to 'rest in order to return again on time' (17 January 1923). By 1925, a deceased Bolshevik could be praised as someone with no personal life: 'Comrade Nesterenko has no personal biography and no personal needs', the author of his obituary observed (15 March 1925).

The obituaries of Frunze, the ill-starred successor to Trotsky, illustrate the mix of old ideals and new patterns emerging among Bolshevik leaders in 1925. As I.S. Unshlikht, Frunze's deputy and the assistant chairman of the War Ministry, an old Bolshevik from 1900, wrote: 'Comrade Frunze did not know any personal life, he strove with all his force toward the social ideals of socialism' (3 November 1925). Even when the self-sacrifice of the deceased hero was not mentioned, the idea of service was stated in a way that strongly implied it. Bukharin wrote: 'Frunze was extremely restrained, almost shy, when the talk was about himself'. Kamenev, in his funeral speech, described Frunze's experience as a tsarist prisoner: 'his life was torture, he lived only because he believed in the final victory of the working class'. Semon Budenny said much the same, stressing how Frunze ruined his health serving the working class.

The Bolsheviks themselves did not have a single formula to describe the object of their devotion, although most of them may have agreed in a general way about what it was, at least into the mid-1920s. The word they commonly used to link their self-sacrifice with its object, however, was *predannost'*, which is usually translated as devotion, with all the religious connotations that implies.

Devotion to whom or to what? During 1921 and 1923 the object of devotion was the revolution, the working class, the ideals of socialism, and somewhat less frequently the party. 'The workers' revolution lost a tested and devoted fighter', wrote the author of Ivanitskaia's obituary (17 July 1921). Lepeshinskaia, the office manager at the Ministry of

Education, was praised as 'exclusively devoted to the affairs of her comrades' (21 January 1923). In the case of a leading Soviet educator, V.L. Nikitin, devotion was to 'Soviet power and to the Communist Party' (8 July 1923).

By the middle 1920s, the party became the usual object of devotion in the formulas used in obituaries, with some variations, as evidenced by the obituaries of Frunze. Although Rykov praised the military leader for 'devotion to the revolution' (5 November 1925) and Trotsky as someone who 'served the cause of the proletariat' (13 November 1925), Zinoviev noted that he had given 'himself fully to his party, his class, and to the cause of the great proletarian revolution' (5 November 1925), and Stalin wrote simply that the party had lost 'one of its truest and most disciplined leaders' (5 November 1925). By 1927, the phrase 'whole-hearted devotion to the party' became standard (30 January 1927).

The meaning of these tributes to loyal service was heightened by a military metaphor, the comparison of party members to soldiers in an army. Preobrazhensky wrote of the revolutionary organizer and head of the miners' union, 'Artem' (F.A. Sergeev), who was killed in a train wreck in 1921: 'This idiotic accident has removed . . . one of the best soldiers from the ranks of the old guard of our party' (14 August 1921). 'Demian Bedny stood in the years of revolution in the most difficult moments at his fighting post', wrote Karl Radek congratulating the writer on his tenth anniversary as a contributor to *Pravda*. 'Yes. Demian Bedny stood courageously at his fighting post . . .' (24 May 1923). Lesser figures were praised in the same way. The obituary of the old Bolshevik A.G. Shvartz, praised for his 'humility and devotion' to the party, concluded, 'One more rank and file soldier of the revolution has left our workers' family' (16 January 1927).

The family metaphor, although less common than the military one, reinforced the notion of an alternative system of loyalties and priorities that completely superseded the personal sphere of life. The revolution-aries promoted a view of the individual life in which family and home counted for little, and in thousands of pages of Soviet newspapers from the 1920s one is hard pressed to find a single picture of a family or even a child with one of its parents. Parents were mentioned occasionally in the biographical sketches but only with reference to an individual's social origins; children and spouses rarely appear. A brief comment on home or family was found in only 7 per cent of the 495 cases, and in these it was almost exclusively negative.

The Bolshevik elite almost never mentioned the families of the deceased when they wrote the obituaries of their comrades. The pro-fessional journalists did so only to heighten a sense of loss, as in the case of a government administrator, who 'left a wife and five small children without support' (3 April 1921), and a military officer who 'left a sick mother and six small children' (2 September 1921).

The commentators in the active sphere portrayed the family more frequently, but largely as a burden, particularly when they wrote of women, and perhaps with good reason. 'Comrade Kabalina is a widow. She has two daughters on her hands, and therefore her life was particularly difficult during the first years of the revolution' (13 January 1923). An exemplary female worker, who has recently lost her husband, 'works with her former energy' despite 'a bunch of children on her hands' (8 March 1923). So irrelevant was the family to the notion of the worth of the individual in this discourse that a teacher named Sechko's abandonment of his family in the chaos of the civil war was described without comment by a local correspondent who was promoting his virtues in the contest for the best red schoolteacher. 'The advance of the Germans and fear of Polish retribution compelled comrade Sechko to leave his family to the mercy of fate and to flee to Bortisovskii uezd, where he was able to establish himself as a teacher', wrote the author of this report (28 April 1923). The story contained no more information about the family, and readers were left to guess their fate. Sechko was praised, however, for devotion to another object. 'Comrade Sechko is not a communist', the author explained, 'but he is faithful to the proletariat to the depths of his soul.' Similarly, a school teacher was lauded for single-minded devotion to work. 'Konopel'ko does not have his own land and he has no family. "The children of the colony are my family", he says about himself' (25 May 1923).

The members of the *aktiv* took up the notion of self-sacrifice with a vengeance, and the authors of reports on exemplary individuals and of the entries in the two contests echoed the ideals of a revolutionary life. There is praise for a factory director, who 'completely forgot about himself' (29 March 1923), for a teacher who had 'no personal concern for himself' (13 April 1923), and for a 'teacher-ascetic' who 'has earned this title' (4 May 1923). Although the lives described in the active sphere echo the self-sacrifice described by the professional journalists and the party elite, the object of loyalty was often different, at least initially. The emphasis in these local reports during first years was on devotion to the locale, the collective, and the place of work, and these notions were reinforced by a lively concern for equality between managers and the rank-and-file.

'Lizavetushka', an exemplary female worker, stayed at the factory every day until eight or nine o'clock. 'At home, her children and husband await her, but she continues to work' (21 January 1923). And why? 'All her strength, despite her weak health, she gives to social work, forgetting about her own "personal" life needs, and finding her sole satisfaction in work among the family of workers.' A self-deprecating school master, who teaches railroad workers, is likewise praised for refusing better paying jobs. He prefers to receive 'the low salary of a teacher, a beggarly ration, and works at his favorite profession' (2 February 1923). A factory director is singled out, in the contest for best director, for his 'love of his factory and his workers' (5 January 1923), a teacher for his 'devotion' to 'the interests of the local peasantry' (17 April 1923), and another for her 'devotion' to 'her school' (25 May 1923).

The emphasis on local loyalties was reinforced in 1921 and 1923 with a kind of egalitarianism, just as the notion of loyalty to the revolution was buttressed with the military metaphor. The equality in these reports was not of a levelling sort, but rather a claim to the right to be respected, to be treated with dignity. Factory directors were praised for keeping their doors open to the workers, for explaining things in terms workers could understand, for performing manual labour themselves in emergencies, in short, for 'comradely relations', and bad directors were condemned for insulting workers or behaving like lords.[13] School directors were singled out for treating their pupils as equals, even when they were children, reflecting, in a similar manner, the egalitarianism of the early educational system as well as that of Soviet society more generally. Asked to do something by local authorities, one school director was cited as replying, 'I cannot resolve this question myself . . . I will have a talk with the children, and then I will reply' (17 May 1923). 'It is necessary to observe', wrote another contributor in the contest for the best schoolteacher, 'that the pupils in the older grades of the school have completely equal rights with Lubentsov [the director]' (18 April 1923).

The differences in these two types of accounts – those coming from the *aktiv* and those from the professional journalists and party leaders – tended to diminish in 1925 and 1927 as the party loomed increasingly large as the officially sanctioned object of devotion. This was particularly evident in the way in which the individuals were identified with a positive group and with a particular kind of achievement. Achievements that were locally significant – improving local conditions, raising the cultural level of the local population, organizing locally – figured prominently in reports and obituaries from the early years, and these were replaced increasingly by identification with the party and with official signs of accomplishment, such as the designation of hero of labour or a job itself. These trends were evident in both spheres.

Despite this tendency to converge, significant differences between the two spheres of discourse remained. The meaning of collective identities and the definitions of a life depend in part on the notion of a cohort, or a shared experience specific to an age. The great experiences or calamities of the early twentieth century that were represented in *Pravda* in these biographical sketches include struggle or suffering under the old regime, the effort to gain an education, participation in the civil war, and entry into the party. Of these, by far the most important in 1921–27 was the experience of struggle or suffering under the old regime. This experience figured not only in obituaries, but also in the lives of contestants and of exemplary people.

The idea of life under the old regime was equally important in the lives described in the active sphere of the newspaper by worker and peasant correspondents, and in accounts written by professional journalists and party leaders. Two types of stories surface here, however, with two very different meanings: the accounts by the Bolshevik elite and professional journalists were most likely to concern struggle, and only secondarily suffering, whereas those from the unofficial correspondents were likely to have these values reversed. A female textile worker and hero of labour was praised in the following way: 'She is a non-party person, but the bitter experience of past exploitation and oppression have made her into a staunch proponent of Soviet power' (8 March 1923).

How different this was from the experience conveyed in an obituary of a Chekist. 'In the person of Shchepansky, who perished before his time, the party has lost one of the most devoted, advanced, and capable workers, who earned the love and respect of all who had come into contact with comrade "Zaria" in underground work up to the revolution and in Soviet Russia' (8 May 1921). In the one case, it was a justification for opinion, whereas in the other, it served as a credential. It is in the sense of the making of an opinion, perhaps, that Bolshevik leaders sometimes spoke regretfully of the fact that young people were growing up without the experience of living under the old regime.

The Civil War counted for much less in these sketches, but not surprisingly it was somewhat more important in the informational sphere than in that dominated by the accounts from the *aktiv*. The elite used this experience when they wrote about themselves and when they wrote for the large audience of common readers. For them, the civil war was more likely to be a credential than an experience of suffering or trial. For example, Smirnov, who died in the attack on Kronstadt, was praised in his obituary by a comrade from that period. 'The deceased comrade was then the humble organizer of the regiment; at the first

sight of him, you at once felt that he commanded a strong will and a firm
hand' (6 May 1921). The local correspondents made the same point, as
in the case of one entry in the teachers' contest, but their perspective
was different, since the past had less meaning to them. 'He was a soldier
of the revolution on the military front. He became a soldier of the
revolution on the peaceful front' (3 February 1923). The local correspondents' more pressing interest in the present was reflected in part in
their stress on peaceful activity. Typically, one correspondent quickly
passed over a factory manager's distinguished wartime experience in an
entry into a contest. 'Comrade Stupnikov was withdrawn from service at
the request of the workers and sent to the Shterskii plant, where the
workers chose him as director' (4 January 1923).

A description of when a person joined the party was slightly more
common in the elite accounts, but as can be expected it greatly increased
in importance after 1925. It was closely linked with the notion of devotion to the party. The author of an obituary explained in 1927, 'In the
year 1919, the twenty-year old Liza had already entered the ranks of our
party' (3 January 1927). Similar reports came from the *aktiv* as well: 'In
the years 1922–23 Comrade Dragunov was already a candidate of the
RKP(b) . . .' (15 May 1923). By 1927 the mention of when a person
entered the party was common in all accounts, as in statements such as
'in 1917 comrade Ispolatov entered the Communist Party' (9 March
1927).

The most important cohort experience in the accounts and reports
from the worker and peasant correspondents and other non-pro-
fessionals was education. If anything showed a gap between the ideals
promoted by the elite during the 1920s and the response from below it
was in these accounts of how people acquired the training that allowed
them to achieve, not because the elite did not promote the mobility of
people of common origins – they did – but because education in these
accounts is often linked with the escape from one's class and with a
dream of personal success, even though the accounts were written by
others.

Typical is a statement of one of the candidates in the teachers' contest: 'Feeling the inadequacy of his general education, Comrade
Mikhailov gave his free time to self-education and after three years he
took the exam for public schoolteacher' (12 April 1923). A worker
promoted to an administrative post (*vydvizhenets*) was similarly described: 'Little Misha passionately wanted to study, but he succeeded in
spending only three years in the school of the Ministry of Education' (14
November 1925). The more educated and better placed professional

journalists, as well as the old Bolshevik leaders themselves, encouraged these aspirations and addressed them, but could not share them.

Public representation of individual and collective identities during the years of the New Economic Policy showed a dichotomy between officially fostered ideals of self-sacrifice and similarly promoted notions of mobility and personal success. On one level this was a split between old Bolsheviks who clung to revolutionary ideals and their memories of the civil war, and energetic upwardly mobile people eager to win a place for themselves in the new order. Yet tensions between official ideals and daily life proved lasting features of the Soviet experience, and a fragmented public image of the respected or notable person long remained a characteristic of Soviet public life.

Notes

1. Although an estimated 88 per cent of the boys and 52 per cent of the girls aged 7 to 14 entered a primary school in 1911, only 39 per cent and 8 per cent respectively began the third year. Jeffrey Brooks, 'The Zemstvo and the education of the people', in *The Zemstvo in Russia*, ed. T. Emmons and Wayne S. Vucinich (Cambridge, 1982), p. 273. See also Ben Eklof, *Russian Peasant Schools* (Berkeley, 1986), and Jeffrey Brooks, 'Literacy and the print media in Russia, 1861–1928', *Communication*, vol. 11 (1988), pp. 47–61. There is no reason to suspect that Soviet schools fared better than tsarist ones.
2. Marcel Mauss, 'A category of the human mind: the notion of person, the notion of self', in *The Category of the Person: Anthropology, Philosophy, History*, ed. Michael Carruthers et al. (Cambridge, 1985), pp. 1–25.
3. See particularly Eric Erikson, *Identity: Youth and Crisis* (New York, 1968).
4. Erving Goffman, *The Presentation of the Self in Everyday Life* (New York, 1959), and *Frame Analysis* (New York, 1974).
5. Quoted in Andrew Weigert et al., *Society and Identity: Toward a Sociological Psychology* (Cambridge, 1986), p. 17; Peter Berger, 'Identity as a problem in the sociology of knowledge', *European Journal of Sociology*, vol. 7 (1966), pp. 105–15.
6. Weigert et al., *Society and Identity*, p. 27. I have relied heavily on this stimulating recent survey of the literature.
7. Regine Robin, *Le réalisme socialiste: une esthétique impossible* (Paris, 1986; forthcoming in English from Stanford University Press).
8. I discuss this aspect of the Soviet press in a preliminary way in 'Public and private values in the Soviet press, 1921–28', *Slavic Review*, vol. 48, no. 1 (spring 1989), pp. 16–35.
9. The lives analyzed from *Pravda* are those that appear in some historical

dimension; i.e. with a reference to the individual's origins or experience in the past. All lives of Lenin were excluded, since these represent a separate problem. So also were the descriptions of the lives of people from the past. Only living people or people who had just died are included in this study. Multiple lives of the same individual were included, however, since each case is equally important in the representation of various qualities of collective identities. The lives are counted individually by cases, although the space allotted to each case is accounted for elsewhere.

10. I did not attempt to distinguish articles in what I have called the inspirational sphere, partly because there were relatively few biographical sketches that fell into this category and partly because of problems with defining the sphere precisely for the purposes of coding.

11. The representations are discussed by article or case rather than by the representation of a given individual, since some individuals were described several times, and sometimes in very different ways.

12. Jeffrey Brooks, *When Russia Learned to Read* (Princeton, 1985), pp. 308–17.

13. See, for example, entries in the contest for the best red factory directors: *Pravda*, 20 October 1923, 4 January 1923 and 5 January 1923.

3   Entertainment or enlightenment? Popular cinema in Soviet society, 1921–1931

Denise J. Youngblood

It's boring, comrade editor, in a country busy replacing the plough with the tractor, where peasants and cooks run the government, where lovers of the electric light bulb don't understand the tales of Baghdad. It's boring, and I'm tired of life. Life has become loathsome. I want to forget myself. I want romance . . .

                    Unpublished letter to Teakinopechat', 1927[1]

The Bolsheviks quickly recognized the advantages cinema had over theatre as a mass art – not only was it mechanically reproducible, it was potentially more intelligible to the marginally educated, an important advantage in a country like Russia.[2] Although I have long wondered whether Lenin's aphorism 'Cinema is for us the most important of all arts' should not be attributed instead to Anatolii Lunacharsky, it can be verified that as early as 1913, Lenin had noted cinema's value as an educational medium.[3] The movies were the new art for the new age.

It was immediately obvious that 'mass art' did not necessarily mean 'popular art' to the Bolshevik regime. When cinema was nationalized in 1919, it was placed under the control of the Commissariat of Enlightenment (Narkompros). That same year Narkompros published the first Soviet cinema manifesto, a slim and sober volume which called on the moving picture to become a 'book for the illiterate', and mentioned entertainment films infrequently and disparagingly.[4]

The Civil War was already underway, and exigencies of war prevented Narkompros from putting its programme for cinema into effect. During the war cinema served almost exclusively as an agent of propaganda.[5] But after the Civil War, although cinema remained under Narkompros's nominal control, official support (whether economic or moral) for the idea of using film exclusively for enlightenment purposes dissipated. Party and government lost interest in film, and under the terms of the New Economic Policy cinema became a commercial commodity on the cost-accounting system. This set-up was tailor-made for conflict. Who would determine the role and purpose of cinema in Soviet society – the 'people' (as consumers in the cinema marketplace) or Narkompros?[6]

The debate over how Soviet cinema should best serve the masses was involved and protracted, and some simplification of the issues and the actors is necessary here. There were three basic 'camps' and two major issues.[7] Narkompros's Main Committee on Political Education (Glavpolitprosvet) was seriously involved in cinema affairs throughout the 1920s. Glavpolitprosvet organized the 'cinefication of the countryside' campaign, was instrumental in founding the first 'mass' cinema organization, the Society of Friends of Soviet Cinema (ODSK), and published its own journal, *Soviet Cinema* (Sovetskoe kino). In some arenas, Glavpolitprosvet's aims were close to those of 'proletarian' organizations, especially to the All-Russian Association of Proletarian Writers (VAPP), and to documentary filmmakers like Grigorii Boltiansky and Nikolai Lebedev. Glavpolitprosvet cinema activists Vladimir Meshcheriakov and Aleksandr Katsigras tirelessly promoted the educational film and the cinefication campaign, and just as indefatigably attacked *both* avant-garde ('art') *and* entertainment films as incompatible with the aims of a socialist society. If they had a favourite enemy, however, it was certainly the entertainment film; 'fun' and 'relaxation' did not appear to be in their vocabularies.

The avant-garde also vociferously attacked entertainment films as 'bourgeois', 'petty-bourgeois', and much worse. Under this general rubric I include directors and writers who made or liked elite films variously labelled 'avant-garde', 'abstract' or 'formalist'. They were not a coherent 'group'; indeed, they sometimes fought bitterly with each other (the Eisenstein–Vertov feud is a good example). But they believed that their films would raise the artistic consciousness of the masses and deplored the continued 'narcotic' influence of the pre-revolutionary and Western taste cultures on film audiences. They also scorned the drab 'formula' films the pedagogues and proletarians believed suitable for the masses.[8]

The third faction consisted of studio heads and film trust administrators, whose charge was to keep the industry solvent. Since no foundations or philanthropists existed to subsidize worthy but dull film projects, the industry had to rely on its own very limited resources. Sovkino's plan for setting the industry right was to give people the movies they wanted to see, whether that meant importing the latest foreign hits or making their Soviet equivalents. Some of the profits from these commercial endeavours could then be channelled into the production of movies less likely to succeed at the box office. Ilya Trainin, the head of the censorship commission (Glavrepertkom) and a member of

Sovkino's board of directors, was a frequent and effective spokesman for the cause of the entertainment film. K.M. Shvedchikov, P.A. Bliakhin, M. Rafes and M.P. Efremov also supported the primacy of the entertainment film.

This tripartite debate took many forms and was played out in many forums (on the screen, in the pages of the press, in the associations), but I will focus here on the conflict between Narkompros and the producers, or more specifically, between Glavpolitprosvet and Sovkino. They agreed that 'futurist' or 'formalist' art was not what people wanted to see, but they disagreed on whether serving the masses meant entertaining them or enlightening them. Implicit in this question is one which had a profound impact on Soviet society. What degree of autonomy is permissible in a revolutionary society? Those very people who talked loudest and most often about 'the masses' seemed to listen to them the least and to distrust their instincts the most. Sovkino's Ilya Trainin was perfectly willing not only to tolerate diversity in theory, but to make it possible in reality by offering viewers actual choices. For a hard-liner like Vladimir Meshcheriakov, on the other hand, cultural pluralism represented an unacceptable compromise with the old order.

The debate over popular culture is not a new one; elite groups over time and across national boundaries have divided the arts into 'high' and 'low', and have believed, to paraphrase Patrick Brantlinger, that mass culture represents social decay and moral decline.[9] Cinema was instantly recognized as an agent of 'corruption' when it appeared in Europe and the US at the turn of the century, enchanting audiences with an endless repertoire of adventure and romance. Nicholas II, who enjoyed films and employed a court cinematographer, made these annotations to a police report about the latest menace to the Empire:

I consider cinematography an empty, useless, and even pernicious diversion. Only an abnormal person could place this sideshow business on a level with art. It is all nonsense, and no importance should be attached to such trash.[10]

This same view was also widely held in early Soviet educational and cultural circles, especially in Glavpolitprosvet and VAPP, and among early avant-gardists like Dziga Vertov and Aleksei Gan. An unsigned editorial in the radical journal *Cinema-photo* (Kino-fot) in 1922, undoubtedly written by Gan, spoke of a cinema in the 'hands of cinema junk dealers, cinema gout sufferers, cinema speculators' as 'poisoning the masses'. In 1924 VAPPist Albert Syrkin characterized the majority of Soviet films as 'hastily-made nonsense, petty-bourgeois, philistine, narrow-minded, loosely draped in red rags'. Narkompros's attacks were usually more circumspect and avoided arousing the curiosity of viewers through such titillating descriptions. Osip Beskin, the editor of *Soviet Cinema*, wrote in 1926 that while a limited entertainment cinema might be permitted, 'we oppose the evaluation of cinema as art'.[11]

I am not, of course, seriously trying to argue that Nicholas II and Albert Syrkin held identical views about cinema. The early Soviet pedagogues and the 'proletarian' artists, unlike Nicholas II, did believe that 'popular' art (art for the masses) was to be encouraged. But they sought, with misplaced idealism and phenomenal energy, to *transform* 'popular cinema' from pictures 'pandering' to the lowest common denominator (through a combination of action and sentiment) into an agent of social, political, and cultural enlightenment.[12]

These cinema revolutionaries faced formidable obstacles. At the end of the Civil War the Soviet film industry, like all sectors of the economy, was in a state of collapse. Twelve feature films were produced in 1921; only sixteen the following year.[13] To rectify this deplorable situation, the Council of People's Commissars authorized the creation of a central cinema enterprise, Goskino, at the end of 1922, but for several reasons (the most important of which were lack of money and leadership) Goskino was never able to turn the situation around.[14]

In the meantime, foreign films dominated the country's decrepit movie theatres, attracting enormous audiences for German films in the early 1920s, for American pictures later.[15] Directors who had been active in Russian cinema began making films again, films which were 'Sovietized' versions of their former work. As early as 1925, it was obvious that these directors (Iakov Protazanov, Cheslav Sabinsky, Petr Chardynin, Konstantin Eggert, Vladimir Gardin, Aleksandr Ivanovsky, Iurii Tarich, and Iurii Zheliabuzhsky) constituted a formidable 'bourgeois front'; their works continued to enjoy great success with the movie-going public.

By late 1924, the ideologues of cultural enlightenment knew that if they did not take action soon, the battle for the cinema audience would be lost. Glavpolitprosvet established a Cinema Section specifically for the purpose of agitating for a cinema designed for the masses, which it defined as peasants rather than proletarians.[16] Goskino, which had no friends and many enemies in the cinema community, was abolished and replaced by a reorganized state film trust, Sovkino. Gifted young directors like Dziga Vertov, Sergei Eisenstein and Lev Kuleshov had made their first pictures, so Soviet cinema no longer had to rely on 'leftovers' from the old regime. In short, conditions seemed right at the end of 1924 for an ideological *coup d'état* in cinema, but it took four long and bitter years before the 'cultural revolution' actually occurred.

Economic (and to a certain extent, political) factors were important impediments to the enlighteners in Glavpolitprosvet, but as crucial in understanding why they stumbled initially is the fact that two articulate and persuasive supporters of the entertainment film emerged to do battle. One was Ilya Trainin, in his capacity as an administrator of the state film trust, Sovkino. The other was Anatolii Lunacharsky, Commissar of Enlightenment, whose attitudes about film and activities on the cinema front put him at odds with members of his own Commissariat.

Trainin's first article on cinema appeared in *Cinema Week* in November 1924. While this essay contrasted sharply with *Cinema Week*'s shrilly 'revolutionary' tenor, it proved to be typical of Trainin's views on film. He discussed the reasons for the success of 'bourgeois' films with viewers, singling out their contemporaneity and human interest. He forthrightly stated that if Soviet cinema was ever to stem the tidal wave of foreign films, Soviet directors would need to make full length entertainment films – and stressed the importance of entertainment value in ensuring a film's success with the public.[17]

The following month *Cinema Week* published one of Lunacharsky's most important articles on cinema, misleadingly titled 'Revolutionary Ideology and Cinema' (Revoliutsionnaia ideologiia i kino). Although Lunacharsky employed revolutionary rhetoric much more liberally than did Trainin, his message was essentially the same and marked a dramatic change from an earlier position on film. (In 1919 Lunacharsky had written in *Cinema* (Kinematograf) that 'the main task of cinema in both its scientific and feature divisions is that of propaganda'.[18]) Though, of course, 'celebration of bourgeois virtues . . . depravity and crime' could never be permitted, Lunacharsky now counselled avoiding 'narrow propaganda', writing that 'our [films] must be no less fascinating and no less entertaining than the bourgeois'.[19]

Anatolii Lunacharsky (1875–1933), one of the best known figures in early Soviet culture, needs no introduction. Yet despite the appearance in 1965 of the documentary collection *Lunacharsky on Cinema* (Lunacharskii o kino), little attention has been paid his role in cinema. Given all that *has* been written about this Bolshevik man of letters, it seems the part he played in cinema was in keeping with his character.[20] Lunacharsky's interest in film, no doubt encouraged by his marriage to actress Nataliia Rozenel, was apparently as genuine as his interest in the other arts. He wrote his first screenplay, *Overcrowding* (Uplotnenie, Aleksandr Panteleev) in 1918. A number of popular films of the 1920s were either based on Lunacharsky's plays or on screenplays the Commissar had written.[21] He appeared in several films playing himself with boyish enthusiasm; the most charming example was his 'role' in the cartoon *Tip Top in Moscow* (Tip Top v Moskve, 1928, A. Ivanov), where he can be seen with the animated character 'Tip Top'.[22] Lunacharsky also wrote an interesting and well-informed book, *Cinema in the West and at Home* (Kino na zapade i u nas), and numerous articles about film.[23]

Ilya Trainin (1887–1949) is a figure of an entirely different order of magnitude than Lunacharsky. Little is known about Trainin, and his role in Soviet culture was confined to the period 1924–30. An Old Bolshevik who joined the party in 1904, Trainin's first recorded jobs in the new government were minor posts in the Commissariat of Nationalities. In 1924 he joined Narkompros as a deputy director of the publications censorship department. That same year he became the chair of the Main Committee on Repertory (Glavrepertkom), which was responsible for film censorship, and he held this key position until 1930. Concurrently he was a member of the board of directors of Sovkino, the state film trust.[24] In these two positions he was uniquely placed to influence the direction of Soviet cinema – but not as a mere bureaucrat.

It happened that Trainin and Lunacharsky had something in common in addition to their longtime party membership. Like Lunacharsky, Trainin had been an 'oppositionist', a member of the *Vpered* deviation, which flourished before World War I. Like Lunacharsky, Trainin's cinematic policies were very much in the *Vpered*ist tradition of encouraging cultural change by non-authoritarian means.[25]

It is not as easy to single out the entertainment film's chief opponents as it is to identify its leading supporters because Glavpolitprosvet seemed to have had an endless supply of reinforcements. It was immediately obvious, however, that Glavpolitprosvet intended to go on the offensive against Trainin's and Lunacharsky's position on entertainment cinema. At the beginning of 1925, Glavpolitprosvet unveiled *Soviet Cinema*, the 'thick journal' of all Soviet film publications, with issues running 80–100 pages. *Soviet Cinema* was long, earnest, and often terribly dull, although occasionally a good piece of film criticism would appear. A glance at the contents of the first four issues reveals themes that would be repeated over and over again. The objects of Glavpolitprosvet's scorn were established early: foreign movies, film critics, the Association of Revolutionary Cinematography (ARK), and Sovkino.[26] Positive concerns included lengthy discussions of practical problems (such as the production of projectors or film stock), studio finances, ODSK, film education, and the 'right' kinds of films (on health, or other edifying subjects).[27]

Soviet Cinema's main topic, however, was the 'cinefication' (*kinofikatsiia*) of the countryside campaign; officially announced in 1924, it was discussed in every issue at great length.[28] The cinefication campaign embodied a number of the agenda items mentioned above. More money and better equipment were needed to create a viable rural film culture. An ideologically acceptable repertory for the countryside would consist of educational films (*kulturfil'my*), newsreels, and documentaries; entertainment feature films, whether of foreign or domestic origin, were condemned as 'bourgeois'.[29] Every failure of the cinefication campaign, real or imagined, was attributed indirectly, and later directly, to one 'wrecker' – Sovkino.

Trainin and Lunacharsky responded to initial sallies cautiously. Lunacharsky, for example, contributed a circumspect piece to the first issue of *Soviet Cinema* which did not press the cause of the entertainment film to any particular degree. Although he insisted that cinema had to be considered an art, he extolled its virtues as a vehicle for popularizing science.[30] Trainin also contributed to this issue, an uncharacteristically accommodating discussion of the present state of cinema affairs, which he characterized as 'chaotic'. Trainin promised to improve the distribution network, especially in the countryside; reduce the importation of foreign films; and to raise standards of film criticism, all of which were commensurate with Glavpolitprosvet's concerns.[31]

The 'real' Trainin soon reemerged; it is not clear why he abandoned a conciliatory route in favour of engaging the enlighteners head on. In a two-part article for *Soviet Cinema* entitled 'The Soviet Film and the Viewer' (Sovetskii fil'm i zritel'), Trainin developed his own programme for the salvation of Soviet cinema. Trainin declared that Soviet films had to compete with foreign films technically in order to win over the viewer, and in the context of the article, 'technical' serves as a code word for 'entertaining'.

The way he illustrated his argument is worth noting, because it demonstrates the subtle hostility to the avant-garde for which Sovkino was noted. He compared Eisenstein's debut feature *Strike* (Stachka, 1925), a film which he characterized as 'ours', to Ivanovsky's *Stepan Khalturin* (1925), a costume drama which Trainin accurately labelled 'old-fashioned'. Yet which film had enjoyed greater popular success – the 'truly Soviet' *Strike* or the 'pseudo-revolutionary' *Stepan Khalturin*? *Stepan Khalturin* made twice as much money as *Strike*, and Trainin believed it was because the supposedly 'old-fashioned' picture had a hero and was not 'dogmatic'. In the second part of the article, Trainin went on to attack overemphasis on *form*, singling out Kuleshov as another example of a Soviet filmmaker who did not understand that films without developed narratives would not attract viewers.[32]

Trainin grew bolder. In a speech to the Moscow Art Workers' Union (Rabis), he characterized Soviet films this way:

From agitfilms, they [viewers] expect pretentious films in which the agitational side predominates, in which numerous intertitles abound, often very revolutionary, but at the same time very boring. This 'revolutionary' zeal often drives them back to foreign 'art' pictures, and so in this fashion, the whole point of such agitfilms is lost. We need to begin a struggle for a really artistic film, in which *its own action and entertainment* would be agitational [emphasis added].[33]

Poverty was a critical factor in the poor quality of most Soviet films, as Trainin freely admitted. The Goskino studio had enough capital to make about ten ordinary films (budgeting 50,000 rubles per film). But 50,000 ruble films could not compete with the lavish foreign productions, and so Trainin proposed several rather radical solutions: solicit foreign investment, develop joint ventures, and make a few big-budget films that could be sold on the international market.[34] He ended piously with a few words about Soviet cinema as a 'weapon of culture', but he had thrown down the gauntlet.[35]

Trainin was not the first person to argue against simplistic (or naive) emphasis on revolutionary content in Soviet films. Aleksandr Voznesensky, a pre-revolutionary scenarist, had written a year earlier in *The Art of the Screen* (Iskusstvo ekrana) that 'man' (not ideas) had to be the main focus of any successful screenplay. Propaganda would not win over the viewer unless the ideas were presented 'like sugar in tea', that is, far more subtly than they had been to date.[36]

Trainin was, however, the first person to be in a position to *do* anything about it, and from 1925 to the beginning of 1928, Soviet cinema *was* transformed – in a way that seemed to mock everything the revolution stood for. The new Soviet film culture was directed toward the middle classes in the major urban centres – NEPmen, *apparatchiki*, 'specialists', and their families. The movie palaces revived and featured buffets, orchestras or jazz bands, souvenir stands – and high ticket prices. Working class viewers sat in the rafters of the commercial theatres or saw their movies in clubs, after the first run.[37]

In terms of sheer volume, importation of foreign films reached its peak in 1925 and dropped steadily thereafter, but the popularity of foreign films cannot be measured by reference to numbers alone. Sovkino imported the latest hits with less delay than earlier, and their popularity was unabated, even though Soviet cinema had entered its fabled Golden Age. Foreign films played the premier theatres, were heavily advertised (even in *Pravda* and *Izvestiia*) and enjoyed runs of at least three months, compared to two or three weeks for a typical Soviet production. *Thief of Baghdad* was probably the biggest box office hit of the 1920s and ran for over a year at one of Moscow's largest theatres, the Malaia Dmitrovka.[38]

Two new popular publications – *Cinema* (Kino) and *Soviet Screen* (Sovetskii ekran) – featured many articles on foreign films and their stars, publicity photos, and letters to the editors from fans waxing enthusiastic about Doug, Mary, Charlie, Conrad (Veidt), and Harry (Piel). Teakinopechat, a state-owned publishing company, churned out innumerable copies of paperback biographies of foreign stars.[39] Yet more evidence of the people's will can be seen in the frenzy with which the masses greeted Douglas Fairbanks and Mary Pickford during their July 1926 visit to Moscow.[40]

Trainin kept his promise that Sovkino would fund big budget films, and he was right that such films would generate good box office returns both at home and abroad.[41] Domestic films which were demonstrable box office successes were typically films on the 'Western' model; if they were to succeed abroad, they also had to be 'exotic'. One of the most famous examples was the lurid melodrama *The Bear's Wedding* (Medvezh'ia svad'ba, 1926, Konstantin Eggert), and the author of the screenplay for this sensational film was none other than Commissar Anatolii Lunacharsky (in collaboration with Georgii Grebner, a professional scenarist). In this film a mad count, transformed into a 'bear', goes on violent rampages. During one of these fits, he savagely murders his bride in their wedding bed. The film was enormously expensive, but also enormously successful.[42]

Trainin's hopes for foreign investments also bore some fruit. The Mezhrabpom studio, which had absorbed the pre-revolutionary studio Rus and was funded by the International Worker's Relief, was known for its commercialism. Although it produced some movies which were ideologically impeccable, like Vsevolod Pudovkin's *Mother* (Mat', 1926), it also made *The Bear's Wedding* and others like it.[43] The left-wing German company, Prometheusfilm, sponsored a few joint productions, which were mostly controversial. *The Salamander* (Salamandra, 1928, Grigorii Roshal), a fictionalized account of the Kammerer scandal, was believed to be too explicit in its depiction of bourgeois decadence.[44] (The script of this troubled film, like *The Bear's Wedding*, was co-authored by Lunacharsky and Grebner.)

As far as Trainin was concerned, these policies and the resultant movies were absolutely necessary to ensure the survival of Soviet cinema. The American cinematic juggernaut had taken over the world market after the Great War, threatening the existence of virtually all national cinemas. All Soviet audience surveys confirmed the external evidence – Soviet viewers, including proletarians, strongly preferred foreign films or their domestic equivalents, i.e. movies that were action-packed and entertaining.[45]

How could Glavpolitprosvet's dour policies compete with a film culture like this? Films about the 'rationalization of production and industrialization', 'mechanization and collectivization', the 'struggle with arson', or the 'struggle to establish a Soviet community' simply could not wean audiences away from *Robin Hood*.[46] Glavpolitprosvet's unpalatable recipes for rural cinema became the butt of jokes in the popular film press, and directors with any film sense avoided such uncinematic assignments.[47]

The situation by 1926 was obviously rather desperate for the enlighteners, and it is at this point that Aleksandr Katsigras and Vladimir Meshcheriakov took charge. Katsigras, the mainstay of the cinefication campaign, was a minor Narkompros functionary, holding posts in Glavpolitprosvet and later in Narkompros's Art and Literature section. Meshcheriakov, on the other hand, was a personage. An Old Bolshevik like his nemeses Lunacharsky and Trainin, Meshcheriakov was a member of the Narkompros Presidium and Glavpolitprosvet's chief; in 1929 he was elected to the party's Central Committee.[48] Although Meshcheriakov wrote less frequently than did Katsigras, it was clear who was in charge – and that Meshcheriakov was no *Vpered*-ist. He would lead the horse to water *and* make him drink.

Glavpolitprosvet refused to give up on its plans to revolutionize the repertory, and in 1926 and 1927, *Soviet Cinema* continued to promote the *kulturfil'm* and the documentary and newsreel. Yet we see changes in tactics that could be interpreted as a result of the Cinema Section's growing pragmatism – or as a skilful feint. Even a die-hard enlightener like Katsigras admitted, for example, that some Soviet-made feature films would have to be approved for rural screenings, and suggested pictures that were fairly 'bourgeois' by anyone's standards, *Cross and Mauser* (Krest i mauzer, 1925, Vladimir Gardin), *The Station Master* (Kollezhskii registrator, 1925, Iurii Zheliabuzhsky), *Palace and Fortress* (Dvorets i krepost', 1924, Aleksandr Ivanovsky), and the picture Trainin had admired for its commercial success, Ivanovsky's *Stepan Khalturin*.[49] (But *The Bear's Wedding* was strictly forbidden, along with foreign films which featured 'sadism, naked lewdness [and] depravity.')[50]

Glavpolitprosvet's Cinema Section also stopped pretending that the masses would automatically go to see *kulturfil'my* and advised the development of extensive promotional campaigns and a special theatre network.[51] *Soviet Cinema* consequently began to focus more attention on proselytizing *kulturfil'my* in the schools on the sound principle that children's tastes were still in the formative stage and could therefore be more easily manipulated than those of adult audiences.[52]

Vladimir Meshcheriakov was never content with half-measures, and in 1926 he launched an offensive specifically directed against Sovkino. The tactics Meshcheriakov and his lieutenants Katsigras and M. S. Veremienko adopted in the polemical pamphlet *Cinema Ulcer* (Kinoiazva) were contradictory, but effective. Meshcheriakov accused Sovkino over and over of being *too* commercial-minded, while Katsigras and Veremienko claimed that Sovkino was not sufficiently aware of the business opportunities awaiting it in the country. Meshcheriakov charged Sovkino with being a 'reactionary' force in the hinterlands, of ignoring the party's cultural policies, of being politically illiterate, and of sabotaging Glavpolitprosvet's cinefication efforts. According to Meshcheriakov, Sovkino's shortsighted and superficial commercialism, exemplified by their alleged slogan, 'To the pocket!' had led to a policy which 'harms the Republic [RFSFR]'s cinema affairs and should be radically changed'.[53]

Whether these charges are true matters little. What is important is that they could not go unanswered, and drew unwelcome attention to Sovkino. Sovkino's administrators had to devote more and more time compiling statistics about their rural distribution networks and preparing rebuttals to such accusations.

Encouraged by their success, Glavpolitprosvet unveiled another campaign against Sovkino at the beginning of 1927. Its subtlety contrasted with the crudeness of the polemics in *Cinema Ulcer*; Sovkino's name was not even mentioned. Glavpolitprosvet called for control over movie theatres and censorship to be transferred to a department under its aegis, the Section on People's Education (ONO). Such a move would effectively have granted Glavpolitprosvet control over repertory and distribution – and therefore over cinema.[54]

The conflict between Glavpolitprosvet and Sovkino soon spilled over into the pages of other film journals and into the cultural community as a whole. Sovkino, like Goskino before it, had few friends. Young directors felt they were not getting the support they needed as they watched the big money going to middle-aged filmmakers who in general had made their names before the revolution. Indeed, many thoughtful observers of the film scene were alarmed at the box office success of a blatantly 'bourgeois' film like *The Bear's Wedding* and by the ample evidence of the audience's fanatic devotion to Western movie stars.[55] In 1927, Sovkino added to the furor by releasing two colossally expensive films, *The Decembrists* (Aleksandr Ivanovsky) and *The Poet and the*

Tsar (Vladimir Gardin and Evgenii Cherviakov), both of which were judged to be horrifying affronts to good taste, the former to the revolutionary tradition, and the latter, to Pushkin.[56]

Poet Vladimir Mayakovsky, still a formidable spokesman for the avant-garde, joined the anti-Sovkino bandwagon. In February 1927 he attacked Sovkino in *New Left* (Novyi lef) for failing to approve a screenplay he had written, and he singled out Trainin, Efremov, and Shvedchikov in his denunciation.[57] Mayakovsky also attended a conference in the autumn of 1927 organized by the Society of Friends of Soviet Cinema (ODSK) and the Komsomol, the ostensible purpose of which was to discuss the future of Soviet cinema. Since cinema's future was intimately connected with Sovkino's fate, any such discussion had to focus on Sovkino, and again the film trust came under scathing attack. When Mayakovsky was charged with seeking to abolish commercial moviemaking, his response was both disingenuous and unequivocal:

Rubbish . . . We're merely saying that the masses who pay to see the films are not the upper stratum of NEP or the more or less well-to-do strata, but the many tens of millions of the masses [. . .] And however much you try, however much profit you make from the public by catering [to] their tastes, you are doing something foul and nasty.[58]

Trainin, P. A. Bliakhin and M. P. Efremov all spoke at this meeting, but they were often interrupted. Many of the speeches attacking them were punctuated with approving laughter and applause. Meshcheriakov's condemnations struck the conferees as particularly witty, especially when he announced that 'the chauffeur [Sovkino] is not taking us where we want to go'.[59] Given the unsavoury atmosphere, it is not surprising that the *Sovkinovtsy* were on the defensive. Bliakhin was far too willing to concede error, and he and Efremov attempted to use figures to 'prove' that Sovkino *had* contributed to dramatic growth in the distribution network in less than three years. Only Trainin really spoke to the point. Arguing that 'contemporaneity' for all films was an unreasonable demand, he added defiantly: 'When they say: here's a worker's film and there's a peasant's film . . . well, I really don't much understand this. A film is either good – or it's bad.'[60]

A few more months remained before the all-important All-Union Conference on Cinema Affairs, scheduled for March 1928, but the stage was set. Efremov was badly shaken, if his abject apology in *Cinema* is any indication. He declared that Sovkino's new slogan was: '100 per cent ideology, 100 per cent entertainment, 100 per cent commerce.'[61] Trainin, however, was uncowed. In *Cinema on the Cultural Front* (Kino na kul'turnom fronte) he made his last stand. Although he adopted the language of the day, his ideas on film remained unchanged. He argued vigorously against the utilitarian aesthetics of his opponents, and pointed out that workers and peasants, no less than the 'petty-bourgeoisie', went to the movies to be entertained.[62] Offering them diverse genres and subject matter was truly serving the people's needs, not 'pandering'. Trainin encouraged adventures and domestic melodramas, in particular.[63] Furthermore, Trainin argued, such a cinema also served the interests of state and party, because 'a dry and conventional approach to the problems of life has frequently turned the viewer (as in the case of the reader) to things and ideas alien to us'.[64]

Anatolii Lunacharsky had more or less stayed on the sidelines while the verbal sparring was going on, but he had made very strong cinematic statements through his screenplays for *The Bear's Wedding* and *Poison* (Iad), a film about a young man who succumbs to the solicitations of a vamp and joins a spy ring. Lunacharsky continued to insist that entertainment could and should be distinct from the 'abominable commercial cinema', because 'a consciously propagandizing cinema that wants to teach is like someone with their legs in irons'. He continued:

One thing is true, namely that [the Soviet public] loves brilliance, a variety of experiences, romance, beauty, rapid actions, an interesting plot, and there is nothing to fear in that.

When the greater and lesser pedants of Soviet cinema start to teach us grandiloquently that all this is essentially trash, and that we should pass as quickly as possible to films without a plot and without a hero, without eroticism, etc., they will be serving us very badly.[65]

In his last major statement on cinema, *Cinema in the West and at Home*, Lunacharsky retreated to a certain extent, which is quite understandable considering the way the 'pedants' had greeted *The Bear's Wedding* and *Poison*.[66] He now admitted that various problems existed regarding the kinds of foreign films imported, the films Glavrepertkom approved and disapproved, the supply of movies for workers' clubs, and so forth. He insisted none the less that making pictures with human interest was essential in order to retain audience support for Soviet cinema; any propaganda content in films must be 'artistic'. And Lunacharsky's admonition to remember that the urban audience was cinema's chief constituency seemed to be directed at his foes in Glavpolitprosvet.[67]

The Party Conference on Cinema Affairs began on 15 March 1928. Lunacharsky, who was conspicuously absent, was one of the main targets, and the conference was as much an indictment of Narkompros and its Commissar as it was of Sovkino and the *Sovkinovtsy*. The rift between Lunacharsky and his deputy Meshcheriakov was out in the

open. Although Meshcheriakov did not give a keynote address, this was
his week of triumph. He spoke in his usual sarcastic fashion of the two
Lunacharskys – the one who passed resolutions condemning Sovkino
when he was in the sanctuary of Narkompros, and the one who dared do
the same in public, presumably because his record as a scenarist would
not stand up to scrutiny. Most speakers, great and small, supported
Meshcheriakov's views on cinema. The *Sovkinovtsy*, even Trainin, had
been subdued.[68]

Although Sovkino's enemies could not immediately claim victory, it
was only a matter of time. The course of Soviet cinema began to change
quickly and dramatically, as the Cultural Revolution engulfed it. The
film press was the first to suffer. *Soviet Cinema* and ARK's journal
Cinema Front (Kino-front) had been shut down before the party conference, and so a significantly reduced film press began a self-criticism
campaign. *Cinema* began to treat movies as secondary to the goals of the
First Five Year Plan, and *Soviet Screen* did the same following the
suicide of its editor, V.P. Uspensky, in spring 1929. (*Soviet Screen* was
'reorganized' as *Cinema and Life* [Kino i zhizn'] the following year.)
The state publishing enterprise Teakinopechat' was purged in 1930, and
published very little during the Cultural Revolution; the last books
about foreign movie stars appeared in 1929.[69]

Continued importation of foreign films was obviously incompatible
with the economic demands of the First Five Year Plan as well as with
the ideological credo of the Cultural Revolution. Although a few foreign films were imported in the 1930s, for all practical purposes importation ended in 1931.[70] (But it took a while to purge all foreign films
from film libraries, and certainly for these movies to fade from public
memory.)[71]

Because of the many films that were already in production, the impact
of the Conference and the Cultural Revolution on domestic filmmaking
was slightly delayed. The year 1928 was in fact the peak year of Soviet
film production, and from 1928 to 1930 a number of interesting films
appeared made by both the 'bourgeois' and the avant-garde directors
targeted by the Cultural Revolution.[72] By 1930, however, the
enlighteners enjoyed uncontested supremacy.

Lunacharsky and several of his supporters had resigned from
Narkompros the year before.[73] Sovkino was abolished in spring 1930,
and under the aegis of the new trust, Soiuzkino, cinema became a
weapon in the class struggle. Soiuzkino promised to focus production on
the impossible: 'the high quality-art-mass film which satisfies the basic
demands of the proletarian viewer'.[74] Feature film production began to
plummet, from 148 films in 1928 to 35 in 1933, and films became over-

whelmingly 'contemporary', addressing the problems of the day (i.e. 'wreckers' and tractors).[75]

Yet as this catastrophic decline in production indicates, the victory for the enlighteners was a pyrrhic one. The first sign that this would be so – the liquidation of *Soviet Cinema* in 1928 – came *before* the Party Conference on Cinema Affairs. From 1929 to 1931, cinema culture was effectively obliterated as well. It took several decades for Soviet cinema to recover fully from the disastrous effects of the Cultural Revolution.

The 'entertainment or enlightenment' debate in cinema illustrates that the elitism and authoritarianism of Bolshevik political culture were widespread and deep-rooted in early Soviet society.[76] Hostility toward pluralism was not confined to the specifically political arena, and in the cultural sphere it took the guise of a bias against entertainment reinforced by the utilitarian aesthetics which were part of the Russian cultural tradition. This debate shows us that in a relatively relaxed period of Soviet cultural history (well before the Cultural Revolution), even lowly popular culture had to be 'directed'.

The debate is significant for a number of other reasons as well. It serves as a vehicle for exploring the impact on Soviet popular culture of the economic competition between haves and have-nots. Sovkino gave, and the blessed received. That the 'blessed' appeared to be representatives of the old order only exacerbated class antagonisms.

It also demonstrates that political tensions between 'Right' and 'Left' were operating at fairly low institutional levels in the 1920s. Vladimir Meshcheriakov can easily be seen as a representative of the party's left-wing, that is, an opponent of NEP. Ilya Trainin, on the other hand, was a representative of the party's right-wing, a supposition supported by the frequency with which he quotes Bukharin in *Cinema on the Cultural Front*.[77] These tensions – political, economic, intellectual – exploded into an interorganizational conflict between Glavpolitprosvet and Sovkino that led to the eventual destruction of both.

Did either party represent the interests of the masses? Glavpolitprosvet cinema activists sincerely believed that they were the people's advocates. Yet they never demonstrated much inclination to find out what the 'people' really wanted, and they shied away from the evidence at hand. Despite Glavpolitprosvet's pragmatic reasons for focusing on the cinefication of the countryside, it is still curious how little the mainstay of the revolution – namely, the proletariat – figured in their plans to bring movies to the 'masses'.

Sovkino was a business, not a bureaucracy, and the *Sovkinovtsy*, like most businessmen, *were* interested in people – if they had the wherewithal to buy tickets for the movies. And so despite its truly

56   *Denise Youngblood*

impressive successes in rebuilding the Soviet film industry, Sovkino was never really interested in the class that formed the vast majority of the population, the peasantry. In its own way, Sovkino was as far removed from Soviet reality as Glavpolitprosvet.

At the beginning of 1935, another major film conference was held in the USSR, the All-Union Creative Conference on Cinematographic Affairs. Surveying the ruins of a once flourishing cinema culture, director Sergei Iutkevich remarked:

the fundamental functions of cinematography are fighting, political functions. From them comes the struggle for the viewer, without whom cinematography cannot exist.
But what happened? What happened was that we lost the viewer.[78]

Notes

The research for, and writing of, this article was supported in part by grants from the American Council of Learned Societies, the International Research & Exchanges Board, the National Endowment for the Humanities, and the University of Vermont. Its presentation at the Congress was made possible by a grant from the ACLS, with funds from the NEH and the John D. & Catherine T. MacArthur Foundation. I wish to express my appreciation to William Chase for running my 'movie moguls' through the Soviet Data Bank at the University of Pittsburgh, and to Richard Taylor and Peter Kenez for their helpful comments on an earlier version.

1. Quoted by Khrisanf Khersonsky, 'Khochu snimat'sia', *Kino-front*, 1927, no. 5, pp. 4–7. The article is about 'cinema psychosis' and how to combat it.
2. As rural cinema workers soon found out, some preparation of the uninitiated (and illiterate) peasantry was necessary, but far less than teaching them to read. See, e.g., A. Katsigras, 'Voprosy derevenskoi kino-raboty', *Sovetskoe kino*, 1925, no. 6, pp. 35–6, and 'Opyty fiksatsii zritel'skikh interesov', in I.N. Bursak, ed., *Kino* (Moscow, 1925), pp. 50–1.
3. Lunacharsky reported his conversation with Lenin in G.M. Boltiansky, *Lenin i kino* (Moscow, 1925); it has been translated in Richard Taylor and Ian Christie, eds., *The Film Factory: Russian and Soviet Cinema in Documents, 1896–1939*, trans. Richard Taylor (Cambridge MA, 1988), pp. 56–7. (An earlier, unattributed reference to the aphorism appears in 'Pochti tezisy', *Proletkino*, 1925, no. 1/2, pp. 3–4, translated in Taylor and Christie, eds., *Film Factory*, p. 84.) Lenin first wrote about cinema in *Pravda*, 26 May 1913; see A.M. Gak, ed., *Samoe vazhnoe iz vsekh iskusstv: Lenin o kino* (Moscow, 1973), p. 13.
4. *Kinematograf: Sbornik statei* (Moscow, 1919), pp. 3–4. For a translation of Lunacharsky's contribution to the volume, see Taylor and Christie, eds.,

Film Factory, pp. 47–9. (The first Soviet film publication appears to have been the repertory list *Kino-biulleten'* [Moscow, 1918].)

5. Richard Taylor has written about this in detail; see, for example, *The Politics of the Soviet Cinema, 1917–1929* (Cambridge, 1979), ch. 3.

6. And who are the 'people'? For the purposes of this article, they are ordinary movie-goers, whose jobs are not related to the film industry. Because film was essentially an urban phenomenon in the 1920s and the available viewer studies concentrated on analyzing the city viewer, peasants will be excluded from such generalizations, unless specifically noted. The ideological implications of this exclusion will be discussed below.

7. In real life, not surprisingly, these factions were far from discrete.

8. Richard Taylor discusses the 'art or entertainment' debate in '*The Kiss of Mary Pickford*: ideology and popular culture in Soviet cinema', in Anna Lawton, ed., *The Red Screen: Art, Politics, & Society in Soviet Cinema* (New York, 1991).

9. Patrick Brantlinger, *Bread and Circuses: Theories of Mass Culture as Social Decay* (Ithaca NY, 1983).

10. Quoted (without source) in Jay Leyda, *Kino: A History of the Russian and Soviet Cinema* (London, 1960; rpt. New York, 1973), p. 69. In *The Politics of the Soviet Cinema*, p. 158 n. 1, Taylor gives the source as I.S. Zil'bershtein, 'Nikolai II o kino', *Sovetskii ekran*, 12 April 1927, p. 10.

11. Editorial, *Kino-fot*, 1922, no. 4, p. 1; Albert Syrkin, 'Mezhdu tekhniki i ideologiei (O kino-poputchikakh i partiinom rukovodstve)', *Kino-nedelia*, 1924, no. 37, p. 1; Osip Beskin, 'Mesto kino', *Sovetskoe kino*, 1926, no. 1, p. 1. Note the front page placement for each of these articles.

12. Popular cinema follows the conventions of narrative realism and combines several of the following ingredients: action (especially violence), heroes and villains (preferably good-looking), love and romance, humour, a happy ending (though in melodrama, the tragic ending can be very satisfying).

13. Denise J. Youngblood, *Soviet Cinema in the Silent Era, 1918–1935* (Ann Arbor MI, 1985; rpt. Austin TX, 1991), appendix 1.

14. See ibid., ch. 2 for a fuller discussion of these problems.

15. For a general discussion of the popularity of foreign films, see Vance Kepley, Jr. and Betty Kepley, 'Foreign films on Soviet screens', *Quarterly Review of Film Studies*, vol. 4, no. 4 (fall 1979), pp. 429–42. The Kepleys have calculated that at least 278 French, German, and American films were imported in 1923; at least 366 in 1924, amounting to over 80 per cent of films shown. (Their calculations were based on analysis of data in E. Kartseva, 'Amerikanskie nemye fil'my v sovetskom prokate', *Kino i vremia*, no. 1 (1960), pp. 193–325; Iu. Greiding, 'Frantsuzkie nemye fil'my v sovetskom prokate', *Kino i vremia*, no. 4 (1965), pp. 348–79; N. Egorova, 'Nemetskie nemye fil'my v sovetskom prokate', *Kino i vremia*, no. 4 (1965), pp. 380–476.)

In 'Americanitis', Lev Kuleshov identified the special appeal of American films as their 'dynamism'. See 'Amerikanshchina', *Kino-fot*, 1922, no. 1, pp. 14–15 (translated in Taylor and Christie, eds., *Film Factory*, pp. 72–3, and in Ronald Levaco, ed., *Kuleshov on Film: Writings of Lev Kuleshov* (Berkeley, 1974), pp. 127–30).

16. V. Meshcheriakov, 'Kino dlia derevni (Rabota kino-sektsii Glavpolit-prosveta)', in S. Syrtsov and A. Kurs, eds., *Sovetskoe kino na pod"eme* (Moscow, 1926), p. 98. Richard Taylor suggests that Glavpolitprosvet may have chosen to focus its efforts in the provinces because it faced no competition from Sovkino there.
17. I. Trainin, 'Puti kino', *Kino-nedelia*, 1924, no. 40–1, pp. 8–10.
18. Translated in Taylor and Christie, eds., *Film Factory*, p. 47.
19. 'Tezisy A. V. Lunacharskogo: Revoliutsionnaia ideologiia i kino', *Kino-nedelia*, 1924, no. 46, p. 11 (translated in Taylor and Christie, eds., *Film Factory*, p. 109).
20. Lunacharsky's most recent biographers – A. Elkin, *Lunacharskii* (Moscow, 1967), and Timothy Edward O'Connor, *The Politics of Soviet Culture: Anatolii Lunacharskii* (Ann Arbor MI, 1983) both ignore his film work entirely.
21. *Locksmith and Chancellor* (Slesar' i kantsler, 1923, Vladimir Gardin); *The Bear's Wedding* (Medvezh'ia svad'ba, 1926, Konstantin Eggert); *Poison* (Iad, 1927, Evgenii Ivanov-Barkov); *The Salamander* (Salamandra, 1928, Grigorii Roshal).
22. See the still in Youngblood, *Soviet Cinema*, p. 103.
23. A. V. Lunacharskiiy, *Kino na zapade i u nas* (n.p., 1928). Other writings have been collected in K. D. Muratova, comp., *Lunacharskii o kino: Stat'i, vyskazyvaniia, stsenarii, dokumenty* (Moscow, 1965). Also see the bibliography *A. V. Lunacharskii o literature i iskusstve: Bibliografcheskii ukazatel', 1902–1963* (Leningrad, 1964).
24. From 1931 to 1947, Trainin worked for the USSR Institute of Law; in the final two years of his life, he held a post at the Academy of Sciences. The third edition of the Soviet encyclopedia *Bol'shaia sovetskaia entsiklopediia* lists Trainin as a 'prominent jurist', with no professional activity before 1931. All other biographical information comes from the Soviet Data Bank project, University of Pittsburgh.
25. See O'Connor's discussion of Lunacharsky's role in the *Vpered* group and his relationship to Bogdanov: *Politics of Soviet Culture*, pp. 7–11.
26. From *Sovetskoe kino*, 1925: on foreign pictures: D. Liianov, 'Blizhe k massam', no. 1, pp. 37–8 and 'Ob upriamoi deistvitel'nosti i bolnykh nervakh', no. 2/3, pp. 18–22; on critics: A. Kurs, 'Kino-kritika v SSSR', no. 4/5, pp. 22–8; on ARK: N. Iakovlev, 'O levom rebiachestve v kino', no. 1, pp. 25–7; on Sovkino: A. Katsigras, 'Voprosy derevenskoi kino raboty', no. 6, pp. 34–8.
27. In *Sovetskoe kino*, 1925, see: P. A., 'Organizatsiia proizvodstva: kino-syr'e i apparatury v SSSR', no. 2/3, pp. 7–12; N. Shapovalenko, 'Ekonomicheskii analysis kino-seansa', no. 2/3, pp. 73–4; K. G., 'Obshchestvo druzei sovetskogo kino', no. 6, p. 59; Valentin Turkin, 'Sostoianie kino obrazovaniya v SSSR', no. 2, pp. 68–72; I. Strashun, 'O sanprosvetitel'nom fil'me', no. 1, pp. 20–2.
28. In *Sovetskoe kino*, 1925, see: A. Abrosimov, 'O prodvizhenii kino v derevne', no. 1, pp. 44–8; G. Lebedev, 'Kino-agropropaganda', no. 2/3, pp. 37–9; A. Katsigras, 'Voprosy kinofikatsii dereveni', no. 4/5, pp. 50–8.
29. For a more detailed discussion of the cinefication campaign, see Young-

blood, *Soviet Cinema*, *passim*, but esp. pp. 47–55, 115–17, and Peter Kenez, 'Peasants and movies', paper presented to the conference on NEP Society and Culture, Indiana University, 1986.

30. A. V. Lunacharsky, 'Mesto kino sredi drugikh iskusstv', *Sovetskoe kino*, 1925, no. 1, pp. 5–7.
31. I. Trainin, 'Na puti k vozrozhdeniiu', *Sovetskoe kino*, 1925, no. 1, pp. 8–14.
32. Trainin, 'Sovetskii fil'm i zritel'', *Sovetskoe kino*, 1925, no. 4/5, pp. 10–18, and no. 6, pp. 16–23. For a discussion of the popularity of *Stepan Khalturin* see Denise Youngblood, ' "History" on film: the historical melodrama in early Soviet cinema', *Historical Journal of Film, Radio and Television*, vol. 11, no. 2 (1991), pp. 173–84.
33. Trainin, *Kino-promyshlennost' i Sovkino: Po dokladu na 8-ii konferentsii moskovskogo gubrabisa, 1925* (Moscow, 1925), p. 16.
34. Ibid., pp. 13, 15–17. A variation of this programme is being put into effect in the USSR today.
35. Ibid., pp. 30–1.
36. Al. Voznesensky, *Iskusstvo ekrana* (Kiev, 1924), p. 103.
37. See, for example, in *Kino*, 1925: Klechatyi, 'Kino-teatry Moskomprom', no. 3, p. 4; 'Moskovskie kino-teatry', no. 4/5, p. 7; 'Po Moskovskim kino-teatram', no. 7, p. 4. On the clubs, see Vance Kepley, 'Cinema and everyday life: Soviet worker clubs of the 1920s', in Robert Sklar and Charles Husser, eds., *Resisting Images* (Philadelphia PA, 1990).
38. My estimate of 'typical' runs is based on studying advertisements to determine how long a film played at any one venue. For confirmation from the contemporary press, see, for example, N. Volkov, 'Sovetskie fil'my', *Izvestiia*, 18 November 1929. On *Thief of Baghdad*, see Kepley and Kepley, 'Foreign films', p. 437; a contemporary Soviet source claimed the run was only 108 days at the Malaia Dmitrovka, still quite impressive; see L., 'Prokat i teatry', *Kino-zhurnal ARK*, 1925, no. 9, p. 21.
39. My analysis of *Knigi o kino (1917–1960): Annotirovannaia bibliografiia* (Moscow, 1962) reveals that in 1926–7, fifty-five separate titles on foreign movie stars were printed in nearly 1.5 million copies, compared to eleven titles about Soviet stars (250,000 print run). This aspect of the cinema press is discussed in more detail in Youngblood, 'The fate of Soviet popular cinema during the Stalin revolution', *The Russian Review*, April 1991.
40. Newsreel coverage was incorporated in the feature film *Mary Pickford's Kiss* (Potselui Meri Pikford, 1927, Sergei Komarov). For a typical account from the press, see 'Ferbenks i Pikford v SSSR!', *Kino*, 1926, no. 30, pp. 1, 3.
41. Little has been written to date about the popular films of the 1920s. See, for example, Taylor, '*The Kiss of Mary Pickford* and Soviet cinema as popular culture: Or the extraordinary adventures of Mr. Nepman in the land of the silver screen', *Revolutionary Russia*, vol. 1, no. 1 (June 1988), pp. 35–6 and Youngblood, ' "History" on film' and 'The return of the native: Yakov Protazanov and Soviet cinema', in Taylor and Christie, eds., *Inside the Film Factory* (London, 1991). I have just finished a book on this subject, 'Movies for the Masses: Popular Cinema and Soviet Society in the 1920s'.
42. On *The Bear's Wedding*, see, for example, I. Falbert, 'Zolotaia seriia

60   *Denise Youngblood*

(*Medvezh'ia svad'ba*), *Kino*, 1926, no. 6, p. 2. This film was so wonderfully outrageous in the Soviet context that critics could not say enough nasty things about it. Viewers, however, loved it; see 'Slovo za chitatelem', *Kino*, no. 14, p. 5 for comments.

43. See Vance Kepley, Jr., 'The Workers' International Relief and the cinema of the Left, 1921–1935', *Cinema Journal*, vol. 23, no. 1 (Fall 1983), pp. 7–23; K. R. M. Short and Richard Taylor, 'Soviet cinema and the international menace', *Historical Journal of Film, Radio and Television*, vol. 6, no. 2 (1986), pp. 131–59.
44. See, for example, Lev Shatov, '*Salamandra*', *Kino*, 1928, no. 51.
45. The most thorough audience survey was A. V. Troianovsky and R. I. Egiazarov, *Izuchenie kino-zritelia: Po materialam issledovatel'skoi teatral'noi masterskoi* (Moscow, 1928).
46. M. Veremienko, 'O kulturfil'me', *Sovetskoe kino*, 1927, no. 4, pp. 14–15; G. Boltiansky, 'Kino v derevne', in Bursak, *Kino*, p. 41.
47. B. L., 'O fil'me dlia derevni', *Kino*, 1925, no. 13 is an especially witty satire.
48. Biographical data on Katsigras and Meshcheriakov comes from the Soviet Data Bank.
49. A. Katsigras, *Kino-rabota v derevne* ([Moscow], 1926), pp. 120–5.
50. Ibid., p. 49; V. P. Uspensky, *ODSK (Obshchestvo druzei sovetskogo kino)* (Moscow, 1926), p. 12.
51. G. Boltiansky, 'Teatr kulturfil'my', *Sovetskoe kino*, 1926, no. 1, pp. 2–3.
52. M. Veremienko, 'Politprosvet kino-rabota: Detskoe kino (Postanovka voprosa)', *Sovetskoe kino*, 1927, no. 2, pp. 18–19.
53. Meshcheriakov, 'Kak aktionernoe obshchestvo Sovkino obratilos' litsom k derevne', in V. Meshcheriakov, M. Veremienko and A. Katsigras, *Kino-iazva (Ob uprazhneniiakh Sovkino nad derevnei)* (Leningrad, 1926), pp. 3–14.
54. I. Piliver, 'K voprosu ob organizatsionno-khoziaistvennykh formakh kino-teatral'nogo dela v RSFSR', *Sovetskoe kino*, 1927, no. 2, pp. 10–11 and A. Katsigras, 'Ne pora li?', *Sovetskoe kino*, 1927, no. 2, p. 23.
55. See, for example, O. M. Brik, 'Kommercheskii raschet', *Kino*, 1926, no. 34, p. 3 and Alexander Dubrovsky, 'Soviet cinema in danger', in Taylor and Christie, eds., *Film Factory*, pp. 49–50.
56. See Youngblood, ' "History" on film'.
57. Vladimir Mayakovsky, 'Karaul!', *Novyi Lef*, 1927, no. 2, pp. 23–5 (translated in Taylor and Christie, eds., *Film Factory*, pp. 160–1).
58. Mayakovsky, 'Karaul', p. 173.
59. *Vokrug Sovkino: Stenogramma disputa organizovannogo TsK VLKM, TsODSK, i redaktsiei gazety Komsomol'skaia Pravda, 8–15 okt. 1926* (n.p., 1927), p. 25.
60. Ibid., p. 48.
61. M. Efremov, 'Nashi sredstva i zadachi', *Kino*, 1927, no. 47, p. 27.
62. I. P. Trainin, *Kino na kul'turnom fronte* ([Leningrad], 1928), pp. 35–6. Based on internal evidence, this appears to be a pre- rather than post-conference polemic.
63. Ibid., pp. 42–3.
64. Ibid., p. 45.

65. A. V. Lunacharsky, 'Cinema – the greatest of the arts', in Taylor and Christie, eds., *Film Factory*, pp. 155–6. This article originally appeared in *Komsomol'skaia pravda*.
66. On the reception of *Poison*, see Iakov Lev, 'Iad', *Kino*, 1927, no. 37, p. 3.
67. Lunacharsky, *Kino na zapade i u nas*, pp. 8–9, 30, 65.
68. B. S. Olkhovy, *Puti kino: Pervoe vsesoiuznoe partiinoe soveshchanie po kinematografii* ([Moscow], 1929). Meshcheriakov, whose speech appears pp. 99–104, also made frequent interjections from the floor.
69. Based on my analysis of *Knigi o kino*, only ten books on any aspect of cinema appeared 1930–2, a dramatic decline; see table 1 in Youngblood, 'Fate of Soviet popular cinema'. For a general discussion of the fate of the press, see Youngblood, *Soviet Cinema*, pp. 163–73.
70. Kepley and Kepley, 'Foreign films', p. 430.
71. The purging of foreign films from libraries began in 1928. See, for example, in *Kino*, 1928: 'Davno pora' and 'Soobshcheniia Glavrepertkoma', no. 20; 'Eshche odna seriia sniatykh kartin', no. 21; 'Udachnaia operatsiia: Ekran ochishchen ot khlama', no. 47.
72. See Peter Kenez, 'The cultural revolution in cinema', *Slavic Review*, vol. 47, no. 3 (Fall 1988), pp. 418–35, and Youngblood, *Soviet Cinema*, ch. 8.
73. Sheila Fitzpatrick, *Education and Social Mobility in the Soviet Union, 1921–1934* (Cambridge, 1979), pp. 133–5.
74. TsGALI, f. 2498, op. 1, ed. khr. 32, 'Biulleten' informbiuro Soiuzkino', p. 2.
75. Youngblood, *Soviet Cinema*, appendices 1–2.
76. For another angle on this issue, see Peter Kenez, *The Birth of the Propaganda State: Soviet Methods of Mass Mobilization, 1917–1929* (Cambridge, 1985).
77. See, for example, Trainin, *Kino na kul'turnom fronte*, p. 45.
78. S. Dinamov, ed., *Za bol'shoe kinoiskusstvo* (Moscow, 1935), p. 83. It must be added, however, that Iutkevich was no particular friend of the people; his remarks may well have been hollow utterances.

4 The centre and the periphery: cultural and social geography in the mass culture of the 1930s

James van Geldern

In the mid-1930s, Soviet society struck a balance that would carry it through the turmoil of the purges, the Great War and reconstruction. The coercive policies of the Cultural Revolution were replaced or supplemented by the use of inducements. Benefits were quickly apparent: education opened professional opportunities;[1] a stable countryside improved dietary standards; increased production and income encouraged consumerism.[2] A lightened mood swept the nation. Women wore make-up; young people revived ballroom dancing.[3] Life, as Stalin said, and Lebedev-Kumach's popular song repeated, had become better and happier.[4]

The stability gave some groups, for example, the new 'middle class', a measure of economic and social security that encouraged them to identify with the Soviet system. Yet it was not founded solely on a rational, if short-sighted, perception of personal advantage. Consumer shortages continued throughout the 1930s; agricultural and housing supplies stayed below 1928 levels.[5] The regime maintained its support during the purges, not only with prospering bureaucrats, but amongst those who fell. The feeling survived the Great War and the years after, when comfort and security were noticeably absent. The most permanent support of Stalinist society was a sense of pride and participation, shared by many social groups, that weathered the gravest tribulations. Society forged a new identity that integrated citizens excluded by the Cultural Revolution.

The nature of this new identity is best sought in mass culture, produced for the people by the state-controlled media. To consider the mass media a reflection of popular attitudes is, of course, problematic.[6] Popular taste was often overriden by political considerations. Discussion was one-sided, dominated by the state; popular participation was limited to the consumer option. Yet the mass media were part of the social fabric. By the mid-1930s, informal social discourse from unofficial gatherings to neighbourly gossip had been subverted. Bilateral forms of communication were cut off, creating a void. If there was a national consciousness, it was informed by the mass media. The party squelched the Cultural Revolution's sectarianism and created a culture shared by the whole country. Restrictions placed on the makers of culture actually opened it to most of the audience: mass culture spoke the language of most people, and used them as its heroes. It represented socialist society in ways that allowed for popular identification.

Media culture was not limited to its political messages which often invited scepticism. Beneath them were less formalized beliefs that help explain the social dynamic.[7] During the mid-1930s, power was centralized; society became increasingly hierarchical; citizens were deprived of many rights. Yet the dissatisfaction aroused by these measures coexisted with a sense of participation. The Cultural Revolution's aggressive political demands had excluded most people from the category of contributing citizens. The mid-1930s redrew the national identity to include them. This chapter will look at the mass media's cultural geography – its representation of relations between centre and periphery, and its ability to integrate parts of the country into the whole – for reflections of the social geography. The attitudes underlying them suggest one cause for popular identification with Soviet society in the mid-1930s: the consolidation of the centre did not exclude those outside, it aided their integration.

The centralization of power, a process observable throughout revolutionary history, was accelerated by the Great Leap. The mid-1930s saw a continuation of the trend, but in ways that often contradicted earlier policies. Investment was shifted from the periphery – the hero projects in the Urals and elsewhere – to the centre. Magnitogorsk found desperately needed funds moving back to Moscow,[8] and fewer projects outside the capital were initiated. Resources were diverted to non-productive construction in an overcrowded capital. Some projects were economically justified (the Moscow Metro, the Moscow–Volga Canal), but others were not: the Exhibition of Economic Achievements and several Lenin monuments among them. An economically sound project like the Moscow Metro mocked utility with its stations clad in semi-precious stone.

Rebuilding Moscow bolstered its symbolic role as centre of the country. It was the capital, focus of political and economic life, and the visible face of the Soviet Union, representing it to Soviet citizens and the world. The plan for a new Moscow had cultural implications beyond its economic consequences. It acted as a model for the state, where power radiated out from the centre to the periphery. The city was to be rebuilt from a medieval to a modern pattern, its crooked alleys replaced by straight thoroughfares. The plan showed the ambiguities of mid-1930s Soviet taste: it facilitated linear communications, but it also preserved a circular structure marking the centre of the city (and thus the country) in the Kremlin. Modern concepts of city planning: the decentralized 'green' city of Barshch and Ginzberg's 1930 Moscow plan, or the linear city of Leonidov's Magnitogorsk plan,[9] were passed over for the ancient model of concentric circles radiating from a fortress centre. The symbolic emphasis on the centre overrode economic need. Removing the Chinatown Wall and Iberian Chapel could have channelled transport efficiently through the city, yet instead the space was devoted to expanding Red Square, an impediment to traffic. Red Square is the ritual centre of the Soviet Union, where May Day and 7 November are celebrated, a role enhanced by the new space.[10]

Moscow centralism was not new to the 1930s; its cultural definition, however, was. The shift of investment from the periphery to the capital signalled a new hierarchy of values, by which society's attention shifted from the many to the one outstanding representative. It was neither democratic nor egalitarian; yet the media encouraged the people to identify with the projects. Grandiose projects in the centre were a source of pride shared by all. The Moscow Metro, for instance, was a constant topic of mass culture, and it was a source of national, not Muscovite pride. The theme ran from newspaper campaigns to children's books.[11] Muscovite youth used the subway as a meeting place for dates; provincial visitors toured the facility as a national landmark. It was incorporated into the culture of the masses.

The strengthening of the centre was to the advantage of all, as was evident in depictions of the centre's counterpart: the periphery. From its inception, Soviet power struggled with huge territorial expanses: by military means during the Civil War, by electrification during NEP, with factories and dams during the industrial revolution. These were, for the most part, lands untouched by civilization. The media showed various attitudes towards the hinterland. The Cultural Revolution typically saw the periphery as savage and hostile. It gained value only when subjugated by the socialist order, that is, when it was industrialized. The cultural geography of the time saw cities – industrial, socialist, the centre of power – as benevolent, and the hinterland malevolent, a place of dark forests, raging rivers, retrograde traditions and socially hostile elements. To the engineer Margulies in Kataev's *Time Forward!*, the great expanses were 'cumbersome'.[12] Nature had no autonomous value;

it was neither romantic nor beautiful. If for another age the phrase 'nocturnal spectres, pathless forest . . . marshy miasmas' would have evoked mystery, in Leonov's *Sot'* (Soviet River) it concealed a hermitage bent on sabotaging the pulp-mill project.[13] The outer regions, with their dark peasants and elemental nature, provided the villains of industrial novels like *Sot'* (1930) and Gladkov's *Energiia* (Energy, 1933). They had to be conquered, usually by representatives of the centre, Komsomol members and workers sent by Moscow.

Hostility to the periphery had softened by the mid-1930s. The mastery of Soviet man over nature was deemed as important as ever in songs, essays and movies. Even the 'March of the Jolly Fellows' (1934) proclaimed *My pokoryaem prostranstvo i vremya, My molodye khozyaeva zemli!* (We conquer space and time, We are young masters of the land!).[14] Yet the attitude was supplemented by a great pride in the vast frontier, which, as it had for nineteenth-century Americans, provided a new source for the national identity. There was consonance between Soviet man and the periphery. The outer bounds of the national identity had shifted from the West, where internationalism had once pointed, to the eastern regions of Soviet Russia. The *Internationale*, the national anthem since the revolution, was replaced unofficially by 'Song of the Motherland' (1936). Its refrain proclaimed the new-found benevolence of uncharted spaces:

> *Shiroka strana moia rodnaia,*
> *Mnogo v nei lesov, polei i rek.*
> *Ia drugoi takoi strany ne znaiu*
> *Gde tak vol'no dyshit chelovek.*[15]

> (Broad is my native land
> It has many forests, fields and rivers
> I don't know of any other country
> Where man breathes so freely.)

The new consciousness helped redefine Soviet notions of heroism, which had often been tied to territorial expansion. Heroes of the Cultural Revolution had been conquerors of open space: the young builders of Magnitogorsk, the collectivizers of virgin lands. Cultural geography mapped the Soviet Union as a set of socialist islands – progressive cities, industrial projects, *kolkhozes* – immersed in a sea of hostile influences – the open spaces. By the mid-1930s the periphery no longer seemed alien or hostile. The map was redrawn to include the great expanses, all in one way or another considered 'Soviet' (in the cultural as well as political sense). The demarcation was not by points – the islands – but by the great outer boundary enclosing the country.

There was a new and powerful consciousness of the border. Socialist conflict arose not when the centre penetrated the periphery, but when outsiders (foreigners) violated the outer boundary. For earlier revolutionaries, the border had been a symbol of enlightenment and sanctuary, but by the mid-1930s it became a symbol of hostility. The border was inviolable, and its sanctity gave mass culture a new adventure hero: the border guard (NKVD *pogranichnik*).[16]

For the mid-30s, heroism lay not so much in subjugating the hinterland as in discovering and exploiting its riches. Mass culture found a new type of hero in geologists searching Siberia and the Arctic for natural resources. They became stock figures in adventure films like *The Bold Seven* (1936), *Gold Lake* (1935), *Moon Stone* (1935), *In the Far East* (1937) and *The Golden Taiga* (1937). The change in attitude touched new industrial projects. Ivan Kataev's account of the building of Khibinogorsk treated open space as a *tabula rasa* for the new socialist culture.[17] As he wrote (in an assumed dialogue with the Second Revolution), 'it turns out that not only historically inhabited regions are fit to be cultivated for socialism, but also regions previously untouched by human hands'. The periphery was no longer hostile; and its affinity to Moscow was represented in the concluding paragraph, when the narrator's gaze travelled over the expanses to the Kremlin Chimes – symbol of Moscow centralism.

The most prominent variations on the pioneer-hero were pilots and polar explorers. The development of an advanced aviation industry and a generation of capable designers had put Soviet aircraft among the world's best; and with them came a generation of daring pilots. Soviet pilots set world records for flight altitude, endurance and distance, and they competed with athletes and movie stars for celebrity status. At the top of the aviation elite was the arctic pilot; in fact the highest Soviet medal, Hero of the Soviet Union, was first awarded to seven fliers who rescued the crew of the Cheliuskin from ice floes.[18] Pilots such as Babushkin provided a new model for the Soviet hero: brave, modest, taciturn – and non-party.[19] The most famous flyer, Valerii Chkalov, became an international hero by leading two flights over the North Pole. A darling of the mid-30s mass media was Professor Otto Schmidt, leader of the Cheliuskin expedition. Schmidt became the subject of newsreels, newspaper essays, even comics.

Aviators and explorers had also earned renown during the Cultural Revolution. What was different about the mid-30s was how they earned celebrity, and how it was described in the media. The Cultural Revolution saw practical purposes for exploration and aviation: opening land for mining and industry, building an air defence against the hostile capitalist world.[20] By the mid-30s, the foremost purpose was national prestige: Chkalov's flight from Moscow to Alaska had marginal military value, but it brought glory to the Soviet Union.[21] A new attitude toward nature could also be seen in the Arctic explorations and flights. Nature remained something to be conquered; yet conquest demanded not subjugation or destruction, but the ability to live in harmony with the elements. Moscow was no longer alien to the periphery.

For Soviet mass culture, as has been true of many other cultures, nature and the periphery stood as metaphors of society. The pattern of classification and association observable in cultural geography, by which consolidating the centre helped reintegrate the periphery, was also applied to social groups. Society became stratified; power and attention were focused on a new elite. Yet coincident with the consolidation of the elite was an attitude of social inclusivity. Classes and institutions deemed hostile by the Cultural Revolution once again found a place in Soviet society.

The evolution of a geographical hierarchy, with Moscow on top, coincided with the stiffening of social hierarchy. Its upper rungs, on the model of Moscow, monopolized attention and investment. The new emphasis on hierarchy was most evident in a tendency to praise leaders of all kinds. Bards wrote paeans to Stalin;[22] films presented him as Lenin's closest comrade. Leadership itself, regardless of its politics, became an object of praise in films like *Peter the Great* (1937–1939), *Alexander Nevsky* (1938) and *Suvorov* (January 1941). The tendency was not limited to political life. Ranks and uniforms, already a norm for the military, were re-introduced to the civil administration, the foreign service, even the railroad.[23] Outstanding workers, artists and scientists were singled out for praise and given economic privileges. The Stakhanovite movement restructured production processes on the model of Moscow centralism: a balanced distribution of responsibilities and privileges was replaced by hierarchy, under which many workers supported the efforts of one. In sports, mass participation, emphasized by the revolution and the Cultural Revolution, was eclipsed by outstanding achievement; investment shifted from mass sports clubs to elite central institutions such as Moscow Spartak.[24] Old sports like production gymnastics and non-competitive mass games were replaced by competitive sports, which called for winners and losers, and thus hierarchy. Athletes were strictly ranked by titles (e.g. Master of Sport), with corresponding uniforms, badges and privileges.

The introduction of hierarchical centralism might have weakened the social position of the average citizen. But closer inspection of the mass media suggests that the new values offered something to all levels of the population. Social legitimacy was concentrated in the centre not as a monopoly, but as a point of distribution. There was a new understanding of Soviet citizenship that allowed for the symbolic distribution of status from the centre to the periphery. The model was mirrored by the cultural geography. Moscow centralism had included greater respect for the periphery. The hierarchy of places was not so much a deprivation of the periphery as a concentration of efforts from all directions on one spot. Elevating Moscow elevated the entire Soviet Union. This vicarious pride was repeated with the accomplishments of the new elite. Soviet citizens basked in the glory of achievements in which they had no direct part. The daring of pilots, the strength of athletes and the productivity of Stakhanovite workers were the effort of an entire nation, and every citizen could justly feel pride in them. Stakhanov was expressing a common sentiment when he said:

every improvement in the work of the individual contributes to the general welfare. The Soviet people know, they see and realize, that the better work progresses, the wealthier the country becomes . . . Loving their homeland, they love their machines, their factories, their work.[25]

Elite status and its attendant celebrity were available to groups excluded by the Cultural Revolution. For the revolution, the path to heroism and celebrity had been through the party. One had first to declare allegiance, then paths were opened. The mid-30s offered celebrity to broader range of citizens; the unspoken guidelines had changed. While the party was still a path to celebrity, celebrity was also a path to the party. The new heroes were not always party members,[26] and their accomplishments were often apolitical. The new success story was fictionalized in the poor shepherd Kostya in *Jolly Fellows*, or the title character of *The Flying Painter* (1936), and it found real-life models in newly celebrated pilots, athletes and workers. Yet the broadening of political standards did not imply a loosening of discipline. The new non-party heroes expressed a stronger appreciation of social hierarchy and political guidance than previous heroes had. The headstrong, politically correct and sometimes arrogant heroes of the Cultural Revolution – Communists and Komsomols – had, despite their acceptance of party discipline, been allowed to resist its restraints. A party organizer sent to the hinterlands to build an industrial complex could act without orders from Moscow, or even ignore them; collectivizers worked independently, and could outdo the political centre in enthusiasm.[27] Heroes of the mid-30s acknowledged the centre's primacy more clearly than their predecessors; it was, in fact, a condition of their celebrity. Citizens were encouraged to pursue and realize their individual potential provided that, in the end, they gave proper credit to the social system. The system condemned those who, after attaining their goals, tried to rise above the collective. The protagonist of the movie *Goalie* (1936) rose from factory-floor worker to star soccer player; yet his final ambition, to represent the Soviet Union in international play, was satisfied only after returning to the team he had abandoned on his rise to the top.

Celebrity in the mid-30s could only be attained with the hierarchy, and it was conferred by the hierarchy. Hierarchy was expressed in a series of personal relationships: leader and people, director and worker, parents and children. Social roles were, in essence, personalized; the apex of the hierarchy was embodied in the person of Stalin. Stalin's personalization of social hierarchy offered average citizens a way to identify with the political system. It bolstered a belief in direct contact between the top of the social order and the masses that institutionalized power had weakened. Even in the most imposing rituals of order, like the Red Square demonstraions, the myth of direct contact was maintained. The event, it must be remembered, was not seen directly by most of the population (entrance was strictly controlled), but through newsreels, which could include a clip of Stalin atop the mausoleum waving to the crowd and acknowledging marchers with a finger or a wink of the eye.

The personalization of politics also contributed to a belief in the direct and immediate transmission of legitimacy and celebrity. Unknown but worthy citizens like Stakhanov or the *kolkhoz* activist Pasha Angelina could win instant recognition from the centre. Mass culture offered countless examples of how the centre – Stalin and the Kremlin – was aware of what was happening throughout the country, and would reward commendable efforts. The transition was always sudden: Stakhanov went straight from simple coal-miner to national hero,[28] the peasant Angelina was given all the trappings of power – from transport in a luxurious Lincoln sedan to election to the Supreme Soviet.[29] Fictional models were provided by Grigorii Alexandrov's popular films, *Jolly Fellows* (1934) and *Volga-Volga* (1938). These were stories of simple musicians living in small towns on the Russian periphery. Local authorities do not recognize their talents; but by a series of fortuitous circumstances, they make their way to Moscow. There they are recognized – the hero of *Fellows* ends up in the Bolshoi Theatre.[30]

The direct transmission of status bolstered the hierarchy by acknowledging its prerogatives. Legitimacy and celebrity were passed on person to person in a mentor–student (*pitomets* or *vospitannik*) relationship; the old notion of party discipline was translated into a new value system.

The system was used by Stalin himself in the *Short Course*, which claimed party leadership had been passed on to him by Lenin; the claim was supported and acted out in sculptures, paintings and movies.[31] A ritual evolved in the mid-30s to represent the transfer of status: individual heroes came to the Kremlin to be acknowledged by the leadership. Stakhanov was called to the Kremlin for a congress of Stakhanovites, Pasha Angelina for a *kolkhoz* workers' congress.[32] Chkalov's famous flights were consecrated by a similar ritual. The flight plans were drawn up by the country's foremost experts, and prepared by a team of pilots and engineers. Yet the flights could not begin until permission was given by Stalin. This moment, when Chkalov's crew was summoned to the Kremlin and granted approval, became a central moment in the retelling of the story. Stalin offered a few words of fatherly advice:

> I explained I fly valuable experimental planes that must be preserved no matter what. During a test flight my thoughts are directed toward bringing the plane back to earth safely.
> 'Your life', said Comrade Stalin, 'is more important to us than any plane. Make sure to use a parachute if needed.'[33]

When social roles were embodied by people rather than collectives, individual lives seemed more valuable.

The ritual of acknowledgement conferred instant status; it allowed average citizens to bypass the middle ranks of society on their way to the top. According to the mass media, the centralization and personalization of power in the mid-30s offered greater opportunities to the masses; it was the middle of the hierarchy that suffered. The defeat of oafish local bureaucrats by popular initiative, usually assisted by the centre, was a standard part of mid-30s success stories: Alexandrov's films, the mythology of Stakhanovism.[34] The middle ranks were a source of mass culture villains, as in *A Great Citizen* (1937); and they were the constant target of media campaigns. Amateur theatre groups attacked bureaucratic ineptitude;[35] satirists like Zoshchenko, Ilf and Petrov, Koltsov mocked institutional inertia. They were free to skewer the bureaucracy as long as they did not attack the centre. The strictures they worked under, which seem obvious to the present-day reader, were not necessarily evident to their audience, who saw satire as a needed avenue of petition. The pattern, as has been observed many times, was a revival of the pre-revolutionary myth of the good tsar and bad civil servants: there was a strong popular fealty to Moscow unshaken by local bungling. In fact it was strengthened by mass media revelations: the belief went that, if only Stalin knew what was going on, the problems would be corrected.[36]

One of the assumed roles of the 1930s mass media was to facilitate direct communication between the leadership and the population in a way that bypassed the bureaucratic middle. One interpretation of the role is consonant with the totalitarian model of Soviet society: the mass media were a transmission belt of party policy to the obedient people. Yet communication ran in two directions: relying on existing institutions, the media published information on middle-level abuse of bureaucratic power. Theatre groups, 'sketch-writers' and worker-correspondents acted as government agents; but they were agents of the centre directed at the middle. They were intermediaries representing the little man and ensuring the just operation of Soviet power.[37] Their work was aided by a remarkable institution, the letter to the editor.[38] Citizens could use this channel of communication to petition higher authorities against the local abuse of power. Extensive publicity was given to instances when justice was served, and people were encouraged to report all abuses.

The centralization of Soviet society in the mid-30s opened a new range of passive roles, like the vigilant letter-writer, to the masses. Mass action in the Cultural Revolution had been a matter of *doing*: collectivizing the countryside and industrializing the periphery, doing mass calisthenics, writing poetry in workers' clubs. For the mid-30s, it was a matter of seeing. The mass media had become the dominant model of social intercourse, and their ability to frame the citizen as a passive viewer penetrated other aspects of social life. The passive spectator became, in many ways, a model of the Soviet citizen. Political and social discourse was redefined by the spectator–performer relationship. During the first decade of the revolution, political communication often occurred where audience participation was encouraged – mass rallies, newspaper readings, mock trials. Contact between performer and audience was direct. A new set of institutions and practices evolved in the mid-30s to accommodate the citizen-spectator. An expensive showplace for the economy, Moscow's VDNKh, was built; voting was ritualized, recorded on newsreel and distributed about the country;[39] show trials afforded a purging of alien elements. The Constitution of 1936 was presented in folk poems and stage tableaux;[40] and, on special occasions, the leaders viewed and were viewed by the nation from atop Lenin's Mausoleum. The leadership took measures to assure citizens that their needs as spectators were given proper weight – even as their passive role was being underlined. Plans for important monuments were exhibited for public review,[41] the Constitution and other legislative acts were subjected to public comment. The public had no more influence in the decision-making process than did a Supreme Soviet ballot, but it was nevertheless an essential ritual of participation.

The role of Soviet citizen found increasingly circumscribed models. When a society stabilizes citizen roles, it also limits social mobility and activism. The mid-30s saw the model Soviet citizen's attention shift from public roles – the workplace and political activism – to private roles, particularly those centred in the family. The family, sorely buffeted by the first fifteen years of Soviet power, was stabilized.[42] Divorce, formerly a matter of one party signing a register, was granted only at the consent of both, and a stiff fee was charged for the proceeding; bigamy, which had been encouraged by light laws and lax prosecution, became subject to stiff penalties. The strongest measure was the controversial 1936 law abolishing abortion.

The revision of marital customs eliminated cherished rights. What was gained in the deal? If the media were to be believed, the life of a model Soviet citizen during the late 1920s and early 30s had been emotionally unrewarding. It seemed that satisfying one's ambition, whether through greed or socialist altruism, impeded personal fulfilment. Communist activists sacrificed their private lives for the good of a society that often distrusted or despised them. What was worse, they could not depend on their families, an institution that they themselves had weakened, for emotional support. One of the stock figures of NEP and the Cultural Revolution was the Communist who sacrificed love for the cause. The prototype was Gleb Chumalov of Gladkov's *Cement* (1925), but the figure was repeated in the engineer Uvadaev of Leonov's *Sot'*; in the heroes of *Time, Forward!*, whose wives leave them or give birth while they break construction records; the loveless Communist of Glebov's *Inga*, who in her devotion to duty ceases to be a woman. The apex of the trend was Pavlik Morozov, who sacrificed his family in the battle for collectivization.[43]

By the mid-30s, this stock figure was an object of condemnation or mockery in films like *The Enthusiasts* (1934) or *A Chance Meeting* (1936). The revolutionary ideal of free sexual relations gave way to monogamous relations. Monogamy was not only encouraged by the government for various policy considerations, it became fashionable. 'Show' marriages were featured in the press.[44] Love and marriage were in effect de-ideologized; romantic love became a standard plot mechanism for films such as *The Rich Bride* (1937). Documents of earlier times were even translated to fit the new tastes; when Furmanov's novel *Chapaev* (1923) was filmed in 1934, a love motif (Petka and Anka the Machine-Gunner) was added.

The new family was cast in the image of the state.[45] The Soviet Union was a great family, in an over-used metaphor of the time. The values of patriotism and family went hand in hand: each assigned similar hierarchical roles and responsibilities. In 1934, the word *rodina*, the country as mother, was revived. Citizens were children, expected to give obedience and loyalty, and to receive parental care and support in return; Stalin was of course the father. The family, like the state, was held together by respect, supported by a hierarchy of obligations extending from the bottom up and the top down. Both parents and children had defined roles. Children were encouraged to respect their parents; hero pioneers of the 30s, like Timur of Gaidar's *Timur and his Squad*, were always considerate of their elders. In return, the duty of parents was to care for their children and raise them as healthy members of the collective. High state officials gave living demonstrations of the ideal: Stalin paid a visit to his old mother in Tiflis;[46] the story of Lenin's New Year visit to a children's colony was revived and given broad publicity.

Women were the mainstay of the new family. They were given new obligations that focused their identity on the roles of wife and mother. The most important role a woman could play was to marry and have children; mass media of the thirties showed these women to be the happiest. Motherhood was the most cherished desire of even the zealous tractor driver Pasha Angelina.[47] Sex roles were increasingly differentiated by the mass media. Rights given by the revolution were taken away, paths to social recognition were cut off. Heroines like the hardened commissar of Vishnevsky's *Optimistic Tragedy* (1933) were replaced by the heroines of *Girl-Friends* (1936), whose contribution was in filling the female role of nurse. A woman's path to recognition was through her unique feminine qualities, as Lebedev-Kumach's 'Merry Girl-Friends' (1937) made clear:

> *Idem, idem, veselye podrugi!*
> *Strana, kak mat', zovet i liubit nas!*
> *Vezde nuzhny zabotlivye ruki*
> *I nash khoziaskii, teplyi zhenskii glaz.*
>
> *A nu-ka, devushki! A nu, krasavitsy!*
> *Puskai poet o nas strana,*
> *I zvonkoi pesneiu puskai proslaviatsia*
> *Sredi geroev nashi imena!*[48]

> (Let's go, let's go, my merry girl-friends!
> Like a mother, our country calls and loves us!
> Caring hands are needed everywhere
> As is our warm and overseeing women's eye.
>
> Well now, girls! Very well, my beauties!
> Let the country sing about us
> And may our names in sonorous song
> Be glorified among the heroes!)

To compensate for the loss of active participation, Soviet society acknowledged passive contributions to the national welfare, and transferred social status to these new roles. Mass culture offered women a path to social recognition inactive since the revolution: tangential status – status awarded for the merit of another. Secondary contributions (similar to the spectator-citizen) to the country were acknowledged. When a famous man was honoured, the supporting role of his wife, which had previously been ignored, was highlighted and commended. The wives of the pilot Chkalov[49] and the shock-worker Stakhanov[50] were used as models for Soviet womanhood; there was a congress of wives of industrial managers in the Kremlin.[51] Wives sacrificed their careers for their husbands, accepted their essential family roles, and freed their husbands for their great exploits.

The role of motherhood received growing recognition. Building a strong family and raising healthy children was a contribution to the state. The child reared in the new Soviet family was a prepared citizen. The most famous child-rearing primer of the Cultural Revolution, Anton Makarenko's *Road to Life* (1933), emphasized the role of the social unit in rearing children. In his second important work, *A Book for Parents* (1937), Makarenko emphasized family roles as the foundation of society.[52] Poorly-raised children could not be good citizens; raising a family depended on mutual love and respect between parents, and the freely given obedience of children. The man who was a good husband and father, and the woman who was a good wife and mother, were making a valued contribution to Soviet society.

The mid-30s redefined the ways a citizen could be integrated into Soviet society. The tendency was evident in changes to a theme prominent since the revolution: redemption. Socialism, it was believed, offered worthless individuals a chance to remake themselves, to give their lives some purpose. For the Cultural Revolution, salvation came from a change of environment. Wreckers and thieves were removed from old associates and brought to the White Sea Canal Project,[53] homeless waifs were resettled in Makarenko's colony. To become a model citizen, a 'Soviet person', one had to surrender one's background and the identity attached to it. Prominent figures like Levinson of Fadeev's *Rout* or Pavel Korchagin of Ostrovsky's *How the Steel was Forged* found an exit from personal difficulties through their social or professional identities. Man was remade by labour, by surrendering personal comfort for the communal welfare; he could, in a most extreme metaphor, become a machine.[54]

Towards the mid-30s the process by which an individual becomes a Soviet person changed. The exclusive standards that kept many groups outside the pale were weakened. Perhaps the most remarkable return was the peasant, who had disappeared from the mass media as a positive image. The typical peasant of the twenties and early thirties was, at best, ignorant: the peasant mother of the literacy campaign's 'Mama, if only you could read you could help me' poster (1923), or the peasant of *smychka* posters gratefully accepting proletarian tutelage.[55] The peasant heroes of Pogodin's *Tempo* (1929), Avdeenko's *I Love* (1933) or Dovzhenko's film *Ivan* (1932) saved themselves by leaving the countryside and becoming proletarians. A peasant could be saved, but only by ceasing to be a peasant.

Cultural Revolution attitudes towards the peasantry resembled attitudes towards the hinterland: industrial activists felt their duty was to destroy nature when it stood in their way; collectivizers believed they were right to crush kulaks. With the consolidation of the *kolkhoz* movement in the mid-30s, the peasantry was rehabilitated, both in law and culture. The 1936 Constitution provided for the equal representation of workers and peasants in the legislature (as opposed to a 1:5 ratio). With new rights came new duties: peasants were subject to civil military training from 1937.[56] Films of the period showed *kolkhoz* peasants defending the frontier alongside border guards.[57] Collectivization created a new range of positive images for female peasants.[58] The outstanding example was Alexandra Sokolova of *Member of the Government* (1939), but the type could be found elsewhere.[59] The figure was a curious amalgam of traditionally feminine qualities and new Soviet ways. Using her fine human understanding and perseverance, she was able to covert the countryside to the Soviet system and win Moscow's recognition. Yet she did not lose her rural identity.

Hybrid identities allowed Soviet society to assimilate folk cultures. The process resembled the redefining of the geographic periphery: the map was redrawn to include most of the population through the intermediacy of the centre. The state patronized the return of folk creativity to national attention; by doing so, it ensured its own primacy. Russian folk culture had been a *bête noire* of the Cultural Revolution. It was seen, like the geographic periphery and the family, as a repository of values antithetical to the Soviet state: patriarchality, the private property instinct, religion. Groups dedicated to its preservation, like the Andreev Orchestra of Russian Folk Instruments or the Piatnitsky Folk Chorus, came in for harsh criticism. The Cultural Revolution saw only one possibility for peripheral cultures: to undergo radical change and accept the ways of the centre.

Hostility towards peripheral cultures eased by the mid-30s. Peasants and nationalities no longer had to surrender their unique identities to become part of the Soviet nation. Folk culture was accepted for a number of reasons, the most obvious being that it supported the surge in nationalist sentiment. Yet it must be remembered that the folk cultures of the nationalities, which were rehabilitated at the same time, did not support great Russian nationalism. Perhaps the only common feature of all Soviet folk cultures, and the one most commonly exploited by the mass media, was that they provided a rhetoric of hierarchy and patriarchality absent in other cultural traditions.[60] Russian and Central Asian bards sang songs in praise of Lenin, Stalin, even the Constitution, in which the Soviet state and its leaders were shown to be benevolent patriarchs creating and distributing benefits to the people – the little children of the Soviet Union.[61] The duties of Soviet citizens were modelled on the family: they demanded a hierarchical system of loyalties, and allowed for status by association. Praise of the state and its leaders was, by association, praise of oneself. Folk poetry represented a social system in which leaders and people were joined by a direct, personal and hierarchical relationship, and it was this relationship that ushered folk culture back into Soviet society.

Once the primacy of the centre was acknowledged, folk culture was no longer contrary to Soviet citizenship. The acknowledgement had its obvious manifestations in paeans to Stalin and Soviet power, but its less obvious and more important facet was that Moscow, represented by the mass media (radio, film, recordings) was now the disseminator of folk culture. Like so many other parts of Soviet culture, folk culture became a spectator entertainment. Traditional folk culture was a local phenomenon: it was transmitted orally within a community, with direct contact between performer and audience. The 1930s assimilation of folk culture was initiated not by the local community, but by the centre. Scholars were sent to the countryside to find outstanding folk performers. They collected anthologies, published them in Moscow, and sent them back to the countryside. Folk performers like Lidia Ruslanova and Maria Kriukova won a nationwide audience for the first time, but their celebrity was won at the expense of removal from the folk community. The centre's ability to control relationships within media culture (which folk culture had become) was demonstrated by a ritual we have already seen: acknowledgement by the Kremlin.

Revived interest in folk culture in 1935 led to a burst of activity. Stalin visited a Bolshoi Theatre performance of popular song and dance on the October anniversary; there was a Moscow Olympiad of folk music; folk companies discovered by researchers were brought to Moscow to perform. Russian folk culture was celebrated, but so were Ukrainian, Transcaucasian and other minority cultures.[62]

The social stability struck in the mid-30s was not dependent on prosperity and opportunity alone; it lasted through times of dire economic need. Its cultural foundations rested on a rethinking of the Soviet national identity. Geographical and social boundaries shifted to include vast expanses of the country excluded by the Cultural Revolution. Previously, the Soviet population had been divided into the small group of faithful and the great grey masses. Now, Soviet citizenship in its ideal sense was extended to the masses, whose support of the state was not always active and not always political, but still valued. New classes and groups were given access to the ranks of the elite without the need to surrender cherished personal and cultural identities. The rights and duties of social initiative were concentrated in the hands of a few, but the acknowledgement of passive contributions and tangential status allowed average citizens to feel they were contributing to the national welfare. They were acknowledged by the state, and were in turn ready to acknowledge its primacy.

Notes

1. See Sheila Fitzpatrick, *Education and Social Mobility in the Soviet Union, 1921–1934* (Cambridge, 1979), pp. 235–49.
2. Vera Dunham, *In Stalin's Time* (Cambridge, 1976), pp. 41–52; Sheila Fitzpatrick, ' "Middle-class values" and social life in the 1930s', in Terry L. Thompson and Richard Sheldon, eds., *Soviet Culture and Society* (Boulder CO, 1989), pp. 20–38.
3. John Scott, *Behind the Urals* (Cambridge MA, 1942), p. 236.
4. I. V. Stalin, *Sochineniia*, vol. 1 (14 of new series) (Stanford, 1967), p. 90.
5. Fitzpatrick, ' "Middle-class values" ', pp. 22–4; Lewis Siegelbaum, *Stakhanovism and the Politics of Productivity in the USSR 1935–1941* (Cambridge, 1988), p. 216.
6. See Dunham, *In Stalin's Time*, pp. 24–8, and Richard Stites, 'Soviet popular culture: entertainment and society in Russia' (unpublished ms., n.d.), pp. 37–9.
7. Good examples of these attitudes can be found in Katerina Clark, *The Soviet Novel: History as Ritual* (Chicago, 1985), or Regine Robin, *Le réalisme socialiste: une esthétique impossible* (Paris, 1986).
8. Scott, *Behind the Urals*, pp. 70–8.
9. Anatole Kopp, *Town and Revolution: Soviet Architecture and City Planning 1917–1935* (New York, 1970), pp. 174–6, 181.
10. Note Lazar Kaganovich's comment: 'My aesthetics demands that the demonstration processions from the six districts of Moscow should all pour into Red Square at the same time'. Richard Stites, *Revolutionary Dreams: Utopian Vision and Experimental Life in the Russian Revolution* (New York, 1989), p. 243.
11. See, for instance, *Gotov! Rasskazy i stikhi o Metro* (Moscow, 1936). Stories

reflecting the mass media's standard viewpoint for peasants and provincial visitors are: E. Tarakhovskaia, 'Song of the stars'; Tarakhovskaia, 'The wonder-stairs'; E. Blaginina, 'Can you really ride like that?'; F. Zamaldinov, 'I too was in Moscow'. The common and probably apocryphal story of the peasant and subway related by Walter Duranty, *I Write as I Please* (New York, 1935), pp. 338–9, is indicative of this sentiment.

12. Valentin Kataev, *Time, Forward!*, trans. Charles Malamuth (Bloomington, IN, 1961), p. 141.
13. Leonid Leonov, *The River* (Moscow, 1983), p. 28.
14. *Russkie-sovetskie pesni 1917–1977* (Moscow, 1977), p. 164.
15. Ibid., p. 167.
16. Border guards appeared in a vast array of films of the mid to late 1930s: e.g. *Aerograd* (1935); *Seekers of Happiness* (1936); *Maritime Post* (1938); *The Commandant of Bird Island* (1939); and *Courage* (1939).
17. Ivan Kataev, 'Lednaya ellada', *Nashi dostizheniya*, no. 7 (1937), with several reprints.
18. See the front page stories of *Pravda*, 13 April 1934. Thanks to Andrew Lowenstein for his research on the Cheliushkin incident.
19. The first of Babushkin's main heroic deeds took place in 1928; he did not join the party until 1935. See his autobiography in *Kak my spasali Cheliuskiktsev* (Moscow, 1934). Of the numerous journalistic accounts, the most interesting are probably 'Nashi letchiki i nashi samolety zasluzhili vsemirnoe priznanie', *Pravda*, 12 April 1934; and 'V lagere Shmidta', *Pravda*, 12 March 1934.
20. Contemporary attitudes towards aviation were expressed in *Ever Higher* (1931, Pavel German): 'My rozhdenny, chtob skazku sdelat' byl'iu, Preodolet', prostranstvo i prostor, Nash razum dal stal'nye ruki-kryl'ia, A vmesto serdtsa plamennyi motor, Vse vyshe, vyshe i vyshe, Stremim my polet nashikh ptits, I v kazhdom propellere dyshit, Spokoistvo nashikh granits': *Russkie-sovetskie pesni*, p. 80.
21. See the congratulatory telegram given Chkalov on landing in Vancouver by the Americans (led by George Marshall!) at the end of the film *Valery Chkalov*, or 'Spasenie Cheliuskiktsev – pobeda vsei strany: svidetel'stvo moshchi proletarskogo gosudarstva', *Pravda*, 13 April 1934.
22. For example, Salomeia Neris (Lithuania), 'Poem of Stalin'; Livia Deleanu (Moldavia), 'The people's love'; Aaly Tokombaev (Kirgizia), 'To Stalin'; Tirzo Tursun-Zade (Tadzhikistan), 'The sun of the world'; Gevork Emin (Armenia), 'I am unswervingly loyal to him'.
23. See Roy Medvedev, *Let History Judge: The Origins and Consequences of Stalinism*, trans. Colleen Taylor (New York, 1972), p. 548.
24. James Riordan, *Sport in Soviet Society* (Cambridge, 1977), pp. 127–35.
25. Aleksei Stakhanov, *The Stakhanov Movement Explained by Its Initiator* (Moscow, 1939), p. 23.
26. Chkalov joined the party in 1936, Stakhanov in 1936 and Pasha Angelina in 1937; all after their rise to celebrity.
27. The pattern could be found in novels like *Sot'* and *Time, Forward!*, or in the collectivization campaign of the '25000ers': see Lynn Viola, *The Best Sons of the Fatherland: Workers in the Vanguard of Soviet Collectivization* (New York, 1987).

28. See Ordzhonikidze's acknowledgements in *Pervoe vsesoiuznoe soveshchanie rabochikh i rabotnits-stakhanovtsev* (Moscow, 1935), pp. 7–8, and the speeches of the Stakhanovites.
29. Sergei Tret'iakov, 'Deviat' devushek', in *Vchera i segodnya* (Moscow, 1960), vol. 1, p. 316.
30. In *Radiant Path* (1939), the plebeian heroine is received by Kalinin in the Kremlin.
31. For example, *Lenin in 1917* (1937), *Lenin in October* (1937), *The Great Dawn* (1938), *The Vyborg Side* (1938).
32. Pasha Angelina told the entire country of her meeting with Stalin in a 9 December 1936 radio broadcast; Prokofiev reported to Stalin by radio on his record-breaking stratospheric flight directly from the dirigible: see TsGAZ SSSR, VIII-136, 01.55, and TsGAZ SSSR, N 44166 (thanks to Richard Stites for these documents). Fictional equivalents of the ritual could be found in *Radiant Path* or *In Search of Happiness* (1939).
33. V. Chkalov, 'Vestrecha so Stalinym', *Rodnaia rech'* (Moscow, 1950), p. 231.
34. See, for instance, *September Night* (1939), in which the sabotage of local authorities is corrected by Ordzhonikidze's intercession, or *A Great Life* (1940). The graphic realism of this film, particularly the second half (1946), brought it under criticism.
35. See Scott, *Behind the Urals*, pp. 236–40, on the activities of the Magnitigorsk TRAM theatre.
36. The attitude was found amongst collectivized peasants (and exploited by Stalin's 'Heads are spinning' article): Maurice Hindus, *Red Bread* (New York, 1931), pp. 149–50; and it was common among sophisticated purge victims: Medvedev, *Let History Judge*, pp. 289–300, or Ilya Erenburg, *Memoirs 1921–1941* (New York, 1964), pp. 426–7.
37. Harriet Borland, *Soviet Literary Theory and Practice during the First Five-Year Plan 1928–1932* (New York, 1950), pp. 38–67; Katerina Clark, 'Little heroes and big deeds: literature responds to the first Five-Year Plan', in Sheila Fitzpatrick, ed., *Cultural Revolution in Russia, 1928–1931* (Bloomington IN, 1978), pp. 197–9.
38. See Merle Fainsod, *Smolensk under Soviet Rule* (Cambridge MA, 1958), pp. 378–408.
39. See, for instance, *Kak budet golosovat' izbiratel'*, dir. Sergei Iutkevich (Mosfilm, 1937). For comment on the practice, see Tatyana Khlopyankina, 'Watching old newsreels', *Moscow News*, 8 March 1989.
40. See, for instance, the anthology *Pod solntsem Stalinskoi konstitutsii* (Moscow, 1951).
41. Such an incident is described in Anatolii Rybakov, *Children of the Arbat*, trans. Harold Shukman (Boston, 1988), p. 492.
42. Gail Lapidus, *Women in Soviet Society: Equality, Development and Social Change* (Berkeley, 1977); Nicholas S. Timasheff, *The Great Retreat* (New York, 1946), pp. 198–201.
43. Later reworkings of the Morozov legend, like Shchipachev's poem 'Pavlik Morozov' (1950), stressed his strong links with his mother.
44. Timasheff, *Great Retreat*, pp. 198–9.
45. Lapidus, *Women in Soviet Society*, p. 112.

46. Timasheff, *Great Retreat*, pp. 202–3. For a fictional equivalent, see the children's film *Siberians* (1940).
47. Tret'iakov, 'Deviat' devushek', p. 314. A fictional equivalent of the same dilemma was to be found in the film *Rich Bride* (1938).
48. *Russkie-sovetskie pesni*, p. 171.
49. Wives were standardly referred to in the many newspaper articles of the time. In addition, see the wives' articles in *Pravda*, 24 July 1936, p. 4.
50. Discussed in Siegelbaum, *Stakhanovism*, pp. 238–42.
51. Ibid., p. 241. See Fitzpatrick, ' "Middle-class values" ', for the middle-class nature of the trend.
52. Translated as A.S. Makarenko, *The Collective Family: A Handbook for Russian Parents* (New York, 1967).
53. See the collective work *White Sea Canal* (London, 1935), or Pogodin's play 'Aristocrats' in Ben Blake, ed., *Four Soviet Plays* (London, 1937).
54. Clark, 'Little heroes and big deeds', pp. 190–2.
55. *The Soviet Political Poster* (Moscow, 1984), vol. 2, nos. 42 and 47.
56. The new attitude towards peasants could be found in the fictional defence film *If War Comes Tomorrow* (1938).
57. *Daughter of the Homeland* (1937); *On the Border* (1938); *Homeland* (1939).
58. See Victoria E. Bonnell, 'The representation of politics and the politics of representation', *Russian Review*, vol. 47 (1988), p. 321.
59. For instance, N. Vigiliansky, 'Velikii perelom' (1934), reprinted in *Vchera i segodnia*, pp. 289–304, or the film *Wonder Worker* (1936). The type was repeated in war posters, and by the same actress in the film *She Defends the Motherland* (1943).
60. Fazil Iskander pokes gentle fun at this connection in *Sandro of Chegem*, trans. Susan Brownsberger (New York, 1983).
61. See, for instance, the poems collected in *Pod solntsem Stalinskoi konstitutsii*.
62. Timasheff, *Great Retreat*, pp. 271–3.

Part III

Politics, Industry and Shopfloor Relations

5 The crisis of productivity in the New Economic Policy: rationalization drives and shopfloor responses in Soviet cotton mills 1924–1929

Chris Ward

> When we talk about the *smychka* it's essential to think of it as a
> material thing. *Smychka* is the endless ribbon of cloth stretching
> between town and countryside . . . *Smychka* without cloth has no con-
> tent. It's merely an empty word.
>> Trotsky speaking to a conference of textile executives in 1926.

The decision to abandon *prodrazvertska* (requisitioning), taken at the 10th Party Congress in 1921, could by itself guarantee neither the economic nor the political stability of the regime. Lenin's 'forced retreat' would not reinvigorate the economy if commodity exchange between the agrarian and industrial sectors of the economy remained in abeyance. Maintaining and strengthening the link between town and countryside therefore had implications for industry. If the Tambov rising and the Kronstadt revolt called forth the *smychka*, the *smychka* in turn conjured up *khozraschet*: factories were enjoined to reduce costs and keep their commodities within the financial reach of the peasantry in order to prevent the recrudescence of mass unrest.

Since the main consumer of finished cloth was the peasantry, all the imperatives of the New Economic Policy (NEP) were refracted through the cotton industry. Throughout the 1920s economic commentators, trade union leaders, party and state officials were united in their recognition of the centrality of cotton to the political and economic stability of the regime.[1] By extension, because cotton was essential to the *smychka*, the shop floor stood at the point of intersection between politics and economics. When commodity exchange between town and countryside was disrupted and the stability of the regime threatened, pressure – in the form of rationalization drives – was brought to bear on the workforce. This happened twice in the 1920s; once after the 1923 scissors

83

crisis and again following the war scare of 1926–7 and grain crisis of 1927–8.

Implementing rationalization, however, was no easy matter. Inside and around the mill the politics of cotton were delineated by an interlocking set of factors which conditioned the nature of the factory regime and the social psychology of the workforce. Here the most salient features of the industry were its long history and intimate relationship to early British industrial capitalism. Complex shopfloor structures crystallized around this matrix of forces, shaping workers' responses to rationalization drives and restricting the scope and impact of central initiatives.

The factory

International capitalism determined the physical structure of the mill – architecture and machinery. Britain's 1842 abrogation of the ban on machine exports and the Oldham bourgeoisie's decision to eschew spinning in favour of light engineering[2] signalled the beginnings of factory production in Russia's cotton industry. In the Ivanovo region Boulton and Watt steam engines appeared quickly and fine spinning was mechanized almost immediately; self-acting mules were installed from the mid-1840s onwards and ring-frames a decade later. Thereafter new equipment for other processes was taken up as fast as it was developed: 'openers' (for stripping baled cotton), scutching machines (for straightening fibres) and carding-frames (for combing cotton) were all located in initial processing rooms. Preparatory departments encompassed drawing-frames (for rolling out thick slivers of cotton) and flyer-frames (for first stage spinning). By the 1880s factory-based spinning dominated the industrial landscape and the internal architecture of the NEP mill had taken final shape (table 1). Weaving was something of an exception. Though large sheds with serried rows of Lancashire power looms steadily encroached on this last stronghold of the artisan, handloom weaving persisted down to and beyond World War I; well into the 1920s trusts in Ivanovo and Moscow *gubernii* recognized a duty to spin thread suitable for domestic workers.[3]

Labour force

Cotton mills employed about 137,000 in 1921, rising to 419,000 in 1926 and 496,000 in 1929. According to the 1926 census 96 per cent of all operatives lived in the RSFSR, concentrated almost exclusively in Leningrad and the Central Industrial Region (CIR). The census also

Table 1. *Machinery in a typical cotton spinning mill, 1924*

Initial processing rooms:	Cotton bale opener	1	
	Scutching machines	4	
	Carding-frames	90	
Preparatory departments:	Drawing-frames	48	
	Flyer-frames – slubbing	580	spindles
	– intermediate	2,000	spindles
	– jack	8,000	spindles
Fine-spinning halls:	Self-actors and ring-frames	80,000	spindles

Source: V. I. Feoktistov, *Ekskursiia na bumagopriadil'nuiu fabriku* (1924), p. 18.

reveals that Soviet mills relied heavily on female labour: women accounted for about 70 per cent of the total workforce.[4] Following the temporary agrarianization of the Russian economy, many operatives returned to their shops after service in the Red Army. For others war and revolution meant flight to the land, but like ex-soldiers the majority of workers who became farmers quickly returned to their mills; virtually all available experienced operatives had been drawn back into production within the first four years of NEP. Increasingly, after the middle of the decade, new workers came from the countryside.[5]

The NEP labour force was thus an amalgam of long-serving operatives and new entrants drawn from the villages, but the former were not always divorced from the land and the latter were not always raw recruits, since many peasants had experience of handloom weaving.[6]

Labour process

Early British industrial capitalism not only dictated the physical structure of the mill and the nature of its equipment, it also shaped the labour process. British expatriates hired by Russian entrepreneurs or foreign concerns replicated the taken-for-granted world of production inside the factory, one constructed on the basis of class conflict and the subsequent compromises worked out in North-Western England from the 1790s onwards.[7] Trade demarcation and the allocation of functions by gender, based on the British model, was rigidly inflected through all shops and departments. Supervisory personnel – overlookers and foremen – were invariably male, the operatives female. Each machine, or machine group, was run by a work team (*komplekt*), and each *komplekt* member linked to a particular aspect of the labour process. There were only three exceptions to these rules, once again reflecting British practice: in weaving sheds power loom tenters and their assistants could be of either sex, and in fine-spinning halls self-actor *komplekty* were always headed by men, as were 'opener' *komplekty*.

The relationship between skill and the labour process was not self-evident. Although the 1926 census gives a detailed skill profile for the cotton workforce,[8] the official categories are virtually useless as a guide to the culture of the mill. Those listed as 'highly-skilled' and 'unskilled' were doubtless service personnel and auxiliary workers respectively, but beyond this the notion of 'skill' had no clear meaning inside the factory. Between 1920 and 1926 the industry was short of the following 'skilled' workers – weaving shed foremen and overlookers, weavers, and flyer-, ring-frame and self-actor spinners.[9] This gamut of 'skilled' operatives represents a good part of the entire range of trades in a cotton mill, so the term is either a social construct which cannot be deduced from technology, or is related to work in some other way.

Here we must return to the work team. *Komplekty* were not just haphazard constructs. They stood at the centre of the operative's working life. The internal dynamics of the *komplekt* defined skill by restricting entry to certain trades, and, to a significant extent, prevented managers and rationalizers from gaining control over labour at the point of production.

In initial processing rooms the 'opener' work team comprised one male and three to four women. The male assessed raw cotton quality and directed the women who fed the machine.[10] Similar patterns obtained on scutchers where the *komplekt* usually consisted of one female operator to one, two or three machines. On carding-frames three women dealt with up to fifteen frames. As in opener and scutching rooms carders were surrounded by considerable numbers of auxiliary workers, ranging from experienced hands to adolescent trainees.[11]

On all these machines skill tended to resolve itself into experience and *komplekt* exerted varying degrees of control over the labour process. Norm setters found it all but impossible to arrive at standard definitions of work routines for the opener, for example, not least because fluctuations in the quality of cotton coming into the mill with each delivery made standard calculations difficult,[12] and while in theory machine speeds and loadings in scutching rooms depended on cotton sort and weight, in practice the 'condition of raw materials and the skill of the workers' were what really mattered.[13] The same was true of preparatory departments: though working the drawing-frame was considered a simple affair, a monograph on industrial accidents in cotton mills asserted that workers were, or should be, 'experienced female operatives'.[14] Matters were even more complex in flyer-frame rooms (table 1). Because thread became progressively finer as it passed down the production chain spindle speeds increased on each subsequent frame group, but were modified to take account of fluctuations in cotton quality and changed depending on whether or not the spinning was for warp or weft threads. On slubbing-frames, prior to 1925 or so, one or two women operated one machine, or two women shared two frames, or one woman worked on two frames alone. Adolescent girl helpers were added to intermediate- and jack-frames because 'doffing' (unloading full spools) occurred more frequently. As in other rooms there were swarms of auxiliaries: bobbin sorters, bobbin strippers, loaders, machine repairers and their assistants, and roving sampler and cleaner teams, each with experienced and ranking members.[15]

Nowhere was the definition of skill more problematic and control over the labour process by the operative more evident than in fine-spinning halls. As already indicated, self-actors, or mule frames, were amongst the first factory-based machines to come to Russia: many Soviet mills had frames well over half-a-century old and some dated from the 1840s.[16] Here British foremen and overlookers brought with them habits and conventions which had evolved in North-Western England throughout the previous century and imposed them on Russia's emerging factory labour force. That their influence persisted can be seen by glancing at materials relating to mule spinning during NEP; 'in spite of the great experience of Russian technicians with the self-actor', notes one source, 'the more experienced technicians and workers' must study nineteenth-century English manuals.[17]

Following Lancashire practice mule *komplekty* were always made up of spinner, piecers (who joined up broken threads) and doffers working a pair of machines, but there were many variations on this basic pattern. Although the hierarchy of work was well established and clearly defined the division of labour was a matter for the individual spinner, and sources are accordingly vague on *komplekt* numbers. One 1925 investigation cites spinner, piecer and creeler/doffer (for doffing and loading rovings) as standard for two 1,200-spindle frames in the CIR prior to the First World War. Another records spinner, piecer, doffer and creeler for the mid-1920s. Four to six to a pair are mentioned in 1924, four in 1926 and 'usually' five in 1927.[18] In fact the *komplekt* could be much larger than these examples suggest. It could include first, second and third piecers and first and second creeler/doffers. These were directly subordinate to the spinner, who also supervised the activities of the following auxiliaries when they touched his machines: one tube sorter, three to four roving carriers, four ropers (supplying ropes and belts) and four thread carriers.[19] Some spinners therefore exerted primary control over more than fifteen operatives at various times throughout the working day.

Lancashire's experience helps us to discover why there were variations in self-actor *komplekt* sizes. Nineteenth-century English craft unions negotiated lists which gave highly detailed guidance to master and spinner alike on how to fix manning levels and the rate for the job,[20] and fragments of this arrangement were carried abroad by expatriates, transplanted to Russia, and embodied in the textile workers' union (VPST) rule books after the revolution.[21]

Thereafter local factors supervened. Self-actors were best for spinning fine to medium thread thickness (counts) with good quality cotton. Although they could spin coarse counts using poor fibres this resulted in 'bad spinning' – rovings were exhausted more quickly, frame speeds accelerated and there were more breakages, which meant more time spent 'piecing up' ends. Consequently, Anglo-Russian practices dictated that *komplekt* sizes should increase.[22] These two factors, the production of coarse counts leading to bad spinning and a fall in the quality of raw cotton coming into the mill, were endemic throughout NEP. War and revolution had swept away the social foundations which underpinned the call for high-count spinning; it is unlikely that the new bourgeoisie which flourished in the guise of the *nepmeny* filled the gaps in the demand for high fashion left by the departed aristocracy and middling ranks. In addition, the disruption of overseas cotton supplies engendered by economic collapse and isolation became a chronic feature of the 1920s. So as cotton quality fell coincidentally with a tendency to concentrate on low counts – *smychka* counts for the peasantry – the cost of mule-spun cloth rose, *komplekt* sizes increased, and consequently the grip of the self-actor spinner on the shop floor tightened.

While the survival of the mule put the industry and the *smychka* at cross purposes because sustained output for the peasant market could be achieved only with a simultaneous rise in labour costs, this was not the case for the other machine found in fine-spinning halls, the ring-frame. The British expatriates who created the mule *komplekt* were not motivated by any wish to defend craft or status; they simply introduced patterns of work which were, for them, self evident. When new technologies came along which gave them the chance to organize things differently, they had no reason to ignore designers' original intentions; thus ring-frame halls were populated by women.

Sources habitually refer to ring-frame spinners as unskilled,[23] but in fact the job did require specific skills. Piecing, doffing and cleaning were often carried out while the frames were still running, and when spinners stopped their banks shut-down time for a full doffing, involving in excess of 700 spindles, was supposed to be three to four minutes. Spinners, therefore, had to be attentive to their work and needed good visual judgement to prevent spindles over-running.[24] As in other rooms, ring-frame spinners were surrounded by a range of fetching and carrying trades. Spinners and doffers, sometimes with assistant spinner, made up the *komplekt* itself, and as on the mule the *komplekt* was more than just a work team: 'the doffers who work under the direction of the ring-frame spinner, these immediate candidates for the post of spinner, are interested in the acquisition of practical skills'.[25]

Bad spinning affected the labour process in weaving sheds because operatives stood at the end of the production chain and were thus completely dependent on the efficiency of all other rooms in the mill.[26] Weavers responded to this difficulty by modifying their work practices. 'In the majority of mills in the Soviet Union', noted one engineer, 'weavers not only work at their machines, they also have to watch over the looms'. Another elaborated the point by complaining of the 'irrational' use of the labour force; weavers had to fetch their own thread and other materials, 'and it even happens that they have to adjust and trim the looms themselves'.[27] The devolution of control to the power loom tenter, however, could occur only in a hesitant, sporadic fashion. Lancashire looms had none of the mystique of craft surrounding the mule, and there was no British tradition of craft which could have been grafted onto the Russian mill.

Machine idiosyncrasy

The labour process was further complicated by machine idiosyncrasy. In 1927 A. A. Nol'de, a frequent commentator on the textile industry, put the issue in its historical context:

The majority of Russian mills grew slowly from small spinning rooms or weaving sheds. As the years passed new extensions were added and new machines installed, but old buildings and equipment continued to function alongside the new. Many mills thus resemble museums of the textile industry spread over many years.[28]

Iaroslavl's biggest mill was a case in point; founded in 1722 and enlarged piecemeal in 1861, 1878 and 1882, it 'violated the elementary rules of the rational distribution of equipment'.[29] Elsewhere, in Moscow *guberniia*, a short history of the Reutovskaia mill published in 1928 includes a fold-out plan showing old and new buildings; self-actors and ring-frames were sometimes in separate rooms, sometimes jumbled together. And in another mill, this time in Ivanovo-Voznesensk, a plethora of spinning and weaving frames were mixed in on the same floors, and even in the same rooms.[30] *Rabkrin*, the Workers' and Peasants' Inspectorate, lamented the 'abnormal distribution of machinery' in the industry at large in 1926, but nothing had changed four years later; mills still had 'in one and the same shop machines of various construction, speed and age'.[31] If anything, the limited market policies of NEP encouraged technological idiosyncrasy and localism: frames offered for sale by Leningrad's Karl Marx enterprise in 1926, for instance, could not be manufactured to one standard pattern. A Supreme Economic Council (Vesenkha) commission noted this curious fact with dismay: 'separatism' arose because trusts insisted on introducing design variations at the behest of particular mills.[32]

The consequences of eclectic capital purchases, technological idiosyncrasy and the gradual accumulation of worn-out machinery were predictable; the extraordinary technological diversity apparent in the industry frustrated managers and technicians who wanted to reform the labour process. 'Methods of work in various trusts and even within enterprises of the same trust are quite different', asserted one technician; in general 'each mill established its own technical norms', observed Nol'de, 'depending on particular circumstances'.[33] Systematic accounting and control over work on the shop floor was thus a real problem for specialists like weaving engineer A. A. Abramov:

The factory shop consists of a collection of operatives engaged in the same work. It is the basic productive unit of the mill, and thus it follows that systematic control of the work of these production cells is the barest minimum required for efficiency's sake. Nevertheless, we know of shops where it is known only that they exist – how they work is known to scarcely anyone.[34]

Control was decentralized, traditional, elusive; something inherited by successive generations of workers of a particular locality or job as they were initiated into the mill: 'in every mill there is some kind of accounting', lamented Abramov in 1926, 'but in many mills things carry on as they were first introduced half-a-century ago. Such methods may be termed "accounting by eye" '.[35] These methods of work were replicated and reinforced by *na glazakh* masters (masters who did things 'by eye'); 'old masters of some kind accepted by the workers in their section', whose relationship with a shop's population, observed another specialist in 1930, had a fundamental effect on output and general attitude. Here, personal idiosyncrasy was the corollary of technological idiosyncrasy. Working by eye meant that foremen kept notebooks drawn from their own experience: 'such notes take, for example, the following form: "weft count sixty sort II on 400-spindle frame turns out in six hours ten minutes" or "five doffers clear 160-spindle ring-frame in three minutes" '. But 'if the master leaves the factory the norm leaves too, and if the master is ill the norm is ill'. Notebooks could not simply be picked up by other foremen and foremen could not transfer their notes to other mills because 'major and minor' differences obtained: 'Master Ivan might give an entirely different output norm to Master Petr – if it were possible to hold a conference of all masters to establish output norms, we should have no norms at all'.[36] Day in and day out men like these passed on traditional work practices to new recruits. This was particularly so because a large minority of workers were illiterate, about one-quarter of the total textile workforce in 1926.[37]

Not only did the mill stamp its image on the recruit, recruits brought their own world to the shop floor. The textile syndicate (VTS) meditated on this point in 1926. Newcomers were 'in the majority of cases domestic workers accustomed to a low return on their work. To expect from such operatives American output levels without creating for them American conditions of life . . . is impossible.'[38] Indeed, there was no shortage of comment on this matter throughout the 1920s. At the seventh VPST congress in 1926 a Moscow delegate complained of the 'great influx of new workers from the countryside. They come to the mill knowing nothing about machinery, and consequently there are many accidents',[39] whilst in the same year another observer reflected on the insouciant attitudes of newcomers to the disciplines of industrial work:

The peasants, given the backward state of our agriculture, have had little con-tact with machinery. They imagine that the workers' tasks are much easier than the peasants', that the machine does all the work, and that looking after the machine is not very difficult.[40]

Family economy

Operatives returning from the land as NEP took hold shared an experi-ence common to all industrial workers, but for cotton hands there are reasons which suggest that the experience was less than traumatic. They were not clearly divorced from the village. Even in 1929 more than 25 per cent of the workforce, drawn almost exclusively from the CIR, had some 'tie with the land' or source of income outside the mill, and most were actively farming with other family members.[41] Moreover, although officials in CIR trusts noted that peasants were coming into the mills after 1922 because they were unable to make ends meet without off-farm income, landed workers were not drawn exclusively from peasant backgrounds, nor were they particularly young.[42] It is therefore possible to deduce that long-serving operatives were holding on to their land in the 1920s, and that land was inherited within cadre worker families. At the end of the decade a wide-ranging sociological investigation elaborated the implications for rationalizers with reference to CIR mills:

A significant fall in output during the summer months is the normal seasonal phenomenon in our mills, and this is partly explained by the fact that workers with an interest in the peasant economy, in our mills more than fifty per cent of the total, reduce their output in the summer months. They come straight from the fields where they've been working . . . usually two to three hours before dawn and the start of the morning shift . . . You can see them in the shops making tea, 'I'm so tired, I come here to rest, not to work'.[43]

Family economy was also inflected into the labour process. Many *komplekt* members were kin, youngsters waiting to inherit jobs which belonged to their families. In July 1927 *Golos tekstilei*, the VPST newspaper, devoted half a page to workers' letters on this issue. Job inheritance necessarily led to the rigid stratification of the workforce, complained one Moscow operative; the unskilled could not break through because 'masters transmit the secrets of their trade only to their own children'. Another remarked that family training inevitably resulted in the reinforcement of traditional work practices. A few years earlier the VPST central committee (TsK) approached the issue from another angle. Two problems beset the industry in the Ivanovo region, asserted one writer, the shortage of skilled workers and the shortage of housing. As many thousands of girls were listed as unskilled in labour exchanges and thus were of no use to the mills, mothers should bring their daughters into the factory to pass on their own skills. Workers' letters in 1927 commented on the 'open secret' that formal methods of training were very bad, and that it was therefore better to let parents instruct their own children: one operative from Ul'ianovsk *guberniia* held that 'youngsters are better taught by their own parents, or by other members of their own family', a sentiment echoed in Leningrad where a correspondent also hinted that the extended family might be the relevant training unit. When new recruits were expected in the Vysh-nevolochek district of Tver' *guberniia* parents petitioned that they should be drawn from amongst their own children. They held that this was the most expedient way of replicating a skilled workforce for the region's mills. Such events were a 'daily occurrence' in Ivanovo *guberniia's* Iakhromskaia mill, particularly as workers objected to the administration hiring peasants[44] – presumably, that is, peasants who did not already have kin on the shopfloor.

Indeed, if families were split up inside the factory production was sometimes disrupted, because kin-based training was inextricably linked to job inheritance. In 1928, when some mills switched to seven-hour/three-shift working, parents in Ramenskoe 'rushed away' from their own machines to instruct their offspring allocated to other rooms. A year earlier an operative from the Ozerskii Textile Trust reported a 'mass demand' from weavers to be allowed to train their own children. 'Parents consider this their right', he continued, and laconically mentioned that family influence embraced the labour exchange and the local insurance office as well. Letters received by *Golos tekstilei* in March that year from the cotton districts confirm the link between the family, direct hiring, shopfloor training and job inheritance: in the northern part of Tver', *guberniia* women operatives passed their looms on to their daughters when they retired, or petitioned the factory committees to let them hire and train members of their own families so they could leave their work 'to rest' for a few months.[45]

Thus the organization of work in the industry at large could be very flexible. Looking back over the decade as a whole one investigator noted that

on a two shift system, that is, where each machine or group of machines is operated by two workers at different times, each shift member can easily estimate the effectiveness of the other's work. Moreover the selection of shift members was comparatively simple, and frequently members of one and the same family worked on the same machines on different shifts.[46]

Moreover, family penetration of *komplekty* gave operatives the chance to arrange time-sharing schemes amongst themselves, a point made explicit by the managers' journal in 1927:

In many factories where women operate the same machines on a two shift system, not unnaturally, they produce half the necessary minimum monthly output each. Furthermore, by private arrangement amongst themselves – and sometimes with the agreement of the foreman – they alter the distribution of their hours so that one or the other of them can attend to some business of her own.[47]

It is also evident from this source that shopfloor managers were not always aware of exactly who was working when, where, or on which machines, and that foremen did not always consider it necessary to control the distribution of labour or gather information on the population of the shopfloor for any given shift.

Pay

In April 1924 Vesenkha and the Central Council of Trades Unions (VTsSPS) tried to force up productivity by imposing piece rates.[48] In fact about half the cotton workforce was already paid by the piece,[49] but existing methods complicated matters considerably. For a start piece rates had existed for decades. They had evolved as a compromise between capitalism and community and family structures in pre-revolutionary Russia, a point noted by R.M. Odell, an American textile specialist visiting Russia in 1912:

Operatives are generally paid by the piece, and in mills working two shifts the production of the spindle or loom is awarded equally to each of the two operatives tending the machine. It would appear that this system would cause complaint amongst the workers, but apparently it does not, and the managers of several mills stated that it actually tended to increase production. The more efficient weaver, for example, 'gets behind' the operative on the same set of looms who is inclined to neglect his work . . . thus increasing the earnings of both weavers. Moreover, wherever possible, two members of the same family operate a set of looms or the same spinning frames, etc. The arrangement is particularly satisfactory in the case of a family with small children; the husband takes one shift and his wife the other, and the children in the home are never left alone.[50]

In addition piece working, whether or not calculated collectively, meant many different things. Pay might be calculated from the value of each unit produced by an operative, the 'direct' piece rate. 'Indirect piece rates', the system described above, applied where individual wages were drawn from the total earnings of a work group. The total wage fund for a *komplekt* might be established by measuring the group's output directly or on the basis of norms derived from comparisons with other teams. On the other hand norms might be set by measuring the productivity of a typical 'skilled' worker on a particular frame, the 'removed piece rate'. Under this dispensation no deductions were made for machine stoppages, provided they were not the operative's fault. Accordingly the accusation was made that the removed piece rate was much favoured by those anxious to keep up their earnings with the minimum of effort; workers who stopped their machines 'for some trifling repair'. A third variant was the 'guaranteed piece rate', where wages depended on the value of output but could fall only to a set minimum should something unforeseen alter conditions of work, like a sharp drop in the quality of raw materials. 'Piece rates with premiums' gave bonuses for exceeding norms. 'Simple or indirect piece rates with premiums for the economic use of materials' added a final complicating touch.

All applied in spinning rooms and weaving sheds in the 1920s, as well as the simple daily rate, sometimes with incentives for productivity. American systems of pay, concluded the author, 'are seldom found'. To add to the general confusion auxiliary workers' pay was often, but not always, linked to the productivity of those operatives to whom they were attached:[51] a source of many conflicts, remarked *Golos tekstilei*, and of all kinds of unofficial additional payments.[52] Finally, each variant had to intermesh somehow or other with the particular wage scale or tariff in use in a given region, and with the type of product under consideration in a given shop. Doubtless machine idiosyncrasy played its part too.

Thus payment by the piece was anything but simple and imposing individual piece rates would be far from easy. This was particularly so because the details of implementation had to be dealt with locally. In Ivanovo *guberniia*, for instance, substantial changes in wage levels appeared within four weeks of 1 April 1924. At the end of June a special commission, with representatives from local government, Ivanovo State Textile Trust, the local economic council, management, the factory committees and the shop floor, met to consider exactly how rates should be worked out for each count and cloth sort. Next month agreed rates were written into collective agreements covering two trusts.[53] Vesenkha and VTsSPS quickly stepped in. In July Dzerzhinsky was appointed head of a special commission to review pay and labour productivity; particular emphasis was to be placed on reducing the number of auxiliary workers.[54] Seemingly indifferent to all these high-level investigations Ivanovo's VPST branch scratched together a 'revision commission' in December made up exclusively of factory committee members. A disingenuous gloss appeared on page twenty-eight of its report:

amongst a mass of various questions . . . of particular significance is the question of raising productivity in the mills. Here [the revision commission] paid special attention to measures directed towards lowering the cost of production, of fixing a norm for the number of auxiliary workers, and of re-organizing the tariff system for some categories of worker.

Immediately below came the recommendations. A mere 421 should be laid off – but spread over six mills. Moreover, each factory should be left to define its own needs in terms of auxiliary workers. Last of all there should be a new tariff sub-division for assistants and production workers on piece rates. All this was supposedly designed to expedite *uplotnenie* – 'speeding up' or 'tightening up' the working day.[55]

Subsequently those VPST branches that had not acted on the April decision reluctantly fell into line: Leningrad sometime in autumn 1924 (comparisons between mills necessary, a six-month research period required); Moscow in September (a feasibility study on machinery, supply of raw materials, quality of workforce, implementation promised for January 1925); Vladimir the same month (caveats about the quality of raw materials and the condition of machines). Like Ivanovo, Leningrad had its own special commission with managers, trust officials, factory committee and shopfloor representatives. The local VPST branch finally ratified individual piece working on 1 December 1924. Like Ivanovo, wages rose when mills in Vladimir district eventually implemented piece rates.[56]

Localism and tradition were thus characteristic of the wage system throughout NEP and attempts to impose individual piece rates met with little success – here is a glimpse of ring-frame halls in the 1920s:

> If work is carried out on two or three shifts, that is, if this or that group of machines is operated at various times by two or three workers, then output and the corresponding wage is calculated collectively and . . . divided between [the workers] equally . . . the absence of individual accounting restrains increases in labour intensification, since every additional effort of a shift member adds to the general store of wages, and [each worker] does not fully receive his own wage from his own efforts.[57]

What is missing from this jaundiced observation, of course, is the link with family structure and family labour inside and outside the mill noticed by Odell, a link which made collective methods of pay and work advantageous to many workers.

Attempts to standardize or equalize pay, which were introduced at the same time as the piece rate reform, met with little success: tradition re-appeared in the wage packet in the familiar guise of gender and trade. Apart from foremen, overlookers and self-actor spinners, few in 1924 earned more than forty roubles a month, and few in these trades less than thirty. Though differentials had been reduced somewhat since 1917, the old shopfloor hierarchy, with self-actor spinners at the top, re-asserted itself.[58]

The *uplotnenie* experiment

Komplekt working, technological and individual idiosyncrasy, diverse wage systems, family economy and kinship networks on the shop floor thus combined to reproduce and transmit a traditional culture of work across generations, and they allowed subtle, fluid arrangements to form and re-form under the official crust of rules and regulations. It was against this unpromising background that the first attempts at rationalization were made.

The scissors crisis of autumn 1923 convinced the government that something would have to be done in the industry if the *smychka* was to be maintained and the regime secured. Engineers and specialists were keen to try out some form of Taylorism,[59] but over the coming months bureaucratic wrangling reduced their ambitions to schemes for *uplotnenie*; as a result, in November 1924 the vice-president of Vesenkha dispatched the following telegram to all cotton trusts:

I order immediately: (1) the transfer from one to three, and where possible to four [looms per weaver]; (2) transfer ring-frame spinners to three spindle banks ... on other machines [transfer workers] to four frames; (3) where explanations are required this telegram is to be made known in my name. If the reasons for the transfer are not fully understood, explain them. On the 1st and 16th of every month each director of each mill is to communicate the progress of this work to me.

                                                                    Piatakov.[60]

To add to the confusion Vesenkha started to back-pedal almost at once. Circular 15, sent to the cotton industry on 10 December 1924, spoke of the need for caution, agitation amongst the workforce and planning,[61] and a few days later Piatakov, VtsSPS, the VPST president and VTS dispatched a soothing letter to all mills and their factory committees. Although *uplotnenie* was necessary there must be no unnecessary haste.[62]

These subsequent instructions were to have no immediate effect. 'Unfortunately', according to one observer, Piatakov's first 'military command',

with its bald and simple demands, made a deeper impression on the minds of some managers than the subsequent circular ... because managers tend to work by applying pressure ... the entire campaign focused on intensifying work on the shop floor and scarcely any attention at all was given to the question of improving, organizing and rationalizing the technical side of production.[63]

The consequence of 'applying pressure' was large-scale unrest in the mills. By summer virtually all factories including *uplotnenie*, encompassing about 25 per cent of the total workforce, were embroiled in strikes. Menshevik correspondents claimed that all affected regions had strike committees. They were not necessarily *ad hoc* bodies; indeed, organization appears to have centred around factory committees. VPST's strongest asset in terms of legitimacy, they were also the weakest link in the transmission belt stretching from Moscow to the most remote mill. In daily contact with operatives and staffed from the shopfloor they were always likely to slip their moorings and break free from central policies. Workers ignored official regulations and captured factory committees by substituting their own candidates. The same thing happened in shop-delegate elections. Local party organizations were 'close to panic'; there was simply no institutional check, no mechanism of control left. Acting as a 'judicial and legal mask' the committees, with freely elected delegates or co-opted strike leaders, started to negotiate with administrators and left other VPST organs 'helpless'.[64]

It appears that strikers wished to see something done about multi-machine working; beyond that we do not know exactly what they wanted. For this reason it is difficult to talk about success or failure, gains or losses, but there were changes in several aspects of workers' lives. For a start several different agencies began to assert that from the very beginning labour intensification was always intended to be a voluntary affair. *Golos tekstilei* reminded its readers that *uplotnenie* was permissible 'only on the basis of the voluntary agreement of the workers and with adequate preparation by trusts and local VPST bodies'.[65]

No less important than the issues surrounding *uplotnenie* were those pertaining to factory committee elections and shop delegate meetings. The second TsK VPST plenum, held in May 1925, signalled a change in policy. Shop delegates were to be given 'real influence' over admission to and expulsion from the union, and over the details of *uplotnenie*. In both instances they were to work closely with factory committees. It took an instruction from the party's TsK to effect more radical change. Prior to 1925 workers elected their factory committees from lists drawn up in advance by the existing committee plenum. In July *Golos tekstilei* announced that lists were abolished. The decision, taken because 'of the general spread of conflicts in some textile mills switching to three-frame working', was manifestly a concession to strikers. VPST clarified the issue at its third plenum in October by observing that lists interfered with the worker's 'right' to democratic participation in the union. Now, where they still existed, they were 'for guidance' only.[66]

At the same time as a renewed emphasis on voluntary *uplotnenie* and a new commitment to shopfloor democracy became evident, pay policy underwent a sea-change. VPST leaders promised a review which would result in wage rises from 1 July 1925. What emerged was a commitment to a 30 per cent increment across the board plus 25–30 per cent again for workers on three looms or three spindle banks. Curiously, Leningrad got only 7 per cent. Everything seemed to revolve around Ivanovo district. Increases were to be paid there first, the union made much of the fact that increments would be higher than elsewhere – 37.5 per cent – and it may be more than coincidental that the announcement was made on the day the *guberniia*'s fifteenth VPST congress convened.[67] Finally, in December a new VPST handbook appeared. 'Experience in the localities' revealed 'mistakes' in the old guide, wrote the TsK secretary in the introduction, now more attention would be paid to the effects of *uplotnenie*. The handbook assigned a scale point for each trade but there was ample scope for local deviation. Frequently a given trade was allotted a range of points; experience, product range and raw material quality were to determine exact placings in the localities.[68]

Although voluntary *uplotnenie*, shopfloor democratization and wage increases were important concessions, this is not to say that discontents entirely abated the following year. As far as cotton operatives were concerned, the Politburo's proclamation of a 'regime of economy' was simply a matter of decanting old wine into new bottles. It is fruitless to try to distinguish between continuing conflicts about piece rates, multi-frame working and speed-ups and new ones arising from the slogan of the day. Pressure for three-spindle bank and three-, or even four-loom working did not cease, and disputes continued to trouble the industry in 1926,[69] but it remains the case that by and large the strike movement faded away in the summer of 1925. Strikers were unable or unwilling to sustain their opposition or to co-ordinate their actions; as one old textile worker put it in conversation with a Menshevik informant, 'we fight one against the other, though each feels that it's necessary to organize'.[70]

There are several reasons why this should have been the case. To start with there were indeed conflicts of interest between workers, and we can start to understand them by looking at mule rooms. Most operatives wished to avoid the shock of *uplotnenie*, but of all production workers only self-actor spinners as a group had the means to deflect the change away from themselves: since no one else understood the workings of a 'pair' except the spinner attached to a given set of 'wheels' the *komplekt* could not be fractured. 'So that the work of the piecer and doffer will be carried out properly', wrote one specialist in 1926, 'so that they can approach the high standards of their English brothers and deal with a greater number of spindles, work on mules must be carried out according to tried and tested methods'.[71] Even the norm setters were at a loss when it came to rationalization. One resolution from their 1925 congress asked Vesenkha 'to give examples of normal manning levels for workers on mule frames'; much depended on 'a subjective opinion of the skill of each spinner', replied the Council.[72] Visions of *uplotnenie* on mules thus boiled down to recommending reductions in *komplekt* numbers and rationalizers fell back on publicizing pre-war manning levels. The net result was that *komplekt* survived 1925.[73] The spinners' ability to avoid *uplotnenie* rested on their control over the labour process; they had little reason to contemplate strike action.

One caveat about self-actor spinning should be mentioned, one which helps to explain another of the strike movement's features. The Menshevik press made no mention of any discontent in Leningrad despite the fact that the city's mill hands did experience change; indeed *uplotnenie* seems to have been enforced there more vigorously than anywhere else – 60 per cent of all spindles affected by the end of 1925.[74] But change took place in special circumstances. In part this had to do with the industry's technical structure and pre-revolutionary history. Since 1850 cotton mills had been migrating from St Petersburg in order to find labour and exploit mass markets by manufacturing cheap cloth. Coarse spinning was therefore very much the preserve of the CIR, a factor naturally reinforced by the NEP. This had important consequences. Working coarse counts on the self-actor required more effort than spinning high counts, thus Leningrad's mule *komplekty* could probably shrug off *uplotnenie* even more easily than their compatriots to the south. In addition, it is also likely that all rooms in Leningrad were insulated from the increased workloads resulting from bad spinning since the city was the *entrepôt* for good quality imported raw cotton.[75] Bad spinning was therefore likely to be more common in the CIR. Not only did this penalize all CIR operatives in all shops when attempts were made to introduce *uplotnenie*, bad spinning also divided workers one against the other. To some extent CIR fine spinners – ring-frame and self-actor – could escape from the burden of working up poor cotton by passing shoddy goods on to weavers, and the CIR was Russia's weaving centre. 'Where all the attention of workers is directed to raising output', wrote a weaver from Moscow *guberniia* in February 1926, discussing mule rooms, 'pre-revolutionary norms have been surpassed', but when thread reached the weavers there were breakages and stoppages, and thus output stayed low.[76]

This brings us on to a much more obvious difference between Leningrad and the CIR. At the 14th Party Congress Tomsky remarked that *uplotnenie* was 'not helped' by the influx of new workers, peasants interested only in material advantage. Two commentators made the vital connection. Looking back, they thought that commuting workers with an interest in agriculture were the 'basic block' to *uplotnenie* because 'the peasant-worker clearly feels that working on three or four machines does not leave him the energy he needs to look after his own farm'.[77] Summaries of factory committee reports exploring the social dimensions of the failure of *uplotnenie* tell the same story. Field work frustrated administrators in Vladimir *guberniia*, rural workers in one district of Moscow *guberniia* were 'mainly interested in their own farms'; the 'greatest response' in another came from those 'cut off from the peasant economy and the peasant family . . . who rarely visit the countryside'. 'I'm not taking on four looms', stated one weaver, 'I've got a lot of work to do on the land.' Some workers around Shchelkovo who owned horses simply gave up the factory for good.[78]

Originally Vesenkha wanted things done all at once, but the drive for labour intensification, though by no means entirely unsuccessful, turned out to be a patchy affair, something like a weather front drifting across the CIR after December 1924. As its leading edge touched now one district, now another, and disturbed established patterns of work in particular mills and rooms, so operatives responded with a ragged strike movement. By spring a series of widely dispersed incidents caused enough worry in Moscow to effect change and compromise – voluntary *uplotnenie*, shopfloor democratization, substantial pay rises. The latter two were doubtless universally popular. The former, a concession to individual circumstances, was important for those with family economy outside the mill.

The events of 1925 had implications stretching far beyond the mill. Cloth was already in short supply in the countryside but in August 1925 VTS had to shut some of its provincial stores. They had nothing to sell. Next month TsK VPST issued a worried statement about the need to maintain the *smychka*, and it is probably no accident that the goods famine, which sparked off another round of grain hoarding and forced the Commissariat of Finance to inflate the note issue, should have come in autumn.[79] Much of this may have been caused by rising demand, but the strikes can only have added to the regime's difficulties. Moreover, the whole confused development of *uplotnenie* brought rationalizers face to face with the problems of changing an industry whose social and technological parameters were so diverse. Here is Kuteishchikov, writing for VTS in 1926: 'one must recall that the campaign . . . did not live up to expectations'.[80] And Markov, a VTS employee, speaking to the fourth plenum of TsK VPST a year later:

In the field of labour intensification we have chaos. In one place they work three looms, in another four, or even six. Here they pay a premium of twenty-five per cent, there thirty or even thirty-eight per cent. In such circumstances it is impossible to speak of a planned transfer to *uplotnenie*.[81]

The seven-hour/three-shift experiment

The second attempt at rationalization was triggered by the war scare and grain crisis at the end of the NEP. Farmers, responding to alarmist press reports predicting foreign invasion, began to withdraw from the market in late 1926 and early 1927,[82] and by autumn 1927 low grain marketings were causing concern in Moscow. The October 1927 jubilee manifesto, which proclaimed reductions in the working day throughout Soviet industry, provided the catalyst for change. In cotton the seven-hour day was to be accompanied by three-shift working and labour intensification in a further attempt to defend the *smychka*: 'as is well known', remarked someone at an arbitration meeting between VPST and management early in January 1928, '*uplotnenie* will occur simultaneously with the transfer to three-shift working'.[83] In November 1927 a VTsSPS commission set up to oversee implementation targeted five mills. Almost immediately the list began to grow including, within a month, four more CIR mills. By 8 January 1928 the commission, now expanded to include representatives from the Council of Peoples' Commissars, had picked out seventeen large mills employing around 104,000 workers.[84] Alarmed by the grain crisis and anxious to tempt the peasantry into the marketplace they suddenly decided to proceed at 'maximum speed'.[85] Directives were issued on the 6th, preparations were to be completed by the 10th, and the change carried out on the 15th.[86]

Prospects for the transition were not good. Almost without exception the mills had only a week or so's grace[87] and the first problem which had to be addressed in the localities was finding workers for the third shift. Little comfort could be drawn from a perusal of labour exchange lists. Although in key trades registrations had been rising slowly for the past two years, totals in the RSFSR were far below requirements.[88] Exchange officials in targeted zones had no clear idea of the skill levels of those on their books and were 'in no condition at all to meet the demands' placed on them.[89] In such circumstances factories had little option but to cast their nets wider and hire 'at the gate'. Unskilled recruits were filling skilled vacancies in Ivanovo-Voznesensk, reported the local paper in January 1928. In Ramenskoe 1,850 new operatives came straight from the villages while VPST officials in Ivanovo *guberniia* scratched together special commissions to scour the countryside for likely recruits.[90]

On the shop floor the new regime was regarded with suspicion. 'From what I've heard', observed one CIR operative, 'no one has spoken against the seven-hour day, but if you're talking about *uplotnenie*, about working four spindle banks or four looms, that's a different matter'.[91] Soon the thunderclouds began to pile up across the cotton districts. During the first four months of 1928 stoppages in the Shuia district's preparatory departments grew apace, and in Vladimir *guberniia*'s Karabanovskii Combine weavers quarrelled violently with management over the details of three-shift working.[92] In December Tomsky addressed the 8th VTsSPS Congress, and, as in 1925, brooded over strikes which occurred without official sanction; the work of the unions in this field was 'hardly commendable'.[93] Nevertheless, despite Tomsky's forebodings, the storm never broke. In 1928 there are no reports of anything like the widespread strikes in the CIR three years previously.

In order to explain why it is necessary to turn our attention to the way changes worked their way through inside the factory. Disparate factors, some deeply embedded in shopfloor culture, others flickering over the mill for no more than a few months, combined to produce a pattern which distorted the entire experiment.

Operatives' responses should be put in the context of a whole range of factors; family ties, machine idiosyncrasy, pay systems, traditional work patterns, social relations at the frame and the disturbing impact of the new workforce. 'They are afraid of losing their own machines', noted one writer, 'their workmates on their shift, or they consider that it would be more convenient to work nights.' Two others acknowledged that women disliked being separated from their husbands who remained on the old shift, feared that their wages would fall if they were moved to unfamiliar frames and generally exhibited 'a feeling of shift solidarity'. *Golos tekstilei* reported the same sentiments in Moscow *guberniia* a year later.[94] Throughout Ivanovo *guberniia* experienced women did not want to work with new recruits: 'the insufficiently skilled nature of the new workforce' in the province, wrote two local specialists,

caused problems over shift placings. Because wages are based on machine output and individual pay is not calculated separately but divided between the shift, operatives were given the right to select their own co-workers. Sometimes misunderstandings arose between shifts. Workers demanded that this or that operative who did not agree or could not work with this loom or that frame . . . should be removed by the administration. There were complaints from old workers that the new workforce, whose productivity was lower than theirs and whose waste rates were higher, lowered their output and pay.[95]

The 'right to select' is significant. So peremptory were the centre's orders that administrators probably had little option but to clinch hurried deals on the shop floor. It was imperative to get things moving. Thus hopes for labour intensification were under threat from the start: 'by introducing *uplotnenie* amongst some operatives (older workers, recent arrivals, those connected with the land)', noted the two specialists mentioned above, 'there arose opposition to these measures (especially in the Seredskaia mill) because of the dread of not being able to cope and the disinclination to change old habits'. Consequently the mill's shifts worked independently, the same machines sometimes had four operatives on one shift and two or three on the others.[96]

In addition, absenteeism amongst new entrants soared alarmingly. In

Ramenskoe, for instance, absences recorded 'for no good reason' were 212 per cent higher for new workers than for established operatives, sickness rates exhibited the same tendency.[97] Much of this resulted from the predilection for field work amongst those fresh from the village: Ivanovo's trades council criticized 'backward' workers who 'pay great attention to the needs of their farms but have little time for the needs and interests of the mill'.[98] Finally, new recruits severely taxed training capacity and schedules had to be reduced. The results were predictable: 'it will be easily understood that such rapid training . . . meant that insufficiently trained workers came onto the shop floor. Output fell, waste rates rose, and experienced workers criticized the poorly trained'.[99]

There had been some attempts at *uplotnenie* over the previous two years or so. Since 1926 trusts had been trying to reorganize the labour process in preparatory departments. *Komplekt* numbers on flyer-frames declined as brigades, each with their own hierarchy, took over the jobs of greasing and cleaning down machines. The process continued into 1928, particularly in transferred mills.[100] As these operatives once belonged to *komplekty* they suffered a singular disadvantage. The chance of advancement narrowed because brigade members were shut out from the traditional world of training; no longer could they learn from the spinners. Their opportunity came in January 1928. Directors had to find competent operatives to man the third shift, and it would be natural for them to prefer workers from these auxiliary groups instead of newcomers, as in fact they did. Contemporaries noticed rapid advancement up the trade ladder for existing *komplekt* members and the consequent promotion of auxiliaries to the frame. Into the vacancies left by promoted auxiliaries stepped raw recruits. The same picture emerges in ring-frame halls.[101] But this did not necessarily result in higher productivity: 'when experienced doffers, upon whom the work of the ring-frame spinner depends, were promoted to the status of spinner', wrote one observer, 'new unskilled workers took their place'. The mills 'suffered conditions of flux', he continued.[102]

Weaving sheds also demonstrate the same pattern of promotion. Established weavers moved up to two, three or four looms along with stand-by operatives and auxiliaries while newcomers took over jobs on single looms, and there were the same complaints about new workers. Incompetent recruits came under fire in Ivanovo *guberniia*,[103] and throughout the seven-hour districts 'not only in each mill, not only in each weaving shed, but even on each group of looms' where the new worked alongside the experienced, the latter's wages declined.[104] But there was an extra problem. Because weaving came at the end of the production process everything depended on the quality of semi-finished goods received from fine-spinning halls. Soon there were a mass of reproaches about bad spinning: 'serious deficiencies' in Iartsevo (sharp wage falls consequent upon poor thread), 'nothing whatsoever done' to improve yarn quality in Serpukhov (a marked increase in loom stoppages), not enough semi-finished goods coming through to weavers (Shuia), and in Orekhovo-Zuevo concern over raw material quality and spinning off the count.[105]

Intricate changes also affected the self-actor *komplekt*. A few months before the jubilee manifesto the journal of the engineers' section of VPST carried an article which recommended establishing brigade cleaning teams, but nothing was said about spinners, piecers, doffers or creelers *per se*; there was no attempt to discuss the *komplekt* as an institution. These proposals elicited almost no response.[106] Nevertheless, spinners were affected by the changes: the influx of new workers into the shops conspired to reduce their pay and the seven-hour/three-shift experiment eventually fractured the internal cohesion of the *komplekt*.[107]

Self-actor halls did not employ stand-by operatives – given the presence of experienced piecers there was no need – so as new *komplekty* were organized for the extra shift senior piecers were the constituency from which new spinners were drawn. Similarly doffers moved up to become piecers and raw recruits found a place on the lowest rung of the trade ladder as doffers or creelers. Thus established spinners had to take on new piecers and – more unsettlingly – raw doffers and creelers who slowed down the work process. As a consequence they may have been asking for more doffers to try to lighten the workload, if so they could well slip a rung on the wage scale. Doffers, however, enjoyed substantial pay rises, most probably a combined result of the new policy of levelling up and their likely promotion to senior doffer.[108]

Perhaps these factors helped to fan the flames smouldering in the Seredskaia mill. On 14 January 1928 someone wrote to the local press criticizing shop solidarity. Since so few skilled workers were available in the labour exchange the most simple method of increasing output in self-actor halls would have been to hive off operatives from existing *komplekty* and form new ones. Nothing, however, was done. Three days later mule spinners went into conference to talk about auxiliary workers because management wanted to form brigades. Discussions did not go well. Next day the self-actor halls stopped work and held impromptu meetings. A compromise emerged. Brigades were formed for the lowest trades only, fetchers and carriers. Encouraged perhaps by the reforming mood, tensions within the *komplekt* began to surface.

Piecers complained that although they could do the work, spinners always controlled operations specific to the end of a production run ('backing off' and 'winding on') – they had 'a traditional view of their skills'.[109] After a long pause discontents exploded on the day work resumed after the summer holidays. On 16 August, in response to a pre-arranged signal, all self-actor spinners shut down their frames and walked out of the mill. They saw 'only one side' of the seven-hour day, hectored *Golos tekstilei*, wages and not productivity; they made 'incorrect and dangerous' demands. In fact their pay had been falling consistently because of poor-quality fibre. A special commission waved aside the figures and blamed the strike on 'opponents of the workers' state' who agitated amongst 'backward' workers. The commission deliberated for five days, the strike was over in two-and-a-half.[110] It found no echo in any other mill, even though mule spinners in nearby factories also felt the shock of falling wages.[111] Moreover, there were no reports of further strikes in the Seredskaia.

The Sereda strike and the unrest which preceded it encapsulate many of the new factors present on the shop floor. If established mule spinners felt themselves threatened, new spinners – a few months ago piecers anxious about training and promotion – might pause and reflect on recent gains as well as losses. Previously they had little chance of inheriting a pair of wheels until someone died or retired: now the seven-hour/three-shift system, by effectively expanding the number of mule pairs by a third or so, presented them with a new opportunity. And the same is true of operatives in all other shops; in preparatory departments, initial processing rooms, ring-frame halls and weaving sheds. Experienced promotees might look askance at raw recruits if they were not kin, but their new condition blunted discontent. Elsewhere established workers were busy keeping strangers away from their frames and out of their *komplekty* by trying to persuade management to juggle the shifts, and new entrants, more than ever before with some source of off-mill income, reacted to *uplotnenie* by taking time off. Interests had diversified to such an extent that it is difficult to imagine any common bond anywhere in the mill strong enough to unite workers, even in a single shop.

If the impact of seven-hour/three-shift working on the cotton workforce was diverse, from the regime's perspective matters had turned out badly. 'For a whole series of reasons', opined a booklet looking back over the first three months of the experiment in Ivanovo *guberniia*, 'the mills . . . were transferred in a forced manner . . . This made it impossible for executives and managers to draw up plans for improving the technical state of machinery, the quality of raw materials and the skill of the workforce.' Another regretted that 'the rural market dictated to the industry', and a third deplored the failure of *uplotnenie*; 'pay has grown *significantly* faster than labour productivity', mainly as the result of the 'mechanical growth of the number of operatives', asserted a fourth.[112] Problems were compounded by VTS's inability to supply good quality cotton and the reluctance of mills to standardize count and cloth sorts.[113] In May 1928 the party's Central Committee turned its gaze on the cotton industry, castigating bad management, poor cotton supply, inept training and the lamentable state of the labour exchanges. The seven-hour/three-shift system had led to 'a series of difficulties' in the factories.[114] The Central Committee of VPST, disenchanted with the experiment by September 1928, did not fail to join in the growing chorus of disapproval:

Economic organs wish to increase production chiefly by tightening up the working day, and particularly by introducing three-shift working in all cotton mills. The TsK is strongly against this . . . From the point of view of efficiency it has scarcely any justification; equipment will be worn out and consequently . . . will have to be replaced at considerable expense . . . On the strength of these observations three-shift working has not, in our opinion, had the expected effect of lowering the cost of production.[115]

Conclusion

Moscow's attempt to utilize seven-hour/three-shift working to reduce the cost of cloth and thus strengthen the *smychka* was undermined by shopfloor culture, but the parameters of implementation, conflict and resolution differed from those obtaining three years previously. In 1925 the government was forced into compromise: so important was the *smychka* to the political economy of the NEP that overt industrial action by part of the CIR workforce resulted in a rapid retreat across a range of disputed territory – *uplotnenie*, pay, shopfloor democracy. By contrast, in 1928, there was no strike movement. Instead, hasty implementation obliged mills to rely on family economy and customary practice inside the mill. The net result was to reinforce traditional labour processes predicated on *komplekty* and so emasculate the drive towards higher labour productivity.

Though they had none of the institutions available to workers elsewhere – free trades unions, independent political parties – operatives were not atomized individuals at the mercy of the party and state. The shaping of tsarist Russia's cotton industry by British expatriates and British equipment, coupled with the Lancashire proletariat's struggles against the early factory regime,[116] unwittingly provided Soviet mill workers with the means of resistance at the point of production. Their inheritance came cheaply. The battles had taken place in a far-away country and another century. Under tsarism the dynamics of class struggle in Oldham, Manchester and the Scottish lowlands were projected in shadow play onto the Russian screen. Thereafter the shadows took on a life of their own. The key to understanding the fate of the rationalization drives of the 1920s lies on the shopfloor, and in particular in the relationship between the labour process in the world's first socialist state and that which evolved in the world's first industrial nation.

Notes

1. See, for example, V.A. Buianov, *Tekstil'shchiku, o trudovoi distsipline* (Moscow, 1929), p. 6; *Na novykh putiakh. Itogi novoi ekonomicheskoi politiki 1921–1922gg.* (Moscow, 1923), vyp. 3, p. 9.
2. See J. Foster, *Class Struggle and the Industrial Revolution: Early Industrial Capitalism in Three English Towns* (London, 1974).
3. *Izvestiia tekstil'noi promyshlennosti i torgovli*, no. 6 (15 February 1926), p. 1 (hereafter *ITPT*).
4. *Sotsialisticheskoe stroitel'stvo SSSR* (Moscow, 1934), p. 134; *Vsesoiuznaia perepis' naseleniia 1926 goda* (Moscow, 1930), vol. 34, table 3, pp. 22–6.
5. A.A. Matiugin, *Rabochii klass SSSR v gody vosstanovleniia narodnogo khoziaistva (1921–1925gg.)* (Moscow, 1962), pp. 212–18, 221, 228–9.
6. *Stenograficheskii otchet 1-go vserossiiskogo s"ezda rabotnikov tekstil'noi promyshlennosti v Moskve, 12–16 okt. 1922g.* (Moscow, 1923), p. 37.
7. See M. Burawoy, *The Politics of Production: Factory Regimes Under Capitalism and Socialism* (London, 1985), and Foster, *Class Struggle*.
8. L.I. Vas'kina, *Rabochii klass SSSR nakanune sotsialisticheskoi industrializatsii (chislennost', sostav, razmeshchenie)* (Moscow, 1981), pp. 116, 123.
9. *Dostizheniia i nedochety tekstil'noi promyshlennosti. (Po materialam tekstil'noi sektsii NK RKI SSSR)* (Moscow, 1926), p. 197; *Rabochii krai*, 21 and 24 November 1920 (hereafter *RK*).
10. A.A. Tikhomirov, *Odin den' na priadil'noi fabrike* (Moscow, 1927), p. 16.
11. V.I. Feoktistov, *Ekskursiia na bumagopriadil'nuiu fabriku* (Moscow, 1924), pp. 27–8.
12. A.F. Ziman, *Tekhnicheskoe normirovanie priadil'nogo proizvodstva. Chast' I. Otdely: sortirovochnyi, trepal'nyi, chesal'nyi* (Moscow, 1928), pp. 11, 17–18, 52–3.
13. *Rezoliutsiia 1-go vsesoiuznogo s"ezda otdelov truda i T.N.B. tekstil'noi promyshlennosti (20–26/IX-1925g.)* (Moscow, 1926), p. 16 (hereafter *TNB 1925*).
14. *Okhrana truda*, no. 3, March 1929, p. 5.

15. *Ozdorovlenie truda i revoliutsiia byta* (Moscow, 1924), vyp. 4, ch. 1, pp. 57–8; *Sistema i organizatsiia*, no. 8, 1925, p. 25 (hereafter *SiI*); A.F. Ziman, *Tekhnicheskoe normirovanie priadil'nogo proizvodstva. Chast' II. Lentochno-bankabroshnyi i vaternyi otdely* (Moscow, 1931), pp. 17–20, 203, 245.
16. *ITPT*, no. 1–2, January–February 1930, p. 49.
17. N.A. Vasil'ev, ed., *Sel'faktor (dlia gladkoi i pushistoi priazhi)* (Moscow, 1922), p. 170.
18. A.M. Buras, *Osnovy tekhnicheskogo normirovania v tekstil'noi promyshlennosti* (Moscow, 1930), pp. 262–4; Feoktistov, *Ekskursiia*, p. 30; N.T. Pavlov, *Sel'faktor* (Moscow, 1926), p. 116; *SiI*, no. 8, 1925, p. 22; Tikhomirov, *Odin den'*, p. 44.
19. *Tarifnyi spravochnik tekstil'shchikov* (Moscow, 1926), pp. 17–18 (hereafter *1925 spravochnik*).
20. W.H. Lazonick, 'Production relations, labor productivity, and choice of technique: British and U.S. cotton spinning', *Journal of Economic History*, vol. 41, no. 3 (September 1981), pp. 493–5.
21. *Tarif tekstil'shchikov* (Moscow, 1922), p. 47.
22. Feoktistov, *Ekskursiia*, pp. 30–1; *SiI*, no. 10, 1925, pp. 7–9; Tikhomirov, *Odin den'*, p. 44.
23. N.A. Rozenbaum, *Gigiena truda v bumagopriadil'nom i bumagotkatskom proizvodstvakh* (Moscow, 1928), pp. 12–13.
24. A.F. Shvarabovich, *Kak uberech' sebia ot neschastnykh sluchaev v khlopchatobumazhnom proizvodstve* (Moscow, 1926), p. 36.
25. Ia. Kvasha, F. Shofman, *Semichasovoi rabochii den' v tekstil'noi promyshlennosti* (Moscow, 1930), pp. 54–5.
26. *Initsiativnyi sovet po nauchnoi organizatsii truda pri tsentral'nom komitete soiuza tekstil'shchikov. Kratkii otchet* (Moscow, 1924), p. 3.
27. A.A. Abramov, *Nagliadnyi uchet v tekstil'noi promyshlennosti* (Moscow, 1926), p. 78; D.D. Budanov, *Obshche poniatiia o NOTe v chasnosti v tekstil'noi promyshlennosti* (Moscow, 1926), pp. 77–8.
28. Ia. Shykhgal'ter, ed., *Vnutrizavodskii kontrol' kachestva. Sbornik statei i instruktsii* (Moscow, 1927), p. 5.
29. *'Krasnyi Perekop.' Priadil'no-tkatskaia fabrika v Iaroslavle. Proizvodstvennyi al'bom* (Iaroslavl', 1926), passim.
30. M.B. Itsikson, *Reutovskaia priadil'naia fabrika. Ocherk* (Moscow, 1928), pp. 12–13.
31. *Dostizheniia*, p. 113; *ITPT*, no. 1–2, January–February 1930, p. 45.
32. *Ekonomicheskaia zhizn'*, 20 July 1928; *Predpriiatie*, no. 10 (October 1927), pp. 60–3.
33. Shykhgal'ter, *Vnutrizavodskii*, pp. 6–7; A.F. Ziman, *Normirovanie tkatskogo stanka. (Kratkoe prakticheskoe rukovodstvo)* (Moscow, 1926), p. 3.
34. Abramov, *Nagliadnyi uchet*, p. 87.
35. Ibid., p. 8.
36. Buras, *Osnovy*, p. 27.
37. Vas'kina, *Rabochii klass*, p. 123.
38. *ITPT*, nos. 33–4, 25 September 1926, p. 3.

110   *Chris Ward*

39. *Golos tekstilei*, 18 May 1926 (hereafter *GT*).
40. A. Lavrova, *Kak zhivut i trudiatsia rabochie-tekstil'shchiki* (Moscow, 1926), p. 2.
41. A.G. Rashin, *Sostav fabrichno-zavodskogo proletariata SSSR* (Moscow, 1930), pp. 24–5, 30, 43, 139.
42. V.V. Il'insky, *Ivanovskii tekstil'shchik. Sostav i sotsial'naia kharakteristika rabochikh-tekstil'shchikov ivanovskoi promyshlennoi oblasti* (Moscow, 1930), p. 31; N.V. Poliakova, 'Bor'ba rabochikh-tekstil'shchikov za povyshenie proizvoditel'nosti truda v 1921–1925gg. (Po materialam Moskvy i moskovskoi gubernii)', *Voprosy istorii*, no. 6, July 1959, p. 22; Rashin, *Sostav*, pp. 35–6, 44–5.
43. N. Semenov, *Litso fabrichnykh rabochikh, prozhivaiushchikh v derevniakh, i politrosvetrabota sredi nikh. Po materialam obsledovaniia rabochikh tekstil'noi promyshlennosti tsentral'no-promyshlennoi oblasti* (Moscow, 1929), pp. 44–5.
44. *GT*, 18 June 1924, 12 March 1927, 18 March 1927, 24 March 1927, 12 July 1927.
45. *GT*, 12 March 1927, 24 March 1927, 21 February 1928; *Trud*, 28 July 1928.
46. Kvasha, Shofman, *Semichasovoi*, p. 73.
47. *Predpriiatie*, no. 2, February 1927, p. 66.
48. *Otchet gubernskogo otdela soiuza 15-mu gubernskomu s"ezdu tekstil'shchikov ivanovo-voznesenskoi gubernii (apr. 1924g.–mart 1925g.)* (Ivanovo-Voznesensk, 1925), pp. 68–9 (hereafter *I-V gubotdel VPST 1924–25*).
49. A.G. Rashin, *Zarabotnaia plata za vosstanovitel'nyi period khoziaistva SSSR. 1922/23–1926/27gg.* (Moscow, 1927), p. 33.
50. R.M. Odell, *Cotton Goods in Russia* (Washington, 1912), pp. 24, 37.
51. Ziman, *Chast' I*, pp. 51–2, 159.
52. *GT*, 11 July 1924.
53. *I-V gubotdel VPST 1924–25*, pp. 57, 69–72, 79.
54. *GT*, 11 July 1924.
55. *Trud i proizvodstvo*, no. 1 (January 1925), p. 28 (hereafter *TiP*).
56. *Otchet leningradskogo gubernskogo otdela vsesoiuznogo professional'nogo soiuza tekstil'shchikov. Okt. 1924–1925gg.* (Leningrad, 1926), p. 60 (hereafter *Lengubotdel VPST 1924–25*); *Otchet TsK vsesoiuznogo professional'nogo soiuza tekstil'shchikov k 7-mu vsesoiuznomu s"ezdu tekstil'shchikov. Iiul' 1924g-ianv. 1926g.* (Moscow, 1926), p. 98 (hereafter *TsK VPST 1924–26*).
57. Kvasha, Shofman, *Semichasovoi*, pp. 42, 73.
58. V.A. Kungurtsev, *Tekstil'naia promyshlennost' SSSR* (Munich, 1957), p. 24.
59. See A.A. Nol'de, *NOT v tekstil'noi promyshlennosti* (Moscow, 1924).
60. *Khoziaistvo i upravlenie*, no. 5 (1925), p. 50 (hereafter *KiU*).
61. *Loc.cit.*
62. *GT*, 19 December 1924.
63. *KiU*, no. 5 (1925), pp. 51, 54.
64. *Sotsialisticheskii vestnik*, 20 June 1925, p. 19; 10 July 1925, p. 15; 25 July 1925, pp. 9–10 (hereafter *SV*).

65. *GT*, 19 May 1925, 26 May 1925.
66. *GT*, 21 July 1925; *TsK VPST 1924–26*, pp. 4–5, 8, 33, 36.
67. *GT*, 16 June 1925, 19 June 1925, 6 October 1925; *Lengubotdel VPST 1924–25*, p. 60; *SV*, 25 July 1925, pp. 9, 14; *TsK VPST 1924–26*, pp. 9, 14, 98–100.
68. *1925 spravochnik*, pp. 3–4.
69. *GT*, 24 June 1926; *SV*, 11 June 1926, p. 13.
70. *SV*, 26 July 1926, p. 14.
71. Pavlov, *Sel'faktor*, p. 120.
72. *SiI*, no. 10 (1925), p. 9; *TNB 1925*, p. 17.
73. See F.E. Dzerzhinsky, et al., eds., *K probleme proizvoditel'nosti truda* (Moscow, 1925), vyp. 3, p. 70; *GT*, 22 May 1925, 2 October 1926.
74. *Lengubotdel VPST 1924–25*, p. 63.
75. *ITPT*, no. 1 (January 1928), p. 43.
76. *GT*, 23 February 1926.
77. *GT*, 8 January 1926; Kvasha, Shofman, *Semichasovoi*, p. 25.
78. Semenov, *Litso*, pp. 52–3, 59–60.
79. R. Day, *Leon Trotsky and the Politics of Economic Isolation* (Cambridge, 1973), p. 114; *GT*, 8 September 1925; *SV*, 18 August 1925, p. 39.
80. *ITPT*, no. 16 (April 1926), p. 1.
81. *GT*, 21 June 1927.
82. V. Kuz'michev, *Organizatsiia obshchestvennogo mneniia. Pechatnaia agitatsiia* (Moscow, 1929), pp. 27–8.
83. *GT*, 12 January 1928.
84. *Biulleten' ivanovo-voznesenskogo gosudarstvennogo tekstil'nogo tresta*, no. 37/4 (February 1928), p. 3 (hereafter *BI-VGTT*).
85. *Sputnik agitatora*, no. 6 (March 1928), p. 25 (hereafter *SA*).
86. *GT*, 7 January 1928; *RK*, 8 January 1928.
87. *Puti industrializatsii*, no. 10 (1928), p. 49.
88. L.E. Mints, I.F. Engel', eds., *Statisticheskie materialy po trudu i sotsial'nomu strakhovaniiu za 1926–27 godu* (Moscow, 1928), vyp. 1, table 4, pp. 15–16; (Moscow, 1928), vyp. 2–3, table 2, p. 6, table 4, pp. 9–10; (Moscow, 1928), vyp. 4, table 4, pp. 15–16.
89. *SA*, no. 6 (March 1928), p. 27.
90. I.S. Belinsky, A.I. Kucherov, *Tri mesiatsa raboty semichasovykh fabrik. (Opyt perevoda i raboty semichasovykh fabrik v ivanovo-voznesenskoi gubernii)* (Moscow, 1928), pp. 19, 35–6; *GT*, 19 January 1928; Kvasha, Shofman, *Semichasovoi*, pp. 15–16; *RK*, 14 January 1928.
91. *Izvestiia*, 17 August 1928.
92. Belinsky, Kucherov, *Tri mesiatsa*, p. 44; *Trud*, 6 October 1928.
93. Cited in J.B. Sorenson, *The Life and Death of Soviet Trade Unionism 1917–28* (New York, 1969), p. 209.
94. *GT*, 15 January 1929; *Kommunistka*, no. 3 (March 1928), p. 29.
95. Belinsky, Kucherov, *Tri mesiatsa*, pp. 19–20.
96. Ibid., pp. 12, 20.
97. *Tekstil'nye novosti*, no. 7 (July 1929), pp. 376–7 (hereafter *TN*).
98. *TiP*, no. 1 (January 1928), p. 6.
99. Belinsky, Kucherov, *Tri mesiatsa*, p. 11.

100. See *BI-VGTT*, no. 5/38 (March 1928), p. 21; *Bol'shevik*, no. 8 (30 April 1928), p. 44; *ITPT*, no. 3 (March 1928), p. 21; *Predpriiatie*, no. 7 (July 1928), p. 18; *TN*, no. 4 (April 1927), p. 148; nos. 6–7 (June–July 1927), pp. 271–2.
101. Belinsky, Kucherov, *Tri mesiatsa*, table 3, p. 16; Kvasha, Shofman, *Semichasovoi*, pp. 16–17, 19, 33, 37, 94–6, 102; *Statistika truda*, nos. 2–3 (February–March 1929), p. 7 (hereafter *ST*).
102. *Ekonomicheskie obozrenie*, no. 8 (August 1928), pp. 48–9 (hereafter *EO*).
103. *GT*, 3 February 1928; *Kommunistka*, no. 4 (April 1928), p. 47; Kvasha, Shofman, *Semichasovoi*, pp. 18–19, 31–2, 35–6, 40, 94–6, 102; *ST*, nos. 2–3 (February–March 1929), p. 7.
104. Kvasha, Shofman, *Semichasovoi*, pp. 104–5.
105. A. Dunaev, Iu. Goriachev, *Iartsevskii khlopchatobumazhnoi kombinat. (Kratkii istoricheskii otchet)* (Iartsevo 1963), p. 68; *Predpriiatie*, no. 4 (April 1928), pp. 35–6; *SA*, no. 6 (March 1928), p. 25.
106. Belinsky, Kucherov, *Tri mesiatsa*, p. 14; *GT*, 3 February 1928; *TN*, no. 4 (April 1927), p. 149.
107. Kvasha, Shofman, *Semichasovoi*, pp. 94–6, 102; *ST*, nos. 2–3 (February–March 1929), pp. 7–9; *TN*, no. 11 (November 1928), p. 527.
108. Kvasha, Shofman, *Semichasovoi*, pp. 18, 94–6, 102; *ST*, nos. 2–3 (February–March 1929), pp. 7–9.
109. Belinsky, Kucherov, *Tri mesiatsa*, p. 17; *RK*, 14 January 1928, 19 January 1928, 20 January 1928, 22 January 1928.
110. *GT*, 8 September 1928; *RK*, 4 September 1928.
111. Belinsky, Kucherov, *Tri mesiatsa*, tables 2 and 3, pp. 15–16; *BI-VGTT*, no. 3/36 (January 1928), p. 3; no. 10/43 (August 1928), p. 3.
112. Belinsky, Kucherov, *Tri mesiatsa*, p. 5; *EO*, no. 8 (August 1928), pp. 51–2; Kvasha, Shofman, *Semichasovoi*, pp. 5–6; *Sputnik kommunista*, no. 12 (30 June 1928), p. 17 (stress in the original).
113. *ITPT*, nos. 8–9 (August–September 1930), p. 110; *Predpriiatie*, no. 2 (February 1929), pp. 15–17.
114. *GT*, 20 May 1928.
115. *Trud*, 23 September 1928.
116. See Burawoy, *Politics*, and Foster, *Class Struggle*.

6   The politics of industrial efficiency during NEP: the 1926 *rezhim ekonomii* campaign in Moscow

John Hatch

In 1926, as Soviet industry was beginning to achieve pre-World War I levels of industrial output,[1] economic policy turned to the tasks of 'socialist industrialization'. The strategy for industrialization adopted in the factory by the Soviet government in the second half of the 1920s was socialist rationalization, and it involved the effort to make production, administration, and distribution more efficient.[2] Socialist rationalization was to be achieved through class collaboration: all dimensions of enterprise and trust life were to become cost efficient, and all social groups were to participate in the campaign, share its costs, and reap its benefits. Difficulties in the practical attainment of this goal brought social and political tensions to the Soviet factory.

The need to present rationalization in the guise of class collaboration points to the presence of powerful constraints on industrial policy. The productivity drive, which began in 1924, had borne this out. Although it achieved some gains, resistance in the working class and the party, along with realities in the labour market and workplace, greatly limited their scope.[3] In fact, by 1926, an impasse of sorts had been reached, with well-paid, skilled workers neutralizing wage and productivity pressures, and with low-paid unskilled workers – who had borne the brunt of wage pressures in the past, and whose numbers were now on the increase – exhibiting a growing intolerance for additional economic sacrifices.[4]

Worker discontent over this one-sided, not always effective approach to productivity was acknowledged by the Moscow Communist Party secretary, Nikolai Uglanov, at the 4th plenum of the Moscow Party Committee (MK) in April 1926. Workers were 'displeased', he noted, 'with the unnecessary delays in construction, with waste . . . embezzlement, plunder, staff inflation, [and] incorrect wage increases for employees of economic organ[s]'. Nevertheless, he asserted, workers supported the policy of industrialization and 'unanimously' agreed that 'economic construction . . . [and] the implementation of the planned economy must be based on the real possibilities of the state . . . consistent with the means at our disposal'. The problem, he said, was that the 'broad masses' did not understand how it was to be achieved:

There is still a rather broad stratum of workers . . . who have the opinion that the development of our economy and the further growth of industry is possible through improving agriculture . . . The line we followed during the first years of NEP – that industrial growth is possible through the growth of the rural economy – now prevails among a well-known group of workers, [especially] lower skilled workers, with connections to the village.

There was considerable nervousness among these workers over the programme of 'socialist construction'. According to Uglanov, clear differences emerged between skilled and unskilled workers, with the former 'certain' of the need for and potential benefits of socialist construction, and the latter 'uncertain' about it, primarily because of their marginal economic position.[5] It is by no means clear, however, that the enthusiasm of well-paid workers extended to the spheres of wage discipline and labour intensification.

The question, then, was how to sell the working class politically on additional labour sacrifices and prod existing factory institutions and social groups into reorienting their practices towards a full-scale assault on the bottlenecks, interests, and shop floor realities that contributed to the high costs of production. This chapter examines the historical experience of the first major rationalization campaign, the *rezhim ekonomii*, which will be given the loose translation 'efficiency regime', of 1926. Its primary focus is on the Moscow region.

The efficiency regime was announced in late April 1926 in a circular signed by Stalin and Kuibyshev (the latter in his capacity as Chairman of the Supreme Council of the National Economy (VSNKh)). It was presented as a collaboration between workers, management and white collar employees. Factory organizations were instructed to participate in it, and the press was mobilized to create enthusiasm for its targets. Management was told to increase labour productivity and to reduce administrative staff, to report regularly to workers on its progress, to take into account workers' suggestions, and to implement them where indicated.[6] The trade unions were entrusted with the politically sensitive task of ensuring the involvement of production conferences and rank-and-file workers in the campaign; party units and other factory groups were also activated.[7]

Although the efficiency regime was presented in terms of class collaboration and management was enjoined to seek savings as much as possible outside of the sphere of labour, the working class was still expected to make sacrifices in the areas of wages, job security, and labour intensity. Before proceeding to a discussion of the politics generated by this campaign, it is pertinent to ask what exactly these sacrifices entailed. According to national figures provided by Gosplan, the first six months of 1926 witnessed a 3.5 per cent fall in wages and a 20.5 per cent increase in productivity.[8] However, according to all-union figures for the 1926/27 economic year cited by Carr and Davies, wage increases actually outpaced productivity gains.[9] Inflation probably undercut some of the increase in real wages; even so, gains in productivity must have been at best marginal. The figures for the Moscow region are also ambiguous about the success of wage discipline, and because of this reinforce the impression that in terms of labour efficiency the campaign was a disappointment.[10]

The attempt to improve labour productivity came up against two obstacles. The first was the need to maintain the economic conditions of various strata of the working class at acceptable levels so as to avoid political complications. A second obstacle was work culture, and since it was an expression of a variety of forces, including the balance between the quality and supply of labour, on the one hand, and the demand for it, on the other, as well as cultural, technological and organizational factors of production, rationalizing that culture was a complicated business – as the Soviet Taylorists had discovered. Of particular notoriety was the poor labour discipline of Soviet workers, usually attributed to their cultural and technical backwardness.[11] In May, echoing common management concerns, Dzerzhinsky attacked the high rates of labour absenteeism in industry, which he blamed on alcoholism and malingering.[12]

Where workers experienced the efficiency regime in a negative fashion was in relation to job loss, deteriorating work conditions, and a shrinking budget for social and cultural entitlements.[13] Severe layoffs occurred in the provincial industries (especially textiles), and lesser cutbacks hit the city. During 1926, the provincial industrial labour force dropped 20 per cent as opposed to only a 2 per cent reduction in the city.[14] Tensions arose when it seemed to workers that they were the only ones laid off, and that white-collar staffs and bureaucrats were exempted from job reductions. Another sore spot for workers was management's attempt to achieve budget discipline by cutting back on labour protection, work clothes, and benefits. Social perceptions were extremely sensitive to any tendency towards the violation of the principle of class collaboration.

The response of local and central party and trade union authorities to worker discontent over social biases in the efficiency regime was to allow the venting of worker concerns and to use this venting to justify criticism of managerial foot dragging. While the trade unions took the lead in voicing criticisms of management,[15] worker complaints became a key reference point also in the developing Communist discourse on the efficiency regime. *Rabochaia Moskva*, the MK organ, reported that at one Khamovniki *raion* factory the white-collar staff remained bloated even though workers agreed to raise their labour productivity.[16] The Moskovskii *uezd* party committee noted 'cases when several managers cut off expenses connected to workers' life', including cuts in firewood and hot water.[17] The Zamoskvorech'e RKK criticized state institutions for avoiding mandated layoffs of white collar staff members.[18] Such views were characteristic of the party's proletarian sections. A meeting of production workers held under MK auspices criticized 'some organizations [that] lay off only door porters and maids who are earning only 20–30 roubles a month and are satisfied with this while the office staff is untouched'.[19] Khamovniki workers criticized the efficiency regime for coming at the expense of workers.[20] A November conference of production line (*ot stanka*) party members cited cases of 'incorrect fulfillment . . . of the efficiency regime in the localities'.[21]

Anti-managerialism, as it was expressed by the trade unions, workers, and party organizations, was provoked by managerial violations of the principle of class collaboration in the implementation of the efficiency regime. The party leadership, meanwhile, was at least as concerned about management foot dragging as it was about class biases. The case against bureaucratism was amply presented in the press, and was a major preoccupation of local politicians. Riutin, who at this time was party secretary of the Krasnaia-Presnia *raikom*, noted resistance of 'some administrators and managers' to the *rezhim*.[22] The Khamovniki *raikom* called attention to the resistance of institution staffs to personnel reduction and criticized trusts for not taking a 'serious approach' to the efficiency regime campaign and for falsifying reports on compliance.[23] The Zamoskvorech'e *orgraspred* director, Zaitsev, commented that the efficiency regime was going 'slow', and that management was carrying it out only in 'details'.[24] Uglanov criticized the reception of the efficiency regime by managers as a 'shock campaign' instead of a lengthy process emphasizing the 'party verification' of the activities of economic organs.[25] A December MKK investigation found that the *rezhim* was feebly administered in a series of enterprises and that management 'overstated cost reductions by 50 per cent or more'. The MKK suggested that a system be established to check the activities of administration and to eliminate bureaucratism.[26]

The chief culprit in all this was bureaucratism and its corollary, the exclusion of rank-and-file workers. The Kolomenskii *ukom* reported in June 1926 that a 'back room' approach was being taken to efficiency regime measures, and that the masses were left uninformed about them.[27] The Moskovskii *ukom* noted that although the regime was advancing, it had not achieved a 'collective characteristic' and that its practical implementation was 'limited to the narrow bounds [of] the factory administration'.[28] The Podol'sk *ukom* criticized management for 'underestimating' the need to involve workers in the regime.[29] The Zamoskvorech'e RKK, amid criticisms that state institutions were avoiding mandated layoffs, called for mass participation in the efficiency regime.[30]

One of the main problems confronting the campaign was the low level of popular participation in the regime. The most commonly cited reason was bureaucratism. According to an article in *Pravda*, workers responded to the indifferent attitude taken by management (and against which the party wanted to struggle) with equal levels of apathy. Disinterest on the part of management persisted despite the fact that workers' suggestions often saved money.[31] The inactivity of the trade unions only compounded this effect. Workers were also discouraged from exposing inefficiencies by the fear of reprisal. This was the case in Khamovniki, where workers criticized the regime for coming at the expense of inner party democracy: the 'general sentiment' was such that 'in the localities they are afraid to talk about waste, afraid to write complaints to the RKK, [and] they demand guarantees and defence' against reprisals.[32]

A third, and often unspoken, reason was the existence of extremely ambivalent attitudes within the working class towards wage and labour discipline which could not but have an influence upon worker responsiveness to the campaign.[33] That wage and job conservatism was a dominant mood in the working class was certainly evident in the response of the Moscow trade union council (MGSPS) to what it described as efforts by economic organs to 'reduce the [work] norms of still functioning collective agreements' and in 'some cases' to use the *rezhim* to worsen the conditions of labour. MGSPS reminded the trusts that such efforts 'resulted in many conflicts' and delayed the completion of the current round of collective agreement negotiations 'by as much as half a year'.[34] The existence of widespread conflict points to the strong resistance in the working class to the implicit and explicit wage and productivity corollaries of the efficiency regime; resistance that was fundamentally organized around economic interests and which constituted a key reference point for the trade unions.

To combat bureaucracy, the party sought to introduce popular forces into the campaign and to step up political pressures on management and the trade unions; in other words, to more fully politicize the factory. The revival of production conferences was seen as a way of involving the masses, but reviving them required the presence of social and organizational forces in the factories capable of doing so; hence, the constant pressure maintained by party leaders on the trade unions and other factory groupings. Their inadequate leadership was in fact viewed as a major problem.[35] Neither the social nor the institutional base of the efficiency regime in the factories offered the kind of energies necessary for its easy implementation.

The failure of the campaign left both the trade unions and management vulnerable to criticism. It came in an August 1926 letter signed by Stalin, Rykov, and Kuibyshev ('On the successes and shortcomings of the campaign for the efficiency regime') which singled out the 'weak participation of the masses' and the insufficient activism of the unions and production conferences as key deficiencies. Its tone was one of castigation. The letter reminded readers that cost cutting was necessary in order to avoid excessive exploitation of the peasantry. It pointed to 'distortions', such as the idea that the efficiency regime was 'a temporary campaign', or that it was purely an industrial matter with no political significance. At the same time, the letter warned against bureaucratism and violations of the principle of collaboration in management's conduct of the efficiency regime, and it cautioned against the tendency to use it to justify violations of collective agreement provisions in the areas of job conditions, cultural funds, and work clothes.[36]

The overall impression of the actual conduct of the efficiency regime is that of reverse class collaboration. That is, all, or at least many, social interests were acting in ways contradictory to the campaign's intent, and instead in ways consistent with the prevailing economic, political, cultural, and technical conditions of production. The findings of a joint MKK-RKI investigation reported upon in September point in this direction. The report criticized the unions for the paralysis of factory committees and production conferences, but it found even more menacing the existence of a pervasive disregard for the efficiency regime's economic goals. The investigation found violations of budgetary discipline by management, including violations of party directives on wages and large amounts of unproductive expenses; for example, 'in a series of trusts, large sums are stolen for the equipping of apartments for white collar employees, for the purchase of furniture'. In almost all institutions the investigation uncovered 'violations of holidays, illegal overtime payments, exceeding discretionary expense limits, increases in [wage] rank, [and] increases in staff'. A joint MKK-RKI plenum insisted upon the 'necessity of strengthening the responsibility for the violation of the efficiency regime and the careful investigation of all matters related to disorders in the disbursement of state funds and violations in budgetary discipline'.[37]

The sharp exchange between management and the trade unions over blame for the difficulties in the campaign appears all the more strained when seen in a context in which failures stemmed from broad collusion between workers, employees, trade union officials, and directors to circumvent the intent of the efficiency regime. Squabbling between trade union and management interests broke out at the September 1926 joint MK-MKK plenum. The head of Moscow's metal workers' union (Strievsky) said that popular perception had it that plans for the efficiency regime were formulated in the offices of management without any worker input. He complained that factory directors left workers in the dark about production conditions.[38] Another delegate agreed: 'Our production conferences do not participate in decisions of questions of the rationalization of production, the work on the efficiency regime is done in the offices; the initiative of workers, in particular, of worker inventors, is not encouraged.'[39] Savvatev, head of the MKK, rebuked those who suggested that 'managers do not carry out the efficiency regime', and he found it 'impermissible to allow the irresponsible criticism of management appearing in the pages of several newspapers'.[40]

The MK took up the complaints of the workers, but it also adopted a critical stance towards the failings of the trade unions. Uglanov reflected upon the fact that 'in the beginning workers greeted the slogan "*rezhim ekonomii*" with great enthusiasm', but that they had turned against it: workers now referred to the campaign as the '*rezhem ekonomiiu*' (a play on verb *rezat'*, to slaughter) and that the authorities 'slaughtered workers' (*rezhut po rabochii*).[41] In light of this, the MK noted the weak participation of administrative-technical personnel in production conferences and criticized enterprise directors who treated the efficiency regime as a one-shot affair, acted against its intent, and damaged workers' material conditions. At the same time, however, the MK cited the inattentiveness of the unions to the campaign, the failure of cells to become involved and the failure of factory organizations to help develop public opinion in support of the efficiency regime.[42]

Management-trade union differences sharpened. At the October 1926 plenum of the Moscow Party Committee, the head of the city's trade union movement, Mikhailov, accused management of attaining the cost cutting goals of the efficiency regime by cutting back on labour protection. He noted that the campaign to lower overhead, administrative and non-production costs met with a warm response from workers, but he criticized the worsening quality of work clothes. Mikhailov called for a 'decisive struggle' with 'the distortions of the efficiency regime'.[43] Tomsky's October 1926 report to the Politburo criticized 'perversions of the efficiency regime by economic organs', including the implementation of rationalization and staff reductions against the interests of workers.[44]

The sources of these squabbles included not only violations of the class collaboration principle, but also the unsatisfactory results of the efficiency regime in the wage/productivity sphere. In October, a front page *Pravda* article cited figures showing the non-fulfillment of directives for increasing the productivity of labour, which grew by 6 per cent as opposed to a planned 10 per cent in the 1925/26 economic year (from 1 October to 30 September). And while in 1924/5 output per worker went up 32 per cent over the previous year, in 1925/6 it went up 11.6 per cent while real wages increased 13 per cent.[45] At the 15th Moscow Party Conference in January 1927, Uglanov blamed lags in productivity for undermining the inflation-fighting, price reduction functions of the efficiency regime. Wages, according to Uglanov, were a prime culprit behind inflation and thus had to be held down.[46] Another delegate, Fedorov, criticized the trusts for their bloated staffs. He singled out one trust for neglecting technical safety conditions, and blamed industrial disturbances that occurred in Sokol'niki *raion* on management. 'Sometimes', he said, 'our party organizations [and] trade union organs run up against a kind of wall [when dealing with] economic authorities that is difficult to get past . . . moreover the unions do not always pay sufficient attention to shortcomings [and] details, a source of worker dissatisfaction'.[47]

In 1927, accordingly, two new initiatives were undertaken by the party. The first, the price reduction campaign, was announced in early February.[48] It was aimed at lowering prices in the co-operative network and was to involve the broad participation of the trade unions and workers, who were also the chief beneficiaries of the hoped-for anti-inflation effects of the effort.[49] The rationalization campaign was also formally initiated at this time. The publication on 10 February 1927 of a circular calling for technical norm determination[50] was followed on 25 March by the Central Committee resolution on the rationalization of production.[51] The indictments listed in this resolution spanned all social groups and aspects of production, implicitly pointing to the failure of the efficiency regime, and signifying the party leadership's growing awareness of the intractability of the problem.[52]

The efficiency regime and subsequent campaigns represented fundamentally a search for political solutions to economic problems: an attempt to substitute politics for underdeveloped, non-existent or politically unacceptable economic forces. That such an effort was made points to the importance the party assigned to the problem of productivity. And that it eluded easy solution speaks eloquently of the obstacles that existed in economy and society to the rationalization of production, distribution, and administration.

The party hoped to mobilize and redirect popular resentment over the failure of management and white collar staff to bear a fair share of the burden of rationalization and transform it into an active and effective oversight of management compliance. However, the party had to contend not only with bureaucratism and scepticism, but also with the defensive orientation of workers on wage and productivity issues. Clearly, it hoped that the combination of 'class collaboration' and anti-bureaucratism would produce political opinions and energies in the working class that were consistent with the needs of industrialization. This strategy ran up against the primacy of economics in the practical vocabulary of working class life. For key sectors of the working class, the main issues were wages and jobs. The divergence between the party and some sectors of the working class over the social costs of industrialization would increasingly determine political alignments in the Soviet factory and fuel the emergent politics of Stalinism.[53]

Notes

1. R. W. Davies, *The Soviet Economy in Turmoil, 1929–1930* (London, 1989), p. 14. Research for this paper was supported by the International Research and Exchanges Board, the Social Science Research Council, and the University of Michigan Center for Russian and East European Studies. None of these organizations is responsible for the views expressed in this article. I would like to thank Hans Rogger for his useful editorial comments.
2. The best discussion of this policy can be found in David Shearer, 'Rationalization and reconstruction in the Soviet machine building industry, 1926–1934', PhD dissertation, University of Pennsylvania, 1988. See also E. H. Carr, *Socialism in One Country*, vol. 1 (London, 1958), and Carr and R. W. Davies, *Foundations of a Planned Economy 1926–1929*, vol. 1 (London, 1969); Hiroaki Kuromiya, *Stalin's Industrial Revolution: Politics and Workers, 1928–1932* (Cambridge, 1988); and William Chase, *Workers, Society,*

and the Soviet State: Labor and Life in Moscow, 1918–1929 (Champaign Il, 1987).
3. See the discussion in Carr and Davies, *Foundations*, vol. 1, part II, p. 521; and Carr, *Socialism*, vol. 1, part I, pp. 397–9; Chase, *Workers*, pp. 235–9; Chris Ward, *Russia's Cotton Workers and the New Economic Policy* (Cambridge, 1990), pp. 141–75. Evidence of these trends may be found in *Pravda*, 11 February, 12 and 16 October and 23 December 1926; *XXIV Moskovskaia uezdnaia partiinaia konferentsiia (30 oktiabria-2 noiabria 1925 g.): stenograficheskii otchet* (Moscow, 1925), p. 40; *Rabota Krasno-Presnenskogo raionnogo komiteta VKP(b) i kontrol'noi komissii s 1 noiabria 1925 g. po 25 noiabria 1926 g.* (Moscow, 1926), pp. 7–9; *Otchet Moskovskogo gubotdela shveinikov s 1 ianvaria 1925 g. po 1 noiabria 1925 g.31* (Moscow, 1925), p. 1; *Tezisy po rabote Moskovskogo gubotdela VSRShP, predstavliaemye k 6-mu gubs"ezdu 6–8 fevralia 1925 g.* (Moscow, 1925), p. 12; *Itogi raboty Moskovskoi uezdnoi partiinoi organizatsii (noiabr' 1925-oktiabr' 1926 g.)* (Moscow, 1926), p. 12; *Izvestiia MK*, no. 12 (December 1926), p. 15; *Rabota Kolomenskogo uezdnogo komiteta V.K.P.(b) s 1-go oktiabria 1926 goda po 1-e oktiabria 1927 goda* (Kolomna, 1927), p. 64; and *Doklady i postanovleniia plenuma Moskovoskogo gubotdela profsoiuza tekstil'shchikov 1-2 oktiabria 1926 goda* (Moscow, 1926), p. 10.
4. At an April 1926 Rogozhko-Simonovskii non-party worker conference, low-paid workers expressed hopes that the *rezhim ekonomii* would not mean lower wages. *Pravda*, 21 April 1926.
5. *Chetvertyi plenum MK VKP(b) 20-22 aprelia 1926 g.: doklady i rezoliutsii* (Moscow, 1926), pp. 4, 6–7, and 22; *Pravda*, 23 April 1926.
6. *Pravda*, 25 April 1926; *Rabochaia Moskva*, 26 March 1926.
7. *Moskovskii proletarii*, nos. 27–8 (28 July 1926), pp. 3–5.
8. *Pravda*, 16 October 1926.
9. Carr and Davies, *Foundations*, p. 488.
10. For the contradictory evidence on real wages and productivity, see MGSPS, *Rabota za 1-e polugodie posle 7-go gubs"ezda profsoiuzov* (Moscow, 1926), p. 14; *Rabochaia Moskva*, 10 July and 19 August 1926; *Moskovskii proletarii*, nos. 27–8 (28 July 1926), and 37–8 (14 October 1926), p. 3; *Rabota uezdnogo komiteta V.K.P.(b) s 1-go noiabria 1925 goda po 1-3 noiabria 1926 goda* (Serpukhov, 1926), p. 10; *Vos'moi plenum MK VKP(b) 18-19 oktiabria 1926: doklady i rezoliutsii* (Moscow, 1926), p. 34; *Sostoianie i deiatel'nost' professional'nykh soiuzov Moskovskoi gubernii v 1926/1927 gg.* (Moscow, 1929), p. 22; *Pravda*, 21 December 1926; *Otchet Moskovskogo komiteta VKP(b) dekabr' 1925-dekabr' 1926 k XV gubpartkonferentsii* (Moscow, 1927), p. 15.
11. Carr and Davies, *Foundations*, p. 509; Shearer, 'Soviet machine building industry'; and Ward, *Russia's Cotton Workers*.
12. Carr and Davies, *Foundations*, p. 486. On increasing rates of shirking, see *Pravda*, 7 April 1927; Central State Archive of the October Revolution (TsGAOR), fond 7952, opis 3, delo 85, list 29; *Rabochaia Moskva*, 3 June 1926; *Semnadtsataia Moskovskaia gubernskaia konferentsiia VKP(b): stenograficheskii biulleten'*, no. 11 (Moscow, 1929), pp. 6–8; *Moskovskii proletarii*, no. 24 (June 1926), p. 5.
13. For example, accusations were raised at a Moscow Textile Workers' Union

that social insurance was 'economized' at expense of workers. *Rabochaia Moskva*, 20 November 1926.

14. *Rabota Moskovskogo komiteta VKP(b) ianvar' 1928–fevral' 1929: otchet XVII gubpartkonferentsii* (Moscow, 1929), p. 42.
15. Speaking at a plenum of the Moscow Provincial Trade Union Council on 10 July 1926, the Moscow trade union chief, Mikhailov, accused some managers of making cuts in areas affecting workers' everyday life. *Rabochaia Moskva*, 10 July 1926.
16. *Rabochaia Moskva*, 6 April 1926.
17. *Itogi raboty Moskovskoi uezdnoi partiinoi organizatsii*, p. 15.
18. *Rabochaia Moskva*, 27 May 1926.
19. *Rabochaia Moskva*, 1 June 1926.
20. *Resheniia plenumov, biuro i sekretariata Khamovnicheskogo raikoma VKP(b) za mart, aprel', i mai 1926 g.* (Moscow, 1926), pp. 77–9.
21. *Izvestiia MK*, no. 11 (November 1926), p. 15.
22. *Pravda*, 21 December 1926.
23. *Izvestiia MK*, no. 5 (May 1926), pp. 11–12.
24. *Pravda*, 15 June 1926.
25. *Pravda*, 4 June 1926. For similar views, see *Rabota Baumanskogo raionnogo komiteta VKP(b) i raionnoi kontrol'noi komissii noiabr' 25 goda-noiabr' 26 goda* (Moscow, 1926), p. 5.
26. *Pravda*, 31 December 1926.
27. *Rabochaia Moskva*, 23 June 1926.
28. *Itogi raboty Moskovskoi uezdnoi partiinoi organizatsii*, p. 15.
29. *Rabota Podol'skogo uezdnogo komiteta Vsesoiuznoi Kommunisticheskoi Partii (bol'shevikov) i UKK VKP(b) oktiabr' 1926 g.-noiabr' 1926 k XXII uezdpartkonferentsii* (Podol'sk, 1926), p. 18.
30. *Rabochaia Moskva*, 27 May 1926.
31. *Pravda*, 2 July 1926.
32. *Resheniia . . . Khamovnicheskogo raikoma*, pp. 77–9.
33. *Pravda*, 30 June 1926.
34. *Otchet Moskovskogo gubernskogo soveta profsoiuzov mart 1926-avgust 1927 k VIII gubernskomu s''ezdu profsoiuzov* (Moscow, 1927), p. 63.
35. *Pravda*, 2 July 1926. Earlier, *Pravda* published an article criticizing 'many' directors for not 'understanding the significance' of the *rezhim* and their lack of attentiveness to details in order to save money. It urged production conferences to play this role. *Pravda*, 8 May 1926.
36. *Pravda*, 17 August 1926.
37. *Pravda*, 17 September 1926.
38. Ibid., 19 September 1926.
39. Ibid.
40. Ibid.
41. Ibid., 21 September 1926.
42. Ibid., 23 September 1926. For additional evidence of bureaucratic indifference, see *Rabochaia Moskva*, 24 September 1926; *Otchet o rabote Bogorodskogo uezdnogo biuro professional'nykh soiuzov i uezdnogo komiteta sotsial'nogo strakhovaniia k VII-mu uezdnomu s''ezdu profsoiuzov* (Bogorodsk, 1927), p. 11.
43. *Vos'moi plenum MK VKP(b)*, pp. 39 and 45. See also MGSPS, *Rabota za 1-*

e polugodie posle 7-go gubs"ezda profsoiuzov, p. 16; *Postanovleniia 6-oi Moskovskoi gubpartkonferentsii soiuza metallistov 12-14 noiabria 1926 g.* (Moscow, 1926), p. 6; *Moskovskii Proletarii*, 17 June 1926, and 7 September 1926.

44. *Pravda*, 22 October 1926. See also *Pravda*, 16 December 1926.
45. *Pravda*, 12 October 1926.
46. At the same time, however, wages of lower paid groups were to be increased. *Pravda*, 18 January 1927; *Piatnadtsataia Moskovskaia gubernskaia konferentsiia VKP(b). Biulleten'*, no. 7 (Moscow, 1927), p. 9.
47. *Piatnadtsataia Moskovskaia gubernskaia konferentsiia VKP(b)*, pp. 8, 43–5.
48. *Pravda*, 8 February 1927; *Rabochaia Moskva*, 25 February 1927.
49. *Pravda*, 25 February and 4 March 1927.
50. Ibid., 10 February 1927.
51. Ibid., 25 March 1927.
52. See 'Difficulties of rationalization and the working class', *Pravda*, 7 April 1927.
53. See Kuromiya, *Stalin's Industrial Revolution*.

7 The Moscow party and the socialist offensive: activists and workers 1928–1931

Catherine Merridale

The relationship between the political elite and the party rank-and-file during the 'great turn' of 1928–32 has always been a controversial subject. Policies like rapid industrialization and enforced collectivization had devastating consequences, and it is difficult to imagine how ordinary people could knowingly have supported them. The idea that substantial sections of the Soviet population might have participated in the barbarous excesses of the first Five Year Plan, and might, indeed, have supported Stalin personally, is difficult to square with the overwhelming evidence of hardship caused by the pace and scale of economic and social change. Moreover, it is clear that the leadership intended to manipulate rank-and-file influence, playing the 'mass card' at crucial turning-points. And yet it stretches credulity to imagine that the first Five Year Plan was carried out at the point of a gun, in the teeth of opposition from everyone outside the party elite and the secret police. This paper will examine the role of Moscow's party members in the campaigns of the first Five Year Plan. It aims to show what kind of people they were, what they tried to achieve, and what contribution they made to the form and scope of Stalin's Great Turn.

It is important to bear in mind that Moscow was not typical of the rest of the USSR. It was the largest industrial centre, and its population included a greater than average number of proletarians and migrant workers. It was also the capital. This meant that its share of government and other public servants was substantial; white-collar workers (including a large number of civil servants of the old regime) made up well over a third of its working population.[1] Moscow also attracted thousands of students,[2] many of them in their mid or late twenties, former members of the Red Army. The city's importance was also reflected in the structure and composition of its party organisation. The Moscow party included a much higher than average proportion of senior party officials; its leaders were among the most influential politicians in the land,

and even its middle-ranking administrators had usually held high office in the provinces in the early 1920s.[3] The gap between the elite and the rank-and-file was greater in Moscow than in many provincial towns. Senior Moscow officials, few of whom, by this stage, were Muscovites, lived near the Kremlin, and had daily contact with their colleagues in the Politburo, as well as enjoying access to the privileges of high party office. Rank-and-filers, Muscovites living and working in the city's industrial districts, must have felt that they lived in another world. Moreover, Moscow's party activists were unlikely to be promoted into this charmed circle. The most successful were moved to responsible posts in the provinces.

In 1928 there were 104,000 party members and candidates in the city of Moscow.[4] As we have seen, these included a large (and so far undisclosed) number of full-time officials, members of the apparatus whose careers depended on their loyalty to the secretariat. But the majority were ordinary people, factory workers, tram drivers, local officials, teachers and students. Over 60 per cent had joined the party after 1924. Their reasons for doing so varied. Some were motivated by the desire to improve their material circumstances; party membership provided the prospect of better accommodation, promotion at work and possibly professional training. But this was most starkly the case for white-collar employees. They had the most to gain by shedding the stigma of 'bourgeois' origins or sympathies, and the best promotion prospects, including the hope of preferment within the party's own apparatus.[5]

For factory and transport workers the benefits of party membership were less clear. Proletarian Muscovites did not rush headlong to join the party during the enrolment campaigns of the 1920s. Some rejected Bolshevism on principle; there were still many former Mensheviks, SRs and others in Moscow's factories, and many also who had supported Bolshevik factions like the Workers' Group in the early 1920s.[6] Merely by outlawing these groups, the party lost a considerable amount of potential support. As one woman worker, critical of the more rigorous aspects of democratic centralism, put it 'I wouldn't join the party. If you're going to join, you have to cut half your tongue out first.'[7]

Even people who were not politically opposed to its overall goals were often put off by the party's image. Depending on the party members they knew, they might regard the vanguard of the proletariat with cynicism, suspicion or outright hostility.[8] Many workers had daily contact with Communists who were arrogant and high-handed. One group of Communists, for example, was caught firing revolvers at workers as they walked home after work.[9] Another rank-and-filer was described as laughing at his non-party colleagues' simple-mindedness, and then refusing to explain the joke.[10] Some Communists openly stated that they had joined the party in pursuit of privileges. Examples were quoted of individuals who hoped to obtain extra ration cards for vodka, or who expected to use their party membership to avoid deployment to unpopular shifts.[11] Older, more experienced workers resented interference from eager party officials keen to apply Marxist-Leninist principles in areas where they had little or no practical experience.[12] And at the same time, party members might themselves be dodging the duties, such as participation in *subbotniki*, which they urged others to take on. Not surprisingly, people expressed fears that if they joined the party they would be ostracized by their friends at the workplace.[13] Finally, party membership was supposed to involve a wide range of extra duties. The members who in fact fulfilled these would find they had no spare time. One survey found that a party activist might expect to attend thirty-three meetings a month, all held outside working hours.[14] Not surprisingly, there was also evidence that such overwork, coming on top of poor diet and after many years of acute stress, left some activists in poor health, the most common problems being digestive and nervous disorders.[15]

The party's own press recorded numerous individual examples of rank-and-file indiscipline. Partly as a result of this, historians have tended to endorse the idea that the Lenin recruits and their successors were mainly 'ballast', or worse, cheer leaders for the Stalinist apparatus in its fight against the opposition. Trotsky and his followers (including historians such as Isaac Deutscher) described them as political illiterates, blank pages awaiting the crude handwriting of the Stalinist clique. Observers at the time of the first Lenin enrolment suggested that it had been designed deliberately to 'flood' the party with supporters of the Stalinist clique in order to outmanoeuvre the Trotskyists in what might otherwise have been an even fight.[16]

But this is hardly fair. The official reports give a distorted picture of the 'average' activist. Many of the worst tales of rank-and-file indiscipline date from 1931 and 1932, when the leadership was on the brink of halting recruitment and curbing grassroots influence within the party structure. Unpublished records, mainly in Soviet archives, give a very different impression. The stenographic reports of party cell meetings, for example, show activists bending every effort to keep the cell running, as well as doing a careful juggling act involving official directives, their sense of local needs, and their own perception of ideological imperatives. Moreover, joining the party did bring problems as well as benefits, as we have seen, and at least until 1929 it required a positive commitment on the part of the recruit.

Clearly it is not enough to write the activists off as careerists or uncritical enthusiasts of socialist construction Stalin-style. As Iurii Poliakov pointed out recently in *Voprosy istorii KPSS*, historians must try to recover the mental world of these rank-and-filers. He suggested that one of the mainsprings of their motivation was a concept of class war, largely inherited from the revolutionary period.[17] Evidence based on Moscow's activists suggests that there is a lot of truth in this assertion, and indeed it goes a long way towards explaining their reactions to events such as the Shakhty and Industrial Party Trials of 1928 and 1930. During the revolutionary period, Communists and their working-class sympathisers knew that they were fighting against enemies who would not spare their lives if they were defeated. Lynch law ruled during the Civil War. And even when the fighting in the Soviet Union ended, the survival of capitalism in Western Europe left Russia encircled by powerful enemies whose intervention was constantly feared.

But the recruits of the 1920s had other, equally powerful, sets of political ideas. Alongside class war, for example, went a vague concept of socialism. Party activists regarded themselves as engaged in a practical task whose goal was attainable in the near future. For obvious reasons, this commitment was something they referred to frequently, although they were no more specific about what socialism meant than were their leaders.[18] In many cases, it probably meant no more than the antithesis of the pre-revolutionary order. Workers might not have been clear about what they wanted, but there was little doubt about what they were trying to avoid. But in the short term their immediate priorities were more concrete. Their first loyalty was to their local community, be it their shift, their shop, or their workplace as a whole. They took on local responsibilities – as early as 1927 the majority of party secretaries in the smaller factories and of shop and shift secretaries were people who had joined the party after 1924[19] – and they devoted their spare time to committees and self-education.

It could be argued that this practical work was of little significance, and also that activists put almost no creative effort into it. There are indeed many reports of poor work – membership dues not collected, propaganda courses cut, cell meetings which were seldom, if ever, convened. And a cumbersome system of administrative supervision bore down on the local cells. Given the party's hierarchical structure and the importance placed on internal discipline and report-writing it might seem that there was very little room for individual initiative. But in fact the administrative hierarchy seldom functioned according to plan. The instructions which were given to local cells were vague, often contradictory and occasionally irrelevant to the immediate problems on the shop floor. As a result, local officials, often working part time for the party, had a genuine contribution to make. They had in the first place to make sense of the stream of different demands from above, work out their own priorities (for there was no chance that everything that was expected of them on paper could be realized in fact), and then adjust the vaguely-worded official policies to suit local conditions.

The propaganda system provides one example of this process in action. In the 1920s party propaganda was a relatively relaxed matter. Former members of other political parties (such as Mensheviks and Socialist Revolutionaries) often found a niche in the new regime as propagandists, and gave their students a varied and not always entirely orthodox view of Marxism-Leninism and the goals of the Communist Party.[20] By 1929, these people had largely disappeared from Moscow's propaganda classes, and the range of texts to be studied had shrunk.[21] Gone were the works of West European Marxists like Kautsky and Luxemburg; dissident Bolsheviks such as Bukharin would soon vanish from the reading lists also. Stalin's letter to the editors of *Proletarskaia revoliutsiia* set out his ideas on political education clearly enough.[22] Throughout the period of the first Five Year Plan propaganda was designed to be simple, uniform and undeviatingly orthodox.

Despite these official plans, however, party propaganda in fact continued to be a rag-bag of half-assimilated information, often poorly presented and inconsistent. Propaganda was frequently seen as a diversion from the pressing tasks of socialist construction (and crisis-management in the factory), and few activities were given a lower priority by the activists themselves.[23] Attendance was not usually consistent, and many classes folded after a few weeks.[24] There were no classrooms (and 'red' corners frequently had to be sacrificed to make space for canteens or enlarged production facilities), no chairs, few textbooks, blackboards or pencils.[25] The material on offer generally consisted of extracts from the latest official speeches and improvised question-and-answer sessions. Propagandists, many of whom had full-time production jobs, were described as preparing their classes 'on the tram on the way in'.[26] The result was that however neat the formal structure of the courses appeared to the casual reader of the Moscow party's journal, *Propagandist*, the reality was a hit-and-miss affair in which propagandists (many of whom had no clearer idea about Marxism-Leninism than their 'students') did not always get the better of the argument. In practice, it was essential for them to adjust their material to suit their audience.[27] The idea that 'Soviet propaganda . . . succeeded in reinforcing the commitment of the propagandists'[28] may need revision in the light of evidence from Moscow before 1932. In this period, they were still part of the community in which they worked, and their message was most effective if it was tailored to local needs.

The activists' role as mediators between the elite and the shop floor has been noted by many historians. But this mediation was seldom simply 'transmission'. Because the practical guidance they were given was so inadequate, local activists were in fact tactical executives at the local level. Their role in industrialization (and collectivization) was a crucial one. In the rest of this chapter, I shall examine the main areas to which they contributed. First, it is important to establish that at the outset they were guardedly enthusiastic about the economic changes proposed by the Stalinist faction in 1928. While not necessarily crucial to the outcome of the Politburo struggle, their enthusiasm helped to facilitate the defeat of the Right in Moscow. They then contributed significantly to the implementation of optimal variants of the plan in Moscow's factories. The collectivization of Moscow province equally could not have been carried out without their active co-operation. Later their enthusiasm began to wane, especially in the winter of 1930–31, but in many factories they continued to play an important role, especially where political circumstances rendered management timorous or ineffective. And finally, although their power was dramatically curbed from the spring of 1932 onwards, it was the recruits of the 1920s who predominated in Moscow's evening classes and summer schools, training as specialists for the professional posts of the next two decades.

In the absence of democratic elections or public opinion polling, the political sympathies of Moscow's activists on the eve of the Great Turn cannot be described exactly. But there is abundant evidence that they were impatient with NEP, and concerned about the future of their revolutionary movement.[29] Local factors played some part in this. Moscow, like Leningrad and a handful of other major cities, had attracted overwhelming numbers of migrant workers during the 1920s, often peasants seeking seasonal employment during the summer.[30] The result had been a dramatic rise in unemployment in the capital (roughly one in four adult members of the workforce was unemployed in 1928) and a squeeze on facilities such as housing and transport. Muscovite party members did not experience high levels of unemployment themselves but suffered from its side-effects, notably pressure on wages, and the deterioration of working conditions (including longer working hours). These problems were not 'caused' by the 'Rightist' Moscow party leadership. But they reflected on it. Nikolai Uglanov, the party secretary, made his situation worse by openly supporting policies like the regime of economy, and by his reluctance to encourage the promotion of workers to administrative jobs within their factories (the main bene-

ficiaries of such promotion would have been rank-and-file party activists).[31] Cadre workers were already impatient with NEP, and when the
crisis came in 1928, they had little sympathy to spare for Uglanov and
his allies.

On the other hand, their support for Stalin was equivocal and ill-
informed. One of the key issues in 1928 was the grain crisis, which
manifested itself in Moscow as an acute shortage of bread. Activists at
meetings were keenly interested in the issue, but in general supported
neither of the solutions on offer.[32] On the one hand, the prospect of
higher procurement prices for grain – and thus, more expensive bread –
was unwelcome. But on the other, most Muscovites, many of whom
retained some link with the villages and peasant life, were unwilling to
support an attack upon the peasantry, were critical of extraordinary
measures, and had doubts about the role of the kulak in engineering the
grain shortage. Those who spoke on the issue at meetings in the late
summer of 1928 commonly blamed the leadership for having exported
quantities of grain the previous year.[33]

Several factors persuaded Moscow's activists to support the Stalinist
option. A powerful one no doubt was the fear of reprisals once it
became clear (in October) that the Right was about to be condemned as
a 'deviation'. Even before that, however, the weight of the lower ranks
in the Moscow Party had been behind the more radical option. Partly
this was because they did not fully appreciate what its consequences
would be.[34] But also it was because they thought they were supporting
change, acceleration, and a chance to lift the revolutionary movement
out of the doldrums of late NEP, to give the proletariat the upper hand
again.[35] They remained critical of all sections of the apparatus, whether
Right or Stalinist, because they were always suspicious of the *verkhi*
(high-ups). But as far as their direct interests, and also those of the
revolutionary movement, were concerned, action seemed preferable to
a continuation of the present difficulties.

The struggle was largely decided in the apparatus, so it could be
argued that this support was immaterial to its outcome. But the next
three years were to show how important rank-and-file support could be.
Few major campaigns of the first Five Year Plan were untouched by
their contributions. Collectivization, for example, was closely watched
from Moscow's factories, and many activists spent time in the
countryside during 1929–30. At first their attitude was fraternal.
Representatives from the Elektrozavod travelled to 'their' *kolkhoz* in
1930 eager to help with the repair and running of machinery, and to
teach the peasants about the benefits of collective life.[36] When they
arrived in the villages, however, they discovered for themselves that the

campaign bore little resemblance to its official images. By 1930 the countryside was near to civil war. A few members of the first Elektrozavod *shefstvo* delegation were shot as they addressed meetings of peasants; others wrote home with tales of violence. No doubt many Communists drew the conclusion that collectivization was an ill-conceived war against the peasants; participants like Viktor Kravchenko report their disgust and claim to have become silent opponents of Stalinism as a result of what they saw.[37] But others decided that violence should be answered with violence. As one Elektrozavod worker wrote back to his comrades, 'sometimes [collectivization] had to be carried out with revolver and whip in hand'.[38]

The excesses of collectivization were not 'caused' by the activists, of course. There is no question of 'shifting the blame'. In Moscow, where the campaign was especially traumatic, responsibility for the catastrophic excesses of the winter of 1929–30 lies with the provincial party leadership (and especially Karl Bauman, the first secretary), with a number of over-zealous *okrug* officials, and most particularly with the Stalinist leadership of the national party secretariat, which was aware of the extent of Bauman's campaign, but which took no steps to curb his activities until it was clear that a major disaster was in the offing.[39] But there is also no doubt that a substantial number of Moscow's party activists, notably young males from proletarian families, and especially those in the metalworking and machine industries, became committed advocates of class war in the countryside. Those who had participated in the campaign knew about the violence it had involved. But few resisted it, and there is no evidence that they encouraged dissent among their non-party colleagues.

The activists' contribution in some factories was even more dramatic. There were numerous cells, of course, which worked poorly. A study conducted by the metalworkers' union in 1930 concluded that party members' low attendance rates at planning meetings suggested to other workers that 'the approach of the administration to the establishment of control figures is not serious'.[40] 'Our meetings', confessed a party member from the Tsindel' factory, 'often lack a businesslike quality.'[41] The strains on party members were enormous, and some could not cope with the endless official pressure or the leadership's equally frustrating refusal to be specific about its demands. Since it was not clear, for example, whether the party should be taking an interest in production matters or not, it was hardly surprising that some cells should scarcely have discussed such issues before 1929.[42]

But despite the pressures, many cells took their duties seriously, although they interpreted them as they saw fit. This does not make them 'good' cells; frequently they were most interested in protecting themselves whatever the cost to the larger community. We have already seen that propaganda was firmly relegated to the bottom of their list of priorities. When they had to provide 'volunteers' to train as propagandists, they tended to send their least able members.[43] Those who returned to the factory were more than likely to be drafted straight back into production work.[44] The pressure to provide potential 'promotees' was also resisted as far as possible. As one factory committee member snapped to his *raikom* secretary, 'If you will take ten people from us every month, you can't really expect us to develop an *aktiv*'.[45]

Another interruption in the cells' daily business was the purge of 1929–30. 'Because of the purge, we'll lose our best activists', was a typical comment.[46] The process could not easily be avoided. Members of the local control commissions and more senior party members from the *raikom* were involved in individual factories, where the process of purging could take several weeks or even months. Unlike city party officials, activists were not officially sheltered from the purge's impact. But they none the less managed to protect themselves in many instances. To avoid public humiliation, for example, one group arranged for the purge commission to sit in a room too small to accommodate any members of the public.[47] *Rabochaia Moskva* noted that many commissions were met in the factories by a 'conspiracy of silence'.[48] In the event, the purge hit Moscow less hard than other centres (partly because there were fewer peasants in the Moscow party than average), although its overall impact was to reduce the proportion of proletarian Communists in the city.[49] And in some cases (no doubt far more than were recorded, even in unpublished sources), key people were quietly reinstated a few months later.[50]

As far as production itself was concerned, the party cells' role was an ambiguous one. Official instructions were typically contradictory. The September 1929 Central Committee resolution on *edinonachalie* (one-man management) stated that the cell's role was 'to implement the leadership of the social-political and economic life of the enterprise so as to ensure the fulfilment of fundamental party directives, without interfering in details of the work of the trade union committee and the director, especially in the operating instructions of the administration'.[51] But although this was designed to strengthen the manager's hand, in practice it was clear to everyone on the spot that bottlenecks could only be cleared by appeals to influential individuals in the political hierarchy.[52] And the leadership appeared to be contradicting its own message. The resolution on *edinonachalie* was accompanied by exhortations to the cells to turn 'face to production'. Cells were criticized in the party press for their failure to discuss production issues. And in 1930 politics was put back in command when the leadership launched a purge of administrative staff, including specialists in factories. For most of the period confusion about who should be in charge of production led to contradictory directives in the press, tensions in the factory and indecision among managers.

As in all other areas, 'the party' in the factory did not speak with a single voice. Apart from the important social differences between its members, there were conflicts between Communists who also happened to be technical specialists, and rank-and-filers whose prime loyalty was often to the workforce. Although forbidden, it was not unknown for Communists to participate in strikes in Moscow factories.[53] More often, the factory cell would split between those who appeared to be on the side of 'management' and those who regarded themselves as the guardians of political rectitude and optimal economic targets.[54]

These divisions made all decisions harder to take, and not surprisingly the cell *buro* or even the secretary alone were commonly accused of 'substituting' themselves for the organization as a whole. But more often what was noticeable was the dedication of a small core of activists within each cell, while a number of recruits and less enthusiastic members around them were more passive. Party members were encouraged to take an interest in all areas of production. 'Our work', remarked one, 'is composed of the minute details of life.'[55] Although official surveys revealed a marked lack of technical expertise among party secretaries in Moscow's factories in the late 1920s, the first Five Year Plan saw thousands of enthusiasts enrolling in the city's night schools and in factory-based classes to improve their knowledge. Whether or not they started out with any familiarity with production techniques, moreover, if, as was often the case, the management could not take full responsibility for production, they had little choice but to take over.

During the uneasy period of the Industrial Party case in 1930, several leading Moscow directors lost their jobs, including two in succession (Prokhorov and Stepanov) from the Krasnyi Proletarii factory. During this period, as its secretary of the time remarked, the party cell 'itself led the struggle for the speediest possible reconstruction of the factory. The cell itself took an active part in seeing that the first diesel shop should be completed, the construction of which had begun in 1914.'[56] The management of Krasnyi Proletarii took several years to recover from the scandal surrounding the destruction of its foundry in 1929. Between 1929 and 1931, decisions were constantly referred to the cell. As a report remarked, 'two corners of the triangle have burned up, one remains – the cell, and therefore the cell has had to take on part of the work of the other two'.[57] In 1929, indeed, it appeared that the cell was assuming responsibility for the appointment of a new director. At the Serp i Molot metalworks, Gaidul', the secretary of the party cell in 1929, listed eight of its economic tasks, including the introduction of a twelve-month working year and seven-day week, the drawing up of control figures for the factory on a monthly, six-monthly and yearly basis, rationalization plans and a number of detailed questions of administration.[58]

But if the cells took their responsibilities seriously, they also took steps to protect themselves against unwelcome attention from the *raion* and city authorities. Each layer in the party hierarchy had an interest in preserving its autonomy against encroachments from above (demands for extra cadres, awkward questions about its performance) and interference from below (often also in the form of awkward questions and demands for full consultation). Partly because the cells were having to take important decisions on their own initiative, they were obliged to conceal their mistakes from superiors. The party cell at Krasnyi Proletarii, for example, systematically deceived the *raikom* about its work.[59] For the most part, bland reporting was an acceptable way of fudging awkward details, and the *raikom*, itself chronically overburdened and incapable of sorting out the problems of individual factories on a day-to-day basis, was unlikely to demand specific information unless it was clear that a scandal was brewing.

The relationship between party members at different levels within the factory was another question. Here again, the handful of 'responsible' officials, often to some extent self-selected from a group of skilled, long-serving workers, passed bland, uninformative reports down to their own shop and shift cells. But where rank-and-filers had an interest in the information, the mere statement that the factory cells work was 'satisfactory' was not enough. Complaints about cell secretaries' 'bureaucratism', directors' 'opportunism', the lack of communication between layers in the factory party organization, and about officials within the cell who 'substituted' themselves for the lower party organs, were common in the press of the period. And the lower cells themselves, though often unclear about the precise boundaries of responsibility, were not afraid on occasion to ask demanding questions.[60]

The result was chaos. No factory was alike; the relationship between the different tiers in the party hierarchy, and between the party and other administrative bodies, depended as much on personalities and specific local circumstances as it did upon official directives. As the Five Year Plan ran into deeper difficulties in the winter of 1930–1, the party leadership began to review the activists' role, and revisions in their status followed. An early sign of this was the increase in OGPU activity in key factories.[61] This was associated partly with the Industrial Party affair. The period saw a renewed emphasis on 'enemies', many of which, it was claimed, were still concealed within the ranks of the working class itself.[62]

Although 'mass' campaigns such as socialist competition continued into 1931, the role of the rank-and-filer was soon to be curbed. From the summer of 1931 the press began to lay renewed emphasis on hierarchy and discipline within the party, as well as stressing the economic importance of specialists.[63] From 1932 the party was restructured.[64] Many of the lowest tiers, such as shift cells, were abolished altogether, and the remaining organs were largely placed in the hands of full-time officials appointed from above. The following year, 1933, proletarian recruitment ceased. The activists' day was over. The 'mass card' would be played again in the form of the Stakhanovite movement, but the party was not restructured to give activists so much leverage within its own ranks again. Indeed, the factory party cell ceased to exercise managerial powers. If it was ever involved in economic matters after 1932, it would principally be, as one historian has remarked, in the guise of *tolkach* for the factory director, using its influence to gain favours from senior officials such as Ordzhonikidze.[65]

The worker activists' importance during the socialist offensive derived largely from the absence of official controls at a time of widespread disruption. However unpopular or heavy-handed they could sometimes be, they were also in the best position to understand and mobilise their fellow-workers. They also contributed to the management of their factories, at least until 1931. They mediated between the shop floor and local politicians, and at times appealed over the heads of the latter directly to the Moscow or national leadership.[66] They could unstop bottlenecks and speed up production in some cases; in others their role was to protect their comrades from undesirable or ill-considered interference. Although their intervention was also often counter-productive, the conditions prevailing during the first Five Year Plan called for people with their qualifications and commitment, and it is difficult to imagine Stalinist industrialization without them. One of their main contributions, after all, was to break the power of the 'bourgeois' specialist, paving the way for a new type of manager to take over, more amenable to political intervention and less concerned to preserve the old forms of accounting and production.

Moscow's activists may not, of course, have been typical of the rest of the Russian republic. They were more isolated from power in the sense that promotion into the local elite was more difficult than elsewhere, but at the same time they often had direct personal access to Politburo members. They were conscious of their duty to set an example to the provinces, but, as they were constantly lamenting, they were also required to provide 'volunteers' for all the major national campaigns and on a regular basis sent cadres off to work in the countryside. This left many factories bereft of experienced political workers, and made the task of the cell secretaries, who had constantly to look for new volunteers if they were not to work alone, much more difficult. But if Moscow's activists, who could expect almost daily visits from national politicians and whose lives were under close scrutiny in a closely-policed city, could exercise autonomous initiative during the first Five Year Plan, their colleagues in the provinces almost certainly had a good deal more freedom to shape Stalinist industrialization. As Soviet archives become more accessible it is to be hoped that more local studies will be written, helping historians to get a better picture of the relationship between the Stalinist elite and the party grass roots.

In conclusion, however, we should note that the idea of participation and commitment 'from below' has received a bad press recently and has been widely misinterpreted. Critics have supposed that historians who demonstrate any kind of autonomous support for Stalinism are somehow 'whitewashing' the Stalinist terror, exonerating its leaders of 'responsibility for mass murder'.[67] If this had ever been the intention of 'revisionist' historians, they would be making a serious error. For the fact of grass-roots activism exonerates the leadership of nothing. It would be futile to suggest that Stalin was not guilty of planning the murder of thousands of his party colleagues in the purges. It would also be fanciful to assume that the excesses of the collectivization campaign were somehow mainly the fault of the local officials and activists who were given the task – on pain of severe punishment – of driving the peasants into collectives.

What the 'revisionist' picture in fact does is to raise some very troubling issues about the mainsprings of social action. For if Stalin was not exclusively responsible, and if the blame for his 'excesses' cannot simply be laid at the door of a terroristic junta exercising totalitarian control, then surely historians have to ask more searching questions about the relationship between post-revolutionary Soviet society and political change. There is not much time left to consult survivors of the period; Soviet historians working on the oral history of Stalinism have only a few hundred respondents to question. But the archives surely contain rich material about the workings of the local cells and their relationship with the leadership. This is one of the most important areas for future research into the origins and dynamics of Stalinism.

Notes

1. In 1931 Moscow's population included 673,000 industrial and 426,600 white-collar workers. The total population was 2,781,300, of whom 1,088,600 were dependants. *Materialy o khozyaistve Moskvy k itoge pervoi pyatiletki* (Moscow, 1934), p. 116.
2. 98,100 in 1931. Ibid.
3. For a more developed survey of the Moscow party elite, see Catherine Merridale, 'Centre–local relations during the rise of Stalin: the case of Moscow, 1925–32', in David Lane, ed., *Elites and Political Power in the USSR* (Aldershot, Hants, 1988).
4. *Moskovskaia gorodskaia i moskovskaia oblastnaia organizatsiia KPSS v tsifrakh* (Moscow, 1972), p. 28.
5. T.H. Rigby, *Communist Party Membership in the USSR 1917–1967* (Princeton NJ, 1968), p. 158.
6. On Moscow's political history before 1921, see R. Sakwa, *Soviet Communists in Power: A Study of Moscow during the Civil War* (London, 1988).
7. Tsentral'nyi gosudarstvennyi arkhiv oktyabr'skoi revoliutsii (TsGAOR), 7952/3/253, 11.
8. For a further discussion of why workers did not join the party in the early 1920s, see J.B. Hatch, 'Workers and the Communist Party in Moscow, 1921–1928', *Slavic Review*, vol. 48, no. 4 (1989), pp. 562–4.
9. K.Ya. Bauman, *General'naia bol'shevistskaia liniia i nasha rabota* (Moscow-Leningrad, 1929), p. 63.
10. *Rabochaia Moskva (RM)*, 10 September 1927.
11. Bauman, *General'naia bol'shevistskaia liniia i nasha rabota*.
12. This point was made in the Serp i Molot factory paper, *Martenovka*, 7 February 1928. Cited in TsGAOR, 7952/3/253, 13.
13. *Sputnik Kommunista (SK)*, 1929, no. 30.
14. *SK*, 1927, nos. 23–4.
15. *Bol'shevik*, 1925, nos. 21–2, pp. 61–74.
16. Walter Duranty, *I Write as I Please* (London, 1935), p. 201.
17. Iu.A. Poliakov, '20-e gody: nastroeniia partiinogo avangarda', *Voprosy istorii KPSS*, 1989, no. 10.
18. Memoirs of the period attest to activists' recollections of their political views. But more immediate evidence can be found in contemporary surveys of activists' views (such as those reproduced in the Trotsky Archive, files T 2167, T 2021, T 2852, which were compiled in the late summer of 1928 by the MK information department) and the collected recollections of factory workers compiled immediately after the first Five Year Plan (see, for example, the memoirs of Krasni Proletarii's factory activists, TsGAOR, 7952/3/96, which were collected in 1933).
19. *SK*, 1927, nos. 19–20.
20. In 1925, roughly a third of Moscow's propagandists were former members of other parties. *RM*, 14 May 1925. For their off-beat ideas, see *SK*, 1929, no. 15, p. 39.

21. For a more detailed discussion of propaganda, including a survey of the texts used, see Catherine Merridale, *Moscow Politics and the Rise of Stalin* (London, 1990), ch. 8.
22. On this, see John Barber, 'Stalin's letter to the editors of *Proletarskaya revolyutsiya*', *Soviet Studies*, vol. 28, no. 1 (February 1976).
23. N.S. Davydova, 'Moskovskaia partiinaia organizatsiia v bor'be za provedenie kursa kommunisticheskoi partii na sotsialisticheskuiu industrializatsiiu (1926–1928 gg.)', unpublished PhD dissertation, Moscow, 1971, p. 422.
24. N. Maslova, *Agitproprabota iacheiki na predpriyatii* (Moscow, 1927), pp. 27–9.
25. See Merridale, *Moscow Politics*, p. 150.
26. *Propagandist*, September 1930, nos. 3–4, p. 30.
27. As they did, for example, when discussing collectivization in the Moscow oblast: *Propagandist*, April 1930, nos. 13–14, p. 66.
28. This assertion was made by Peter Kenez in his *The Birth of the Propaganda State: Soviet Methods of Mass Mobilisation* (Cambridge, 1985), p. 254.
29. For an elaboration of this argument, see Catherine Merridale, 'The reluctant opposition: the right "deviation" in Moscow, 1928', *Soviet Studies*, vol. 41, no. 3 (July 1989).
30. See William Chase, *Workers, Society and the Soviet State: Labor and Life in Moscow, 1918–1929* (Urbana, 1987), pp. 79–88.
31. On Uglanov's unpopularity, see Merridale, *Moscow Politics*, pp. 50–1.
32. Summaries of activists' views (as expressed at party meetings in July and November 1928) can be found in the Trotsky Archive, T 2167, T 2021 and T 2852.
33. T 2167.
34. They had no idea, for example, that collectivization would be taking place within the next few months. Stalin was silent about his plans until the following autumn.
35. As one Muscovite remarked, 'What did we fight for, why did we allow our blood to flow, if our conditions are so bad?' (T 2021).
36. Extracts from the letters appear in TsGAOR, 7952/3/493.
37. 'The village horrors', Kravchenko wrote later, 'left psychological lesions which never healed.' *I Chose Freedom* (New York, 1947), p. 132.
38. TsGAOR, 7952/3/493, 10.
39. See Merridale, *Moscow Politics*, ch. 3.
40. TsGAOR 5469/14/242, 20.
41. *RM*, 10 September 1927.
42. *Pravda* noted this in 1928, singling out the Dinamo factory for particular criticism. *Pravda*, 28 October 1928.
43. *Partiinoe stroitel'stvo*, 1931, no. 2.
44. *RM*, 4 July 1932.
45. TsGAOR 7952/3/82, 153.
46. TsGAOR, 7952/3/253, 25.
47. *Pravda*, 22 May 1929.
48. *RM*, 24 October 1929.
49. 6.9 per cent of the Moscow organization (as opposed to the national average of 11 per cent) were purged in 1929. The proportion of workers purged was

7.3 per cent, while of white-collar workers, only 6.7 per cent lost their party cards. *Ocherki istorii Moskovskoi organizatsii KPSS*, first edn (Moscow, 1979), p. 454.

50. This was especially the case with specialists. For an example, see TsGAOR 7952/3/96, 85–6.

51. *KPSS v rezoliutsiiakh i resheniiakh*, 9th edn, vol. 4 (Moscow, 1984), p. 559.

52. Such direct petitions were common in Moscow. For an example (the appeal came from Elektrozavod's party members and was sent directly to Krzhizhanovsky), see TsGAOR 7952/3/490, 77.

53. On the early 1920s, see Merridale, *Moscow Politics*, p. 116, and Hatch, 'Workers and the Community Party', p. 567. For the period after 1928, see Donald Filtzer, *Soviet Workers and Stalinist Industrialization* (London, 1986), pp. 81–4.

54. These divisions came out clearly in the debates of the Krasnyi Proletarii party cell, whose secretary sided several times against the cell and with the director. See TsGAOR 7952/3/82.

55. *RM*, 3 September 1927.

56. TsGAOR, 7952/3/96, 78.

57. TsGAOR, 7952/3/82, 27.

58. L. Gaidul', *Litsom k proizvodstvu. Opyt raboty partkomiteta zavoda 'Serp i Molot'* (Moscow, 1930), p. 8.

59. See Merridale, *Moscow Politics*, pp. 184–5.

60. For examples, see TsGAOR, 7952/3/82, 71–5.

61. See Hiroaki Kuromiya, *Stalin's Industrial Revolution. Politics and Workers, 1928–1932* (New York, 1988), p. 264.

62. 'Our enemies', remarked one report, 'conceal themselves in a worker's blouse.' TsGAOR, 7952/3/253, 105, citing *Martenovka*.

63. The classic statement of this new emphasis was Stalin's speech to the economic managers of July 1931. *Sochineniia*, vol. 13 (Moscow, 1951), pp. 51–80.

64. This restructuring in fact began with a speech by Kaganovich, who was then Moscow party first secretary. He based his plans on evidence from Moscow factories. The speech was published in *Pravda*, 7 June 1932.

65. M. Lewin, *The Making of the Soviet System* (London, 1985), p. 252. And for an example, see Kravchenko, *I Chose Freedom*, pp. 196–7, where he describes Ordzhonikidze as 'one of my protecting angels'.

66. Many larger Moscow factories had direct links with individuals in the leadership. Serp i Molot, for example, looked on Kaganovich as its sponsor, while Mikoian and Molotov were both regular visitors to the party cell at the Krasnyi Proletarii factory and Krzhizhanovsky was an 'honorary shock worker' at the Elektrozavod.

67. See *Russian Review*, vol. 45 (1986), contributions by Meyer and Kenez.

8   The demise of the shock-worker brigades in Soviet industry, 1931–1936

John Russell

Introduction

On 1 January 1936, the management newspaper *Za industrializatsiiu* printed an open letter from the Stakhanovites of Moscow's Serp i Molot (Hammer and Sickle) metalworks to all Stakhanovites in heavy industry, calling for the Day of the Shock Worker planned for Saturday 11 January to be transformed into an All-Union Day of the Stakhanovite, demanding that '1936 must become a Stakhanovite year, a year of unprecedented new achievements'. The slogans of the eight workers (whose signatures were preceded by those of the factory director, party secretary and union representative) formed the basis of a mass campaign as the weight of the Communist Party, management and union organs was shifted behind the movement of industrial record breakers.[1] This had been started just three months previously by the young Donbass coalminer, Aleksei Stakhanov.[2]

With the personal blessing of no less a superior than 'comrade STALIN [*sic*]', the Stakhanovite (i.e. a young worker who had mastered her/his trade sufficiently well to introduce innovatory techniques and thus smash the existing work norms) became the central figure of socialist competition and, as such, of shopfloor input into the management of Soviet industry. By comparison, the 'ordinary' shock workers, who worked intensively but utilized 'old' techniques, paled into insignificance and, as was made clear by the middle of 1936,[3] they were forgotten. The day of the shock worker was effectively over. Yet, how different the situation had been just six years previously. In January 1930, at the height of the optimistic phase of *the* Five Year Plan (not yet first of many), the Soviet trade unions had launched the Lenin Enrolment (*leninskii prizyv*) during which, it was claimed, up to one-and-a-half million people in Soviet industry became shock workers within a few weeks.[4] Indeed, 1930 was to become the year of the shock workers, and the year of their most widespread and popular form of organization – the shock brigade.

This chapter traces the demise of this specific form of socialist competition from the first Shock Worker Day in October 1930 to its eventual absorption by the Stakhanovite movement in early 1936. Rather than covering anew such well-researched aspects of this problem as the struggle for labour discipline,[5] the atomization of the workforce, the imposition of strict one-man management and the influx of rural migrants into Soviet industry,[6] I shall focus on three connected issues in an attempt to evaluate the impact of the shock brigades during this critical period of Soviet development. These are (1) the numbers game – an analysis not only of the absolute numbers of shock workers between 1929 and 1936, but also an examination of the use made of these data in presenting shock work as a growing phenomenon; (2) the erosion of the practical influence of shopfloor organizations capable of providing a genuinely collective worker input into the management of Soviet industry; and (3) the interplay between two competing images of the Soviet worker, the 'heroic' – representing a sentimentalized bureaucratic view, and the 'realistic' – objectively seeking efficiency, stability and sustainable methods of work (and more likely to emanate from line management or shopfloor workers). The first image will tend to sanction forms of work organization that are both task-orientated and campaign-led, whereas the second favours longer-term strategies. The decisive victory of the former during the period under review, it will be argued, has cost the Soviet economy dear.

Stages in the growth of shock work 1929–1936

One of the problems besetting the pre-glasnost school of Soviet history has been the persistence of a 'socialist realist' approach which interprets events 'in their revolutionary development'. This requires that such phenomena as socialist competition and shock work be portrayed as developing 'naturally' (*zakonomerno*) and their growth as even and consistent. Thus direct links between competition and shock work during the revolution and civil war (1919–1921) and the spread of the mass movement from 1929 are exaggerated.[7] Similarly, one might conclude, on reading Soviet histories of socialist competition, that shock work (*udarnichestvo*) evolved naturally and evenly between 1929 and 1935 into the Stakhanovite movement.[8] However, a closer examination of the facts will reveal that the links here, too, were equally tenuous and that, in fact, this period witnessed a succession of disparate campaigns. These, especially after the collapse of the 'optimistic' phase of the

industrialization drive during the economic crisis of mid-1930, appeared
to emanate progressively less from genuine initiatives by the workers
and more from party and management orchestration.

This uneven development is reflected in the paucity of comprehensive
data on the growth of shock work (and socialist competition as a whole)
between 1929 and 1936. More surprisingly, for such an avowedly collec-
tivist society, there are very few details on the size and number of the
shock brigades themselves. From the first surveys of shock work in 1929
and 1930 until the growth of cost-accounting brigades in 1932, the average number of workers per brigade appeared to average between nine
and twelve.[9] As a rule, brigades in heavy industry were smaller than in
light industry. Moreover, under the continuous working week, the five-
person brigade system became widespread, utilizing a worker from each
shift plus a relief for every machine tool.[10]

Even allowing for the lack of precision and reliability of Soviet data
on shock work and competition during the period, the following table
illustrates the ebb and flow of the movement between 1929 and 1936:

Table 1. *Percentage of workers in Soviet industry engaged in shock
work and competition, 1929–1936*

Year (on 1 Jan)	No. of workers[a] (in thousands)	% in shock work[b]	% in competition[c]
1929	2,788.0	—	—
1930	3,116.2	29.0	65.0
1931	4,256.4	57.8	65.5
1932	5,271.3	64.2	67.6
1933	5,139.7	56.2	70.6
1934	5,215.0	43.0	73.4
1935	5,658.3	48.0	72.0
1936	6,173.0	43.0	64.0

Sources:
[a]   *Trud v SSSR: statisticheskii spravochnik*, Moscow, 1936, p. 94.
[b] 1930   *Materialy k otchetu VTsSPS IX s"ezdu profsoiuzov*, Moscow, 1932, p. 32.
   & 1932
   1931   *Narodnoe khoziaistvo SSSR: statisticheskii spravochnik*, Moscow, 1932, p. 452.
   1933   Calculated from *Profsoiuznaia perepis', 1932–33gg.*, Moscow, 1934.
   1934   *Profsoiuzy SSSR: dokumenty i materialy*, vol. 3, Moscow, 1963, p. 737.
   1935/6   *Voprosy profdvizheniia*, 1936, no. 6, p. 24.
[c] 1930   *Materialy k otchetu VTsSPS IX s"ezdu profsoiuzov*, p. 32.
   1931/5   *Istoriia sotsialisticheskogo sorevnovaniia v SSSR*, Moscow, 1980, p. 97.
   1936   *Voprosy profdvizheniia*, 1936, no. 6, p. 24.

Thus the proportion of shock workers during the period of their apparent ascendancy (1929–1935) rose from zero to 64.2 per cent, then fell back to under half. Indeed, after the trade union survey of 1932/3 until the spread of Stakhanovism in 1936, separate figures for shock work ceased to be given on a regular basis within the overall data for participation in competition; evidence, perhaps, of the dramatic decline in numbers of shock workers.[11] This decline is not reflected so graphically in the figures for socialist competition, although the proportion of workers competing in 1936 is actually lower than in 1930. This embarrassing statistic has been circumvented, since 1934,[12] by replacing the 1930 figure of 65 per cent with one of 29 per cent,[13] i.e. the figure hitherto applied to shock workers.[14] Accordingly, the percentage of shock workers also had to be marked down – to 10 per cent, a reduction of almost two-thirds![15]

Soviet historians might maintain that the revised figures provide a truer picture as the earlier statistics were inflated. This is most certainly the case. However, given the relative wealth of data on competition in 1930–2 compared to subsequent years, one should have as much confidence in the 1930 figure as in any other, and might suspect the massaging of statistics for political purposes. So dubious, indeed, are the figures for competition and shock work throughout the period that one must be most careful in drawing definite conclusions from them. None the less, table 2, it seems to me, still succeeds in illustrating just how levels of shock work fluctuated even within given years, pointing to the short-term nature of the successive campaigns.

What clearly emerges from table 2 is that, following a significant fall-off in mid-1930, shock work had become consolidated as a feature of Soviet industry by the beginning of 1931, numbers appearing to peak in 1932 and then fall towards the end of the period. The number of shock brigades would have peaked at over 300,000 in 1932 and also fallen thereafter.[16] Not explicit in the figures are the forms of shock work that were undertaken.

The critical year was 1930, for it clearly produced the highest number of new shock workers (1,546,900), considerably more than either 1929 (903,100) or 1931 (790,000). Yet, the proportion fluctuated during the year considerably, there being two major influxes (in the first and last two-month periods) and a significant falling-off in between. The influxes represent respectively the Lenin Enrolment launched on 21 January[17] and the autumn campaign for labour discipline initiated by the party appeal of 3 September.[18] The two appeals were quite different, the first triumphantly addressed to the workers at large and evoking a huge, albeit short-lived wave of enthusiasm (marked by brigades, workshops and factories declaring themselves shock), and the second aimed

Table 2. *Estimates of total number of shock workers in Soviet industry, 1929–1936*

Date	Total no. of workers[a] (in thousands)	Total no. of shock workers[b] (in thousands)	% of shock workers[c]	% in competition
1.10.29	2,856.9	290	10	—
1. 1.30	3,116.2	903	29	65
1. 3.30	3,269.8	1,815	55.5	72
1. 5.30	3,479.1	1,663	47.8	72.3
1.11.30	4,035.7	1,973	48.9	58.1
1. 1.31	4,256.4	2,460	57.8	65.5
1. 4.31	4,236.3	2,720	64.2	73.3
1. 5.31	4,237.6	2,754	65.0	71.1
1. 6.31	4,393.2	2,873	65.4	71.3
1.10.31	4,771.0	2,963	62.1	74.3
1. 1.32	5,271.3	3,240	64.2	67.6
1. 4.32	4,904.7	3,146	64.1	76.5
1. 1.33	5,139.7	2,889	56.2	71.3
1. 1.34	5,215.0	2,786	43	73.4
1. 1.35	5,658.3	2,716	48	72.1
1. 1.36	6,173.0	2,654	43	64

Sources: (as for Table 1 except where stated)

[a] 1930 (except 1.1) *Industrializatsiia SSSR, 1929–32gg.: dokumenty i materialy*, & 1931   Moscow, 1970, p. 435.
          (for 1 October 1929, *ibid*., p. 517).

1932 (except 1.1) *Sotsialisticheskoe stroitel'stvo SSSR*, Moscow, 1934, p. 325.

[b, c] 1/3/30   *Materialy k otchetu VTsSPS* (1932), p.35.

& [d] 1/5/30   *Sotsialisticheskoe sorevnovanive v promyshlennosti SSSR*, Moscow, 1930, p. 11.

1/11/30 & 1/6/31 *Narodnoe khoziaistvo SSSR (1932)*, p. 452.

1/5/31 & 1/10/31 *Sotsialisticheskoe sorevnovanie v SSR, 1918–1964: dokumenty i materialy profsoiuzov*, Moscow, 1965, pp. 60–1.

1/4/32   S. Kheinman, *K voprosu o proizvoditel'nosti truda v SSSR*, Moscow, 1933.
          (N.B. the author gives the proportion of shock workers as 76.5 per cent)

primarily at party, union and Komsomol organizations urging them to mobilize the workers through moral appeals (to rebuff the class enemy and tighten discipline) and material incentives (tying preferential provisions to participation in shock work). From then on the shock worker's card was to become, first and foremost, a meal ticket and/or a pass to a better job,[19] and reasons for engaging in shock work became more individual than collective.

The watershed between the two appeals was the industrial crisis of mid-1930. The enthusiasm generated in the optimistic phase of industrialization in the last quarter of 1929 to early 1930[20] had dissipated largely by the time the 16th Party Congress met in June 1930. It was at this forum, however, that Stalin chose to comment:[21]

The most remarkable thing about competition is that it effects a radical change in people's attitudes to work, for it transforms work from a despised and heavy burden, as it used to be regarded, into a matter of honour, a matter of glory, a matter of valour and heroism.

That this yawning gap between desire and reality became a permanent feature of Soviet life is revealed by the terms of Gorbachev's address to veterans of the Stakhanovite movement as recently as September 1985:[22]

Allow me on behalf of the party Central Committee to sincerely greet you veteran Stakhanovites, who stood at the source of the movement which epitomized valour, honour and heroism of the worker and you front rankers and innovators, who are worthily continuing the unfading tradition of labour achievement.

Compare such lofty rhetoric with the realism voiced in the autumn of 1930 by such political opponents of Stalin as Syrtsov, leader of the so-called right–'leftist' bloc within the party. Conceding that socialist competition had certain positive features, he complained that it was being implemented[23]

with a degree of unhealthy moral and political pressure that distorts discussion and drives valuable groups of workers and managers towards passivity . . . in an auction-room atmosphere of agiotage, figures plucked from the air are imposed . . . attempts to defend the business-like elaboration of plans evoke stomps of disapproval and flippant accusations and suspicions of factionalism, wrecking, 'underestimation', 'overestimation', 'failure to grasp' and so on . . . by some sort of automatic process just about every creative political idea of the working class, after a while, is unfailingly distorted . . .

Under conditions of 'the sharpening of the class struggle', such realism was to be outlawed and found, subsequently, only on the pages of Opposition journals. As early as mid-1931 a correspondent to the Menshevik journal encapsulated thus the shift from moral to material incentives in shock work:[24]

There are no ideological reasons for becoming a shock worker any more. Some are talked into it, others by threats, others just don't want to be left out, but the majority join for material well-being or for a good job. They are mainly the most backward workers and semi-mature youngsters . . . there are shock workers and there are ordinary workers and the differences between these two groups are growing all the time.

By early 1932, according to reports in the same journal, even the party faithful were fired less by enthusiasm than by prospects for self-advancement:[25]

And notice, even among our Communists and Komsomol members, one comes across all the more rarely sincere enthusiasm, a genuine burning desire. And as for the rank and file millions of 'enthusiasts', when all is said and done, they are just like our entire Soviet output: full of defects and, all too often, good for nothing! . . . both the youngsters and the Communists, even the most active, are more and more infected by the same individualistic, the same egoistic moods and aspirations.

Why, then, should workers continue to join the shock brigades in such numbers? In the winter of 1931/32, another correspondent was in no doubt:[26]

When the food rations for the shock workers are raised, those of the ordinary workers are lowered. Hunger is forcing the workers into shock work. And they are going.

In other words, by the end of the first Five Year Plan in 1932, the reasons for engaging in shock work were significantly different from those existing during the optimistic phase of 1929/30. However, the need to portray shock work as riding a growing wave of enthusiasm remained a political priority. If one traces the development in 1930/1 of many of the original shock brigades into production communes and then in 1931/2 into cost-accounting brigades (the last truly significant form of collective work organization prior to the Stakhanovites), the changes in the organization, aims and authority of the brigades become apparent. The critical factor was the evolving (or degenerating) role of the brigade in the process of management. This, in turn, was determined by the perceived priorities of the Stalinist leadership, which it has become customary to equate with slogans popularized at various stages of the industrialization drive. The scheme below illustrates how a different form of shock work was deemed most suitable for each successive period:

1929 to mid-1931	'Tempos are decisive'	– shock brigades
1931–1934	'Technology is decisive'	– cost-accounting brigades
1935–	'Cadres are decisive'	– Stakhanovism

As the command-administrative approach to industry was the 'red thread' connecting these three periods, one would expect that both management and worker inputs into the production process would have to be subordinated to this principle. In the event, this came to mean that, although managers were given the sole right to fix work norms, socialist competition (especially in the form of rate-busting) remained a means of keeping production in the sphere of 'heroic' target-setting, while any form of shock work that hindered the command approach could be scrapped. Thus, the data are given for shock brigades until 1931/2, for cost-accounting between 1931–4 and for Stakhanovites from 1935.

The shock brigade and the *promfinplan*

Significantly, the form of competition that Syrtsov was referring to specifically above was counter planning, a product of the party's September appeal. It is worth examining the link between the shock brigade and the industrial and financial plan (*promfinplan*) at the level of the factory for, I would argue, the former represented in organizational form a mass workers' response to rapid industrialization, whereas the latter was restricted largely to a minority of management-minded workers. By 1935, strict implementation of one-man management and the individualization of the *promfinplan* had rendered the shock brigades superfluous (even counter planning, by which workers, brigades, shifts etc. would counter – i.e. raise – planned management targets, had virtually died out with the cost-accounting brigades by 1934).[27]

A contradiction between the brigades and the plan occurred because shock work was vaunted primarily by Stalin's faction as the means by which the *political* battle over the pace of industrialization and the social struggle for labour discipline could be won. On the shop-floor this involved emasculating the unions and smashing craft attitudes and existing work norms. The economic value of shock work was often secondary, for it did not guarantee good results in production. For example, in 1931, despite an upsurge in shock work, productivity per industrial worker rose by only 5.6 per cent against the 28 per cent that had been planned.[28]

That shock work built upon a wave of enthusiasm alone was of little utility appears to have been recognized by the Soviet authorities at an early stage. This is shown by two decrees issued on the same day in April 1930 (usually taken as the end of the optimistic phase of industrialization). The party decree 'On the Results of the Lenin Enrolment of Shock Workers'[29] criticized 'sham shock work' (*lzheudarnichestvo*) and the 'razzamatazz' (*paradnaia shumikha*) surrounding so many competition pacts. It called for the *promfinplan* to be brought down to the level of the brigade (so that each shock group would have concrete responsibilities, tasks and targets), as well as the introduction of rewards for outstanding shock workers. The trade union decree 'On the Involvement of Trade Unions in Compiling Control Figures for 1930/1'[30] advocated more tangible ways of involving workers in cutting costs and raising productivity and lay the foundation for the counter-planning movement later in the year.

From surveys conducted at this time (May 1930) it is clear that there were approximately 1.6 million shock workers engaged in Soviet industry.[31] In other words, almost half of the workforce was enrolled, albeit nominally, in shock brigades. Within the brigades an interesting development was occurring for, in response to party and union calls for more productivity and efficiency, the leading brigades were transforming themselves into production collectives and communes, sharing their earnings in one form or another.[32] From a base of approximately just 150,000 industrial workers in May 1930, the number of communards doubled (to 306,000 or 7.2 per cent) by May 1931,[33] despite meeting with considerable opposition and receiving no encouragement from the authorities. There is ample evidence that the best communes consistently produced good results and represented the most genuinely popular form of shock brigade.[34] However, in the chaotic conditions of the first Five Year Plan, they were unsustainable as a viable form of shop-floor organization for the workforce at large. Finally, they came to be regarded as constituting a threat to one-man management, wage differentiation and individual responsibility, were denounced as 'SR demagogy' and proscribed in September 1931.[35]

The fall of the communes and their enforced conversion into cost-accounting brigades (with brigade leaders henceforward appointed by management rather than elected by its members[36]) marked the end of the spontaneous growth of shock work, the last 'grass roots' attempt to transform Soviet industry. Significantly, a feature of the cost-accounting brigades was the individual accounting of each member's work, an essential difference from the collective approach of the communes but a valuable weapon in the struggle against 'lack of responsibility' (*obezlichka*) launched by Stalin's 'six conditions' of June 1931.

This is not to say that elements of enthusiasm and commitment died out with the communes. Indeed, sufficient cadres could be found in each succeeding generation to perpetuate the myth that competition manifested the dominance of a 'socialist attitude to work' in Soviet factories. All subsequent forms of socialist competition, however, seemed to lack the spontaneity of the early shock brigades and communes, were often initiated by party officials, fitted into the scheme of one-man management or represented an heroic response to a critical situation. For example, the party decree of September 1930, while failing to encourage the communes, gave the class struggle a sharp new edge by ushering in a new epoch of 'heroic' labour as a rebuff to the defendants in the forthcoming Promparty trial. 'Red Guards of the Five-Year Plan', 'Battalions of Enthusiasts' and 'Komsomol Battalions' were all mobilized in response[37] and individual cases of heroism were widely publicized. Similarly, the popularizing of the fifteen leading shock workers in March 1931 (at least one of whom, Anton Ol'shevsky, had been leader of a production commune) coincided exactly with the Menshevik trial.[38] The prevailing atmosphere of class hate was vital in order to mobilise public opinion against those who attempted to hinder the great leap forward into socialism, be it by means of appeals for rational planning or physical attacks on shock workers.[39]

Thus, after the founder of the first cost-accounting brigade – Piotr Kapkov – was badly beaten up by two fellow-workers following the Leningrad obkom decree in May 1931 spreading this form of competition, the Supreme Court of the RSFSR was moved to issue a clarification 'On Responsibility for Threats Aimed at Shock Workers in Connection with their Production Activity from Backward and Alien Class Elements that have Infiltrated Enterprises'.[40] This made the persecution of shock workers a criminal offence. In reality, of course, the motivation for such attacks was usually cuts in rates of pay or increases in work norms initiated by the shock workers in their quest to fulfil the *promfinplan*. However, the system's support proved an extra incentive (to material benefits) for the rate-buster to ignore pressures of worker solidarity. This was to become an essential prerequisite for Stakhanovism.

We have seen how the cost-accounting brigades neatly fitted Stalin's switch of emphasis in the industrialization drive to 'technology is decisive'. Indeed, the decrees 'On Cost-Accounting Brigades'[41] that established the movement nationwide was promulgated by the top management (*Vesenkha*) and union (VTsSPS) organs. All workers and brigades were to be assigned to a specific machine or workplace and put on piece-rates. The *promfinplan* was to be brought down to the individual worker. Management would then establish standards for output, costs and wastage and the brigade would submit a counter plan. Just two days after the publication of the decree *Pravda* endorsed the new movement thus:[42]

With the cost-accounting brigades there ends a given period of searching for the organizational form of shock work that most closely conforms to the current tasks of socialist society.

Further evidence that the unions stood square behind the party was provided following the All-Union Meeting of Cost-Accounting Brigades in March 1932, when in the preamble to a new decree on the brigades it was stated:[43]

Being the highest form of socialist competition and a new form of labour organization that combines socialist competition and shock work with material incentives at work, and realising in practice the six historical conditions of comrade Stalin, cost-accounting brigades are called upon by the will of the party and the working class to resolve the historic task of teaching millions of people to run the economy.

How very different was this concept of the workers being 'genuine masters of production' to that of the communards.[44] Despite rising to more than two million members (about 40 per cent of the entire work-force) by mid-1932,[45] the brigades never really took root and had virtu-ally died out by 1934.[46] The absence of reliable accounting in the workshop as a whole as well as a lack of will to involve the workers at large in the planning process called into question the *raison d'être* of the brigades. The mastering of technology replaced counter planning as the top priority in competition and this was reflected in the subsequent forms of shock work that appeared between 1932 and 1935. Although both the DiP ('Catch Up and Surpass') and Izotov movements[47] worked on the brigade principle, neither had the impact of the early shock brigades. The individualization of both work and pay facilitated the growth of forms of individual shock work, such as the *otlichniki* (excel-lers). This, together with the ending of rationing in 1934 and 1935,[48] served as a necessary precondition for the spread of the Stakhanovite movement.

Tamed and emasculated, some shock brigades survived to 1935 as 'the most simple form of competition'.[49] However, as *Pravda* commen-ted in February of that year, 'workers no longer endeavour to interfere in management'.[50]

Images of shock work

From the first posters of the October Revolution to the present the most enduring image of the Soviet worker is a young giant with hammer in hand striding purposefully towards a radiant future. For more than fifty years the quintessential example of this image has been the worker in Vera Mukhina's monumental 'Worker and Collective Farm Girl' statue completed for the 1937 Paris International Exhibition and subsequently erected in Moscow. The healthy young *bogatyr'* (Hercules) was held to represent the youth, dynamism and optimism of the USSR during an epic period of derring-do and achievement, when real-life young giants in the Stakhanovite movement were being lauded as heroes of the modern age. It performed an important function in symbolizing the workers as 'masters of production'. After all, which other country erect-ed massive monuments to its workforce? Five decades on, how dated and inappropriate this rhetoric in stainless steel appears when set beside the problems currently bedevilling an aged and ailing Soviet industry.

How misdirected seems that resolute stride into communism, now that the USSR is back in the realm of reality.

As I have suggested, it was precisely in the Stalin Revolution during the period under review that the struggle between 'heroic' and 'realistic' images of the workers was resolved unambiguously in favour of the former. Compare the difference in approach to the average worker embodied in the speech of the old trade-union leader, Tomsky, delivered in December 1928:[51]

Trade unions unite workers irrespective of their political or religious beliefs. If we exclude all believers, who are we left with? The borders of our unions would not be much wider than those of the Communist Party, i.e. one hundred per cent orthodox communists. A worker is a worker in spite of his prejudices.

with that of the Stalinist union official, Veinberg, expressed in the trade union daily in January 1933:[52]

We must treat trade unionists who repudiate the directions of the Communist Party in the matter of wages with the same severity as the party applies to members who disorganize the grain front or any other battlefront of the socialist economy. Trade unionists are sometimes heard to ask whether, as unionists, they ought to protest when wages above the standard rates are paid. These unionists are afraid of what the workers will think of them. This is an absolute disgrace and reveals a complete misunderstanding of the duties of Soviet trade unions. It is typical 'trade unionism'. We must put an end to this sort of 'protection of the workers' interests'.

One should bear in mind that it was Tomsky, in December 1928, who called into question the viability of shock work, and his former colleague Veinberg who followed faithfully each twist and turn of party policy on socialist competition.

Prior to the first Five Year Plan this conflict had been largely of a generational nature, between wise old heads and impatient youngsters. The difference of approach is captured by the author, Fiodor Gladkov, in his novel 'The Exuberant Sun' (written in 1927) when an experienced management representative and party member explains to a Komsomol secretary recuperating in a rest home from a nervous breakdown (due to intensive work):[53]

Enthusiasm is a tempest. It is fed not on day-to-day work, but by the fire of struggle and by inspiring images of the future which set us alight today. When enthusiasm dissolves into business-like pressures and the tedium of day upon days that recede into infinity, then it is transformed into so-called love for the task in hand and unseen creative processes. To live by this, to feel this, demands great self-discipline and profound experience, but this is now characteristic of the few. Such things as the reconstruction of the economy, the raising of labour productivity, conveyors, output norms, rates for the job and so on – these are all cold and weighty words, not the stuff for a triumphal march. Given our universal level of cultural backwardness, work remains for the masses an obligatory burden, joyless conscript labour (not for nothing do many workers call the conveyor the convoy). Work will only be a source of joy, of creative delights when it merges with art. But as yet work, far from inspiring the masses, wears them out and mechanises them. From this comes the need to escape from the daily grind through a kind of anarchistic revolt, and the forms that revolt takes are drunkenness, hooliganism, sexual promiscuity and so on. How else do you explain such a general state of mass exhaustion?

With the mass spread of shock work in 1929, this story was withdrawn from the author's collected works in print. The heroic image of the worker was gaining ground, however, as this contemporary observation by a cadre worker makes clear:[54]

We have many members of the party who perceive the workers as muscular, strapping chaps in blue overalls with rolled up sleeves and with massive hammers (the like of which the world has never seen) in their hands, or robust lads, stripped bare to the waist, shifting great hunks of rock. They look at the worker thus depicted and sigh 'Ah! a worker, *batiushka!*'

To give the Soviet press its due, the portraits of shock workers that adorned the pages of the dailies and periodicals at this time were realistic enough: wrinkled faces in flat caps or kerchiefs, whiskered old-timers, young men and women. Contemporary accounts of shock workers' exploits in this period were similarly matter of fact.[55] By 1931, the switch towards the mastering of technology in the factories had somewhat compromised the image of the hammer-toting hero. However, at the showpiece project of the first Five Year Plan – the Stalingrad Tractor Works – the gung-ho attitude to shock work was causing havoc, as this observer ruefully recalled:[56]

Technology will not be taken by storm. No amount of jerking will make the conveyor work properly. You cannot launch a factory by means of a headlong charge. This is clear to everyone now. These are simple truths, but ones that had to be learned through suffering. And thousands of workers had to endure this. Backwardness reduced their heroism to naught.

Yet this was precisely the attitude to production that Syrtsov had ridiculed in the autumn of 1930 (and had been roundly condemned as a politically harmful element for so doing).[57]

With him were swept away not only those who opposed the exposed fallacies of the heroic heave to socialism, but also those who pleaded for genuine efficiency. As the editor of the factory newspaper at the Stalingrad Tractor Works lamented:[58]

Sometimes elements of folkloric rapture creep into an author's attitude to shock workers. They write about a shock worker as if he was a super-Hercules (*chudo-bogatyr'*) who can stop a troika of horses with one hand. Sometimes a romantic passion for 'production prowess' creeps in, such as working overtime for one-

and-a-half to two months. But how the shock workers achieved their successes, what they did for them – a calm, business-like story which would teach others how to organize their work properly, without overtime, but productively and economically, is hard to find.

In other words, the older experienced workers conscientiously but quietly fulfilling their plan came to be less the stuff that heroes were made of than were bright-eyed youngsters willing to shift mountains or raw recruits from the countryside who were used to bouts of intensive work. The September 1930 appeal had broken the link between work experience and rewards by making participaton in shock work the prime criterion. The biographies of many Stakhanovites reveal strong, young peasant lads who came to the construction sites of the first Five Year Plan to earn their pot of gold, but who stayed on to work in the factories they had helped build.[59] The Soviet Constitution of 1936 took this one stage further as, by proclaiming a society free of class antagonisms, the children of kulaks and other class enemies could redeem themselves through participation in the Stakhanovite movement.

The predictable outcome of ignoring the 'realistic' worker and encouraging the myth of heroic labour was that shock work itself had become largely a myth by the end of the period under review. A survey of nearly 2,000 enterprises at the beginning of 1934 revealed that only 57.4 per cent of those engaged in competition were fulfilling their output norms. The same report claimed that, in December 1933, only 6.6 per cent of those competing, and 12.2 per cent of the shock workers had received material rewards, these averaging 52 roubles 80 kopecks.[60] The remaining cost-accounting brigades were performing no better. Of the 209 functioning at the Chelyabinsk Tractor Works in December 1933, only 98 had fulfilled their plan with an average reward per member of 30 roubles 41 kopecks.[61] Shock worker cards were handed out irrespective of plan fulfilment and, conversely, shock workers who had fulfilled plans were denied cards.[62] In general, socialist competition and shock work were not being monitored.[63]

Management was obliged, therefore, to concentrate its attention on those trades that were central to the *promfinplan*. Shock workers in the leading industries had enjoyed preferential rates of pay and rewards since October 1931,[64] but now leading trades were identified within these industries and, by 1933, these were accorded special rates of pay and provisions.[65]

By 1935, the production conferences (through which shock workers nominally ran competition) were switched to management control, thus placing in management hands all levers controlling worker input except improvements to the production process (rate-busting, rationalization, inventions etc.).[66] At last the system, and not the workers themselves, could determine who was and who was not a 'genuine' worker.

Conclusions

In reassessing the course of Stalin's industrial revolution in the light of the changes effected in Soviet society in the Gorbachev era, one is tempted to dismiss shock work in particular, and socialist competition in general, as an integral part of the Stalinist myth of a new socialist society. Certainly, the shock brigades were an extremely premature and ill-judged experiment given the composition of the Soviet workforce in the 1930s. Equally as certainly, however, the movement did generate great enthusiasm and did mobilize groups of workers not only to achieve impressive results in production, but also to improve their skills. Moreover, Stalin was perceived as standing at the head of this movement (he had been elected an honorary shock worker as early as 1929)[67] and the USSR regarded itself, and was perceived by workers abroad, as being 'the shock brigade of the world's proletariat'.[68]

However, the dead hand of Stalinism stifled any genuine enthusiasm and autonomy at an early stage, swept aside opponents and silenced the most rational criticism. In a Manichaean atmosphere of suspicion and suppression, reality was replaced by a kind of ideal image under which figures, facts and images were distorted. The rot had set in by the autumn of 1930 when ironically, in the wake of the party appeal of 3 September, the first Shock Worker Day had been proclaimed (to mark the first day of the special 'shock' quarter from October to December 1930).[69] Further Shock Worker Days ushered in the second Five Year Plan on 1 January 1933 and the New Year of 1934.[70] Anniversaries of socialist competition became another pretext for mobilizing shock work, as did the major events in the 'socialist' calendar. Stakhanov's feat, for example, was meant to mark International Youth Day on 30 August 1935.

Support for shock work alone was not enough, as the experience of the production communes proved, for the form as well as the content of shock work had to fit Stalin's definition of 'socialist'. By the same logic, the composer Dmitrii Shostakovich was obliged to scrap his plans for an opera in which Yevgeniia Roman'ko, leader of the celebrated women's shock brigade of cement-layers at the Dnieper Hydroelectric Dam, was to represent the modern Soviet heroine in the concluding work of a tetralogy devoted to the revolutionary spirit of Russian women. Unfortunately for him, Stalin had visited a performance of the first work in this epic cycle 'Lady Macbeth of Mtsensk District' in December 1935 and appears to have prompted the celebrated article 'Chaos instead of Music' printed in *Pravda* on 28 January 1936, which lambasted the composer and cut short his operatic career.

So, the year of 1936 witnessed the death of a musical monument to a real live shock worker and the birth of Mukhina's celebrated statue. Myth had triumphed over reality once more. The mighty symbol of the hammer and sickle stands to this day in Moscow at the entrance to the Permanent Exhibition of Economic Achievements. How long, I wonder, will it be before a young wag from an artists' co-operative on the old Arbat sneaks up to the monolith and sprays the word 'Ozymandias' on its base? The modern Soviet worker must look at the economic achievements and despair.

Notes

1. See also *Za industrializatsiiu*, 14 January 1936 for the announcement of the first Stakhanovite 'five-day' campaign.
2. On 30 August 1935, Stakhanov mined a record 102 tons of coal in a single shift. *Pravda*, 6 September 1935.
3. 'The majority of trade union organizations . . . have forgotten other forms of socialist competition, especially shock work . . . In the Urals they have virtually eliminated shock work the words "shock worker" have been dropped from the vocabulary' (V. Malakha, 'O sotsialisticheskom sorevnovanii', *Voprosy profdvizheniia*, 1936, no. 6, p. 23).
4. *Istoriia sovetskogo rabochego klassa v shesti tomakh*, vol. 2 (Moscow, 1984), p. 266.
5. See John Russell, 'The role of socialist competition in establishing labour discipline in the Soviet working class, 1928–1934', unpublished PhD dissertation, University of Birmingham, 1987.
6. See, for example, D. Filtzer, *Soviet Workers and Stalinist Industrialization* (London, 1986); V. Andrle, *Workers in Stalin's Russia: Industrialization and Social Change in a Planned Economy* (New York, 1988); and H. Kuromiya, *Stalin's Industrial Revolution: the Formation of Modern Soviet Production Relations, 1928–1941* (Cambridge, 1988).
7. The classical Soviet periodization is:
   1917–1928 Maturing of the Prerequisites for Competition
   1929–1935 The Shock Worker Movement
   1935–1957 The Stakhanovite and Innovators Movement
   See N. B. Lebedeva, *Voprosy istorii*, 1976, no. 2, p. 49.
8. See, for example, *Istoriia sotsialisticheskogo sorevnovaniia v SSSR* (Moscow, 1980), chs. 2 and 3.
9. A major survey of shock brigades on 1 January 1930 found an average of 11.7 members per brigade (9 for metalworkers and miners): *Trud v SSSR. Spravochnik 1926–1930 gg.* (Moscow, 1930), p. 25. A survey of communes in May 1930 found an average of 7.3 workers per brigade in metalworking and 14.1 in textiles: *Sotsialisticheskoe sorevnovanie v promyshlennosti SSSR*,

1930, p. 90. A survey of nearly 2,500 enterprises on 1 January 1933 found an average of 11.66 members in each cost-accounting brigade: *Sotsialisticheskoe sorevnovanie v SSSR, 1918–1964: dokumenty i materialy* (Moscow, 1965), p. 106.

10. For discussion of implications see *Voprosy truda*, 1930, no. 3, pp. 71–81.

11. Thus, some sources maintain that the percentage engaged in shock work was over 70 by April 1932; see note to table 2 concerning Kheinman's estimate of shock workers.

12. This switch first occurred in the article by A. Devyakovich, 'Sotssorevnovanie i udarnichestvo' in *Voprosy profdvizheniia*, 1934, no. 5, p. 83. A leading article in the same journal earlier that year (no. 1, p. 5) gives 29 per cent shock workers.

13. See, for example, *Istoriya sots. sorevnovaniia*, p. 97.

14. The accepted figure of 903,100 shock workers represents 28.98 per cent of the workforce (3,116,200); see table 2.

15. This figure is usually that given for 1 October 1929; see *Industrializatsiia SSSR, 1929–1932 gg.* (Moscow, 1970), p. 517.

16. Based on an average of 10 members per brigade (see note 9).

17. *Trud*, 21 January 1930.

18. *Pravda*, 3 September 1930.

19. For introduction of these cards, see N. B. Lebedeva and O. I. Shkaratan, *Ocherki istorii sotsialisticheskogo sorevnovaniia* (Leningrad, 1966), p. 116.

20. Best exemplified in Mayakovsky's poetry at this time; see his 'Zastrel'shchiki' (Trailblazers), published in *Na trudovom fronte*, 1930, no. 1. Mayakovsky's suicide in April 1930 may be taken as symbolizing the end of the optimistic period of industrialization.

21. *XVI s"ezd VKP(b): stenograficheskii otchet*, 2nd edn (Moscow-Leningrad, 1930), p. 39.

22. *Pravda*, 21 September 1985.

23. 'Sotsialisticheskoe stroitel'stvo i pravo-"levyi" blok', *Puti industrializatsii*, 1930, no. 20, p. 9.

24. *Sotsialisticheskii vestnik*, 2 June 1931 (Iu.L).

25. Ibid., 23 January 1932 (letter from L [Moscow]).

26. Ibid., 27 February 1932 (letter from P).

27. *Sots. sorevnovanie v SSSR, 1918–1964*, p. 476.

28. *KPSS v rezoliutsiiakh, chast' III* (Moscow, 1954), p. 135.

29. *Partiinoe stroitel'stvo*, 1930, no. 9, p. 59.

30. *Sots. sorevnovanie v SSSR, 1918–1964*, pp. 75–7.

31. See table 2.

32. For surveys of the communes, see Russell, *Role*, ch. 6; and L. Siegelbaum, 'Production collectives and communes and the "imperatives" of Soviet industrialization, 1929–1931', in *Slavic Review*, vol. 45, no. 1 (spring 1986).

33. Russell, *Role*, p. 277; Siegelbaum, 'Production collectives', p. 70.

34. See P. P. Semyachkin, 'V bor'be za vstrechnuiu' in *Neizvedannymi putiami: vospominaniia uchastnikov sotsialisticheskogo stroitel'stva* (Leningrad, 1967), p. 192.

35. *Pravda*, 12 September 1931.

36. In 1930, more than 60 per cent of Leningrad shock brigades had elected their own leaders: *Statistika i narodnoe khoziaistvo*, vyp. 4–5 (1930), p. 11.

37. *Na trudovom fronte*, 1930, no. 29, p. 2; *Sotsialisticheskoe sorevnovanie v promyshlennosti SSSR* (Moscow, 1973), p. 112; *Promyshlennost' i rabochii klass Ukrainskoi SSR v period postroeniia fundamenta sotsialisticheskoi ekonomiki, 1926–1932* (Kiev, 1966), p. 326.
38. Details of the trial were on the front page, the article on the shock workers on page three: *Pravda*, 6 March 1931.
39. For murders of shock workers, see A. I. Vdovin and V. Z. Drobizhev, *Rost rabochego klassa SSSR, 1918–1940* (Moscow, 1976), p. 230.
40. *Sbornik vazhneishikh postanovlenii po trudu*, 4th edn (Moscow, 1932), p. 121.
41. *Pravda*, 12 September 1931.
42. *Pravda*, 14 September 1931.
43. *Sbornik vazhneishikh postanovlenii*, p. 35.
44. See, for example, S. Zarkhii, *Kommuna v tsekhe* (Moscow-Leningrad, 1930), p. 62.
45. I. P. Ostapenko, *Uchastie rabochego klassa SSSR v upravlenii proizvodstvom* (Moscow, 1964), p. 187.
46. Lebedeva and Shkaratan, *Ocherki*, p. 111.
47. The 'DiP (*Dognat' i peregnat'*) brigades began in December 1931, setting themselves the task of catching up and surpassing foreign production indices. See ibid., pp. 112–13. The Izotov movement was begun by the Donbass miner (and future Stakhanovite) Nikita Izotov, who had studied the technology of his pneumatic drill and increased output by up to 500 per cent. He took over groups of young workers and taught them his methods. N. Izotov, 'Rabochaia initsiativa' in *Govoriat stroiteli sotsializma: vospominaniia uchastnikov sotsialisticheskogo stroitel'stva v SSSR* (Moscow, 1959), pp. 243–56.
48. *KPSS v resoliutsiiakh, chast' III*, p. 258; *Sobranie zakonov SSSR*, 1935, no. 51, art. 421.
49. *Voprosy profdvizheniia*, 1936, no. 6 (Malakha), p. 22.
50. *Pravda*, 3 February 1935.
51. *Vos'moi s"ezd profsoiuzov SSSR: sten. otchet* (Moscow, 1929), p. 186.
52. *Trud*, 24 January 1933.
53. Fiodor Gladkov, *Sobranie sochinenii*, vol. 3 (Moscow-Leningrad, 1929), p. 207.
54. I. Zhiga, *Novye rabochie* (Moscow-Leningrad, 1929), pp. 59–60.
55. See I. Povalyaev, 'Avtobiografiia udarnika' in *Bor'ba klassov*, 1931, nos. 3–4, pp. 77–83.
56. *Liudi stalingradskogo traktornogo* (Moscow, 1934), pp. 476–7.
57. B. Markus, 'K voprosu o traktovke problem ekonomiki truda', in *Voprosy truda*, 1930, nos. 10–11, p. 30. Syrtsov characterized socialist competition and shock brigades as sometimes just: 'a sign over an empty place. There is something wrong with the mathematics: you pile up the plusses and somehow end up with a minus.' See S. Syrtsov, *O nashikh uspekhakh, nedostatkakh i zadachakh* (Moscow-Leningrad, 1930), pp. 8–9.
58. *Liudi stalingradskogo traktornogo*, p. 435.
59. Most notably, the 'Stakhanov' of the automobile industry, Aleksandr Busygin. See his 'My vse kuznetsy svoego schast'ia' in *Govoriat stroiteli*, pp. 266–7.

60. *Voprosy profdvizheniia*, 1934, no. 5 (Deviakovich), p. 84.
61. Ibid., p. 86.
62. Ibid., p. 85.
63. Khitrov, 'Rabota profsoiuzov s peredovymi udarnikami i geroiami sotsialisticheskogo stroitel'stva', in *Voprosy profdvizheniia*, 1933, nos. 1–2, pp. 45–8.
64. *Trud*, 23 September 1931.
65. I. Koliashin, 'Opyt raboty s vedushchimi professiiami v avto-traktornoi promyshlennosti', *Voprosy profdvizheniia*, 1933, no. 13, pp. 31–9.
66. S. Rastorguev, 'Novoe v rukovodstve sotssorevnovaniem na predpriiatii', *Voprosy profdvizheniia*, 1936, no. 5, pp. 50–1.
67. *XVI s"ezd*, p. 528.
68. See the 1931 poster by G. Klutsis in *The Soviet Political Poster* (Harmondsworth, 1985), p. 54.
69. *Pravda*, 1 October 1930.
70. *Sots. sorevnovanie v SSSR, 1918–64*, p. 115; *Istoriia rabochikh Leningrada v dvukh tomakh*, vol. 2 (Leningrad, 1972), p. 241.

9   Reassessing the history of Soviet workers: opportunities to criticize and participate in decision-making, 1935–1941

Robert W. Thurston

Only in recent years have Soviet industrial workers of the 1930s been described in the West as anything more than slaves or victims of a brutal dictatorship.[1] Like many depictions of the Soviet people as a whole during the 'Great Terror', the mass arrests of 1935–1939, the older treatments have been at once ennobling and demeaning: ennobling because for many suffering evokes sympathy and demonstrates the innocence of the sufferer, so that workers become virtual saints through their martyrdom; demeaning because older studies have shown workers only as passive, meek recipients of actions, utterly without initiative or influence in their environment. In turn, this view is essential to the totalitarian model, in which the omnipotent state dominates the impotent society.[2]

Studies taking this view of Soviet workers have typically not delved beyond sources like law codes and leaders' statements; ironically, inquiries into the lives of proletarians have only rarely featured their voices. In part this reflected the notion that, since the state supposedly controlled everything, only it was worthy of attention in writing the story. The result was something of a self-fulfilling prophecy, since on the basis of this kind of evidence the state did appear to be all-powerful.[3] A law might be adopted, a policy announced – Western and Soviet writers alike agreed, without supporting their conclusions, that workers then leaped to fulfil the state's wishes. In the USSR, this obedience was described as stemming from enthusiasm, in the West from fear. Soviet studies of workers in this span, now thoroughly denounced in the USSR, have therefore also dehumanized them and have been terribly dull to boot.[4]

Another reason for the statist emphasis in earlier Western works was the problem of access to sources in the USSR, particularly archival materials, but also local newspapers and journals. All of these reveal a greatly more complex picture than previously described. With the advent of glasnost, availability of sources has improved considerably. However, older studies also ignored the reminiscences of workers already available in the United States in the form of interviews with ex-Soviet citizens.[5]

More recent Western investigations have substantially modified the older picture by offering considerable insight into, for example, the difficulties encountered by the regime in controlling the turnover of workers, labour-management relations, and the Stakhanovite or model worker movement. There is a valuable study of the politics of production in the sense used by Michael Burawoy; that is, the focus is the important roles workers played in the day-to-day determination of production, wages, and job assignments.[6] Another recent monograph examines shop-floor culture and the adaptive mechanisms workers used to make life more bearable in the factories.[7] Much remains to be done; for example, there is still no usable study of an individual Soviet factory or industry in the 1930s. Another area ripe for inquiry is the impact of mass arrests during the Terror on factory life.

This chapter examines the spectrum of ways in which workers voiced complaints and influenced decision-making regarding their own environment at this time. 'Participation' and 'criticism' in this context refer to both formal opportunities, through established organizations and forums, and informal possibilities, through contacts and influence on the shop floor. The nature, limits and results of tolerated criticism expressed by workers are also discussed. Several of the recent investigations touch on these areas,[8] but largely as peripheral concerns. They merit direct attention, however, since they are at the heart of workers' sense of whether the regime responded to them meaningfully and positively.

Obviously there were limits to the objections anyone could make, yet that simple truth also conceals much. The view of an émigré construction engineer on criticism in general, which applies to his experience before World War II, is worth quoting at some length.

The Soviet system is a dictatorship, but on the other side you must recognize that there exists a big criticism of the small and responsible workers excluding criticism of the regime, the party or the Politburo. No doubt in their authority can be expressed, and a word against the regime, the Politburo or the party and this is the end of you. You can criticize the secretary of a *raikom* [district party committee] but it is fairly dangerous. Also you can criticize comrade Ivanov [the equivalent of Mr Smith] who works as a [second or lower] secretary of the *raikom*. If you criticize him nothing will come to you.

The engineer maintained that such a man was open to criticism even regarding official duties. 'If you do this you defend the Soviet regime by criticizing the way he does his party work.'[9] To this one might add that speaking out was a good deal safer if the critic had a desirable social background as a child of the former oppressed classes.

It may be that workers did not widely want to criticize Stalin or the system as a whole; there is insufficient evidence to judge. None the less, in a broad sense fear defined the parameters of permitted speech. But within the obvious constraints lay a great many important concerns open to criticism and not conditioned by fear; this area is the subject of this chapter.

Workers did sometimes suffer arrest, for example in several cases when they produced too much waste on the job.[10] They also entered prison as 'babblers', those who, usually when drunk, transgressed the unwritten rules about criticism.[11] But taken together, the sources reveal relatively few cases of this type. On the other hand, there are instances in which workers spoke against broad policies but were not punished; these will be discussed below. At other times close links to superiors meant that workers were swept up in arrests which began at a higher level. Hence when the chief of the Donbass mine trust entered jail in 1937, fifteen others in the same organization followed, down to two or three workers.[12] Finally, workers were also charged as 'wreckers', particularly in the worst years for arrests, 1937–8. Yet the sources indicate overwhelmingly that industrial toilers were the least likely of any social group to be arrested in the Great Terror; this was the consensus of the thousands of émigrés, for example, who answered questionnaires in the Harvard Project survey after the war.[13] Since considerable evidence argues against the view that the population generally feared arrest,[14] it follows that workers would have felt even less of a threat from the state than other individuals.

While coercion and manipulation of workers certainly existed on a large scale, much more went on in the factories. Workers often did not behave as though they had been conditioned by a 'system of repression'.[15] Rather than accepting such assertions about the context, it is necessary to establish that context in the first place, through the use of detailed evidence. The larger questions here are to what degree workers had any meaningful input and influence in the factory environment, and to what extent the influence they possessed imparted to them a sense of the regime's legitimacy. If something is now known about the politics of Soviet productivity, there is still little understanding of the broader subject of workers' politics.

Former Soviet workers sometimes described their situation in the late

1930s using terms that support the view of their peers as fear-ridden slaves. Virtually all of the twenty-six émigré factory workers or employees interviewed by J. K. Zawodny in the early 1950s said that they had been afraid to complain about anything. For instance, a former coal miner spoke of 'this horrible fear of being arrested'.[16] Many analyses of the period rest upon such generalizations, but in fact this is only the beginning of the story, for the very same people who made these statements sometimes offered specific evidence from their own experiences which undermines their general observations. Were this inquiry a legal trial, any court would rule that the second kind of evidence (if the first is really evidence at all) is considerably more important.

The regime regularly urged its people to criticize local conditions and their leaders, at least below a certain exalted level. For example, in March 1937 Stalin emphasized the importance of the party's 'ties to the masses'. To maintain them, it was necessary 'to listen carefully to the voice of the masses, to the voice of rank and file members of the party, to the voice of the so-called "little people", to the voice of ordinary folk [narod]'.[17] The party newspaper Pravda went so far as to identify lack of criticism with enemies of the people: '*Only an enemy* is interested in seeing that we, the Bolsheviks . . . do not notice actual reality . . . Only an enemy . . . *strives to put the rose-coloured glasses of self-satisfaction* over the eyes of our people.'[18]

But were not these calls merely a vicious sham, so that only carefully chosen, reliable individuals could make 'safe' criticisms?[19] The evidence suggests otherwise.

One of the men Zawodny interviewed offered a curious story from 1939, by which time the 'Great Terror' had supposedly 'broken' the entire nation or reduced it to a 'scrap heap of humanity'.[20] Once a lathe operator, at the time of the incident this respondent was second in charge of his shop. During one of the endless bond drives, the party committee of the factory called in all the workers to sign up. Here is the tale:

There was even a man we knew worked for [the] NKVD [the political police] at the table. A girl came in – a Komsomolka. They gave her the standard speech – she had to work for nothing for a while. She just turned around, bent down, put her skirt over her head, and she said, 'Comrade Stalin and you all can kiss me whenever it is most convenient for you,' and she left. I am telling you, I saw that and I was numb with fear. All those men behind the table, they just sat silently. Finally, one of them said, 'Did you notice, she didn't have pants on?' and everybody started to laugh.

The girl got away with her act; she was not arrested.[21]

Among the same interviews is one with a former furnace operator who insisted that 'nobody really complained' and said that he did not express criticism even to his own wife, for fear she might say something to a neighbour which would lead to his arrest. But this same man recalled that once he went to the 'head of the Ukrainian government', presumably the president of the Ukrainian republic. The worker and his wife had been denied passports because of her social origin, and the authorities had told them to move at least 100 kilometres from their city of residence. But the president ordered that passports be issued to the couple, and they never had to move.[22]

In fact, the Zawodny file contains numerous reports of cases in which workers were not at all reluctant to complain. Some respondents even had a positive view of the way grievances were handled in general: 'honestly, I have to say that the People's Court usually rendered just sentences favouring the workers, particularly with regard to housing cases', said a former accountant.[23] A man who had been a worker, rising to become an electrical engineer and finally chief of a shift in a power station, reported that 'Anyone could complain in a formal way, especially when he had the law behind him. He could even write to a paper, and in this way to let the higher officials know about his complaint.'[24] This often happened: for example, in the first half of 1935 workers sent 2,000 letters, many of which undoubtedly contained criticisms, to *Voroshilovets*, the newspaper of the Voroshilov factory in Vladivostok.[25]

What resulted when ordinary people took their complaints to the press? A civil engineer interviewed after the war remembered that people frequently complained about the poor quality of construction and that he had to spend a considerable amount of time responding. Citizens protested to the city soviet, 'and then when they see that it doesn't help they write direct to Stalin'. Answers would come back to his organization from Stalin's secretariat with a standard message, 'We send these complaints to you for investigation and taking of necessary measures'. The chief of the whole housing administration in the area would then tell the engineer, 'Let me know in three days what has been done'.[26]

The Smolensk Archive contains numerous examples of both these standardized replies from central organs concerned with complaints, which besides Stalin's secretariat included such bodies as the Party Control Commission and the Special Sector of the Central Committee, and of the actions subsequently taken in Smolensk *oblast'* (the rough equivalent of a province).[27] In early 1936 a worker at the Red Handicraft factory complained, apparently to various officers, about corruption, delays in pay, and rudeness by the officials of his *artel'*, a voluntary, cooperative association of workers. Four separate investigations followed, two by the *oblast'* party committee, one by an official of the relevant union, and one by the *oblast'* procuracy. Several of these confirmed the accusations, and the *artel'* leaders had to take steps to correct the situation, while the *raion* (approximately the equivalent of an American county) party secretary had to go to Smolensk and report to *oblast'* authorities on his monitoring of the affair.[28] Surely the *artel'* officials in question then behaved better toward workers.

Sometimes complaining did not go well for the initiator. Zawodny's lathe operator, working as an instructor in 1936, had a conflict with the *raion* party committee over his housing. He had gone to the party and his labour union about the problem but had obtained the impression that they wanted bribes from him. At that point he wrote to *Trud*, the national trade union newspaper, which published his letter. Immediately the town party committee called him in. 'Do you know that it is forbidden to write a letter like that?' an official asked him. The question seems almost surreal, since a national periodical would hardly publish a 'forbidden' complaint. The incident instead reveals the attitudes of local officials, who were unhappy at interference from above. Hence it is necessary to ask whom, exactly, did workers fear, if they were apprehensive? Local satraps had the power either to make life extremely uncomfortable for people or to grant them favours; to offend the authorities on the spot was clearly dangerous at times, as it is in many a society. But central officials did not welcome that situation, judging by this and other evidence.[29]

One of Zawodny's respondents expressed dismay at the idea that a worker would have made use of any organization to protest about a problem. 'No. Man! This would be like putting your head into the lion's mouth. It would be silly. I wanted to be alive.'[30] But specific evidence again belies a general opinion. Besides offering informal verbal criticisms and writing to newspapers, workers utilized other means of expressing dissatisfaction. First, they could go to the Rates and Conflicts Commissions (RKKs) within each factory to challenge decisions regarding pay, job classification or dismissal. These bodies had an equal number of representatives from the employer and from the factory or shop union committee. If workers failed to win their cases at that level, they could appeal to the people's courts or to the central committees of their unions.[31] To cite one illustration of the way this system worked, in 1938 the Central Committee of the paper workers' union considered 796 appeals of RKK decisions, of which 263 were resolved in favour of workers. 1939 saw even more protests to the union central committee, 1,002 in all;[32] obviously workers were not afraid to use this means of defending their rights. The fact that so many appeals reached the highest body of this union indicates that a vastly greater number of cases went through the RKKs themselves.

Union officials called *instruktory* often travelled from the organization's headquarters to factories, where they listened to complaints from workers. For example, in March 1936 an instructor heard about problems from workers in the mechanical and pouring shops of the Orenburg metallurgical plant. They complained about poor materials, lack of supplies, and production norms that had been set too high. In his report to the presidium of the union central committee the instructor urged it to suggest to the relevant trust, the next level of industrial organization, that the 'mistakes' he had heard about needed correction. The affair had dangerous overtones, as workers had suggested that wrecking was responsible for the problems.[33] In this instance labour unions, usually pronounced all but dead by this time in Western literature,[34] in fact still had some power to act on workers' behalf. Other examples of the same point will be given below.

This account also shows that workers considered it possible to complain about a subject as sensitive as production norms. They objected to new norms in the Khar'kov tractor factory in January 1936, too, with remarkable results. A normer had reduced the time allotted to a job from eight to four minutes. Workers in a tool shop challenged the decision and presented the old rate to the normer, who then reversed his change. In another shop of the same factory a normer set pay at a 'low' rate for a job. 'At the insistence of the union group the one guilty of these [second] mistakes', the normer Nikitin, was fired from the factory and remanded to a court. Published in the official journal of the Central Trade Union Council (VTsSPS), the report of these incidents depicted them with complete approval.[35] Such articles undoubtedly encouraged other workers to protest in the same manner.

The Commissariat of Justice also heard and responded to workers' appeals. In August 1935 the Saratov city prosecutor reported that of 118 cases regarding pay recently handled by his office, 90 or 76.3 per cent had been resolved in favour of workers.[36] Representatives of the Commissariat occasionally went to factories to solicit or respond to complaints, as happened in Khabarovsk in July 1936.[37]

Workers participated by the hundreds of thousands in special inspectorates, commissions, and brigades which checked the work of managers and institutions. These agencies sometimes wielded substantial power. For instance, the former worker turned inspector V. R. Balkan, together with a union official, investigated an accident at his Moscow factory in 1937. Finding the cause in improper testing of materials, the two fined the head of the production shop 100 roubles, about a week's pay, and placed a reprimand in the foreman's record.[38] The book which recounted this story was published as a guide to action for other union officials and inspectors and therefore also encouraged similar action by workers.

The Stakhanovite movement and workers' criticism

During the night of 30–1 August 1935, a slim and pleasant-looking twenty-nine year old, Aleksei Stakhanov, cut 102 tons of coal in one shift at a mine in the Don River basin (Donbass). This amounted to 14 times the prescribed norm. Though at first the achievement received only moderate publicity, within weeks the 'Stakhanovite movement' spread across the country, through many branches of the economy.[39] Everywhere workers scrambled to set production records. Eventually there were even Stakhanovite mail carriers and waiters,[40] an idea which would have appealed to many a visitor to the USSR in later years.

The Stakhanovite movement has usually been described as a drive by the state to squeeze more production out of the workers.[41] This is certainly true, as the regime utilized the new production records as examples of how much workers could achieve and then proceeded to raise norms in various industries during 1936 and subsequent years as well.

Yet this point is only a minor part of the story. In the first place, Soviet industry had already witnessed various 'movements' intended to boost productivity. Workers had long been used to such campaigns.[42] A second important point about the impact of Stakhanovism, one contrary to the old image that all workers somehow suffered from the movement, is that a relatively small percentage of the labour force was directly affected by the raised norms. Although many discussions of norms have been published,[43] their significance in practice requires further clarification. To begin with, some workers earned straight hourly wages; obviously the concept of a work norm did not apply to this group at all. For the rest, pay depended not only on norms (*normy vyrabotki*) but on rates (*rastsenki*) and job classification (*razriad*) as well. A portion of industrial workers were paid according to progressive piece rates, meaning that wages increased progressively above a fixed level of production, the norm. Still other workers earned by flat piece rates, a system in which norms had no direct impact, since by definition pay depended only on the amount produced. Sometimes rates increased along with or independently of norms, so that those on flat rates immediately earned more even when norms when up.[44] Those on progressive rates might also lose little or nothing with an increase in norms provided that the rates stayed the same or rose.[45] A sympathetic foreman could raise the classification of a worker, granting a higher rate for some kinds of work.

Although for those on flat rates, falling short of or exceeding the norm made no difference by itself in terms of income, it could affect promotion and status, particularly whether one became a 'Stakhanovite' or not. There was never a clear policy to determine who gained the title; in some cases it was applied to workers who merely fulfilled their norms, while in a few plants supervisors simply designated workers wholesale as Stakhanovites.[46] Sometimes the title had nothing at all to do with norms, but simply with working well or suggesting innovations.[47] Among Iaroslavl' weavers, the term referred merely to 'a worker who has mastered new technology well and has learned how to utilize all its potential.'[48] Achieving Stakhanovite status meant a wide range of things, from better access to apartments and consumer goods down to having a favoured place in the factory cafeteria or one's name on an honour roll.

Subtracting the workers on hourly wages and flat piece rates leaves 32 per cent of all industrial toilers paid on the progressive piece rate system as of 1 January 1938.[49] To give a hypothetical example of the last scheme, a lathe operator might have had a norm of 10 fittings per hour. Making those 10 earned the worker a certain rate per piece. If he or she produced 11, or 110 per cent, a bonus would come into effect – say, 10 per cent extra for the eleventh piece. At 15 fittings per hour the next level of bonuses would begin, at 20 fittings yet a higher level started, and so forth. Such a worker obviously had a great incentive to exceed the norm; and to reiterate a point, only such workers had reason to care directly about norms.

Stakhanovism did not represent an entirely new departure regarding norms; they had regularly been raised before, though admittedly not by so much. However, the new norms of 1936 and succeeding years were often not especially difficult to reach, so that many workers quickly met the new targets. For example, in one group of four Far Eastern coal mines, the range of those miners not fulfilling the new norms by May 1936 was from 5.4 to 15.4 per cent.[50] By June 1938, despite further rises in norms, only 0.7 per cent of workers in electrical power could not fulfill them. The same figures for selected other industries were 4.8 per cent in coal, 11 per cent in chemicals and 27.9 per cent in paper, the highest proportion among available figures.[51] In October of the same year, *average* fulfilment of the norms in four factories involved in heavy industry ranged from 147.6 to 172.6 per cent.[52] Often the workers who could not quickly achieve the new norms were those who had just been hired and thus had not yet gained sufficient experience or on-the-job training to work effectively.

New norms were not always introduced into practice, despite orders from above to do so. At the Voroshilov factory in Vladivostok in May 1936 a turner was still working according to the old norms. His foreman signed work orders without filling in pay rates or specifying the time allotted for completion of the job.[53]

Set too high, norms would impel workers like the turner to take another job, something frequently easy to accomplish in view of the constant labour shortage. After another round of norm increases in 1939, the Elektrosila plant in Leningrad 'lost 7,000 workers. Almost the whole body of workers changed.' Both norms and the premium system changed at the same time at Elektrosila, causing pay for some proletarians to fall 30–40 per cent.[54] Obviously the effect of such thorough turnover on production was devastating. To avoid this outcome executives of two weaving trusts sent thirty-eight requests to have norms lowered to the Commissariat of Light Industry in 1938. In a few cases the Commissariat allowed the changes.[55] Acting completely on their own, managers in the Donbass in 'very many' cases raised job rates and lowered norms; in one group of mines this happened four times in 1937 alone.[56]

Managers abused the pay system so much, generally to keep workers on the job, that the national trade union chief, N. M. Shvernik, complained publicly about the situation in August 1938. Citing two factories that had developed elaborate premium systems, he charged that the pay schemes 'were thought up especially to get around the directives of the party and the government and that an increase in wages must be accompanied by a growth in productivity and a rise in the skill of the worker'.[57] But executives faced a hard choice: they could either act strictly according to the rules on pay, in which case they could lose workers and fall into the very dangerous position of not fulfilling their factories' production plans, or they could accommodate workers by paying them more whenever that could be done quietly. Usually the second course was safer, at least as long as the enterprise fulfilled the plan. Thus workers exercised yet another kind of influence within the factories, circuitous but powerful, by virtue of their ability to leave. As the example of Elektrosila shows, they maintained this possibility even after the adoption of a law in December 1938 intended to tie them to their workplaces.[58] The forces of the market for labour were simply too strong to yield to socialist directives.

The problem of labour turnover leads to another point about norms: it was neither desirable nor possible to introduce new ones without consulting workers. For this reason in April 1935 the head of the Moscow *oblast'* trade union council insisted that there 'should not be one worker touched by the review of norms with whom no one [from the union] has spoken, to whom it has not been explained why his norm is being examined. It is forbidden to take such measures administratively.'[59]

Each major branch of industry, some ninety altogether, held a conference in early 1936 to discuss the course of the Stakhanovite movement and its impact on production, focusing specifically on norms. These conferences and the discussions on norms throughout Soviet industry at this time provided further new opportunities for workers to be heard. In preparation for the conferences, workers in various enterprises at least made recommendations regarding norms, while some reports indicate that very broad discussions took place among the hands.[60] To cite one example of how the new norms were actually determined, 70 per cent of the new ones adopted in early 1936 at the Voroshilov factory in Vladivostok were set by technical personnel on the basis of their observations of workers.[61] This practice facilitated slowdowns by workers who wished to minimize the increases in norms; as a proletarian from the Stalingrad tractor factory admitted, when being observed for norm-setting, 'any worker will deceive at every step'.[62] There were also opportunities for communication and connivance between supervisors and workers while setting norms.

Still, involving workers in determining new standards was now to be standard practice, as underscored by the Moscow *oblast'* union council in April 1936 when it strongly criticized the administration of the Krasnaia Presnia factory for not doing so. The council resolved to inform the central committee of the relevant union and the Commissariat of Heavy Industry of the transgression, which made it impossible for workers to earn premiums.[63]

Worker involvement in determining norms sometimes resulted in proposals to raise some but lower others, for example at the Ordzhonikidze lathe factory.[64] Several branch conferences recommended retaining certain norms at their current level,[65] while others reduced the increases urged by individual factories.[66] Therefore the fact that Stakhanovites typically represented workers at the conferences did not mean that the trend-setters could think only of how to boost norms rapidly and steeply. The basic constraints of work by norms still applied.[67]

The problems inherent in setting norms without considering the practical impact or involving workers again became evident at another Far Eastern factory, the Kaganovich works, in the summer of 1937. According to a newspaper report, two engineers had determined new norms in their offices during the spring of 1936. Management then demanded fulfilment but did not create the necessary conditions, a failure labelled 'the blow of an enemy'. By September 1937 about 50 per cent of the factory's workers still could not fulfil the 1936 norms. Then, 'after broad consideration by Stakhanovites, masters, and shop heads', lower standards were established. Although at the time of the article the two engineers were still employed in the area,[68] it seems likely that the secret police soon arrested them.

For all these reasons, the Stakhanovite movement was not a crude bludgeon used to beat all workers into vastly greater production, despite the drive to raise norms. However, it did accomplish something else for the industrial labour force which was of grave importance. The movement provided new status for workers in voicing criticism, urging and even demanding changes in production processes, and getting supervisors' attention in general. New forums appeared in which Stakhanovites could speak out, while some old and weak mechanisms for input now revived.

Strident criticisms of working and living conditions quickly began to surface, drawing on support from the highest level. In May 1935 Stalin had offered a new slogan: instead of the old 'technology decides everything', he now said that 'cadres decide everything'. In context, 'cadres' meant almost anyone. For, he continued, this slogan 'demands that our leaders display the most careful attitude toward our workers, toward the "small" and the "big", no matter what area they work in'.[69] Taking advantage of Stalin's emphasis and referring to his words, an article in the major trade union journal in September 1935 lashed out at housing conditions for workers at the electrical stations of Uzbekistan. In one room of four square metres lived six workers, while three different families totalling seven people occupied a room of seven square metres. Some employees had to sleep on bare earthen floors.[70]

Workers themselves, undoubtedly bolstered by the title of Stakhanovite that many now bore, began to speak frankly. A major early move in this campaign was the First All-Union Conference of Male and Female Stakhanovites, held in Moscow in mid-November. One of the leading worker-speakers was Nikita Izotov, like Stakhanov a coal miner. Indeed, there had already been an 'Izotov movement' to raise productivity and norms in 1932–3. But that idea never spread widely, since at that point the party had other concerns in mind, particularly bolstering managers' authority after a long assault on it in the 'Cultural Revolution' of 1928–32.[71] However, by 1935 the leadership was prepared to foster a vast productivity movement. The key problem of the second Five Year Plan period, 1933–7, was how to get more out of the newly-built industries rather than how to construct plants and bring in labour in the first place.[72]

Worker enthusiasm was essential to boosting productivity. In order to help whip up zeal, the party leaders were quite willing to encourage workers to speak out; workers needed to feel that the Stakhanovite movement was theirs in a meaningful way. Therefore with Stalin, Molotov, and other top officials sitting behind him, Izotov was blunt:

Stakhanovites spoke to me and asked me to convey the following to the government: they earn a lot, but there is little to buy. One says: I need a piano, another – a bicycle, a third, a record player, radio and all sorts of cultural goods, which are necessary, but which are not [available] in the Donbass.[73]

Aleksandr Busygin, a stamping press operator with a stature in the movement almost as high as that of Stakhanov himself, made an indirect but clear comment at the conference on the economic situation of most workers. Earlier almost all his money went for food, 'but now, I think, it will be necessary to improve the food, and I'll be able to get new clothes, and even to furnish the apartment better'.[74] Thus the leading Stakhanovites took the new opportunity to address the national leadership in person about the general plight of workers. Even if, as may well have been the case, the Stakhanovites who spoke at the conference were selected and prompted from above, that does not matter; the importance of their statements was that they constituted a signal to the country that a policy of soliciting and listening to workers' complaints was now in place. More precisely, an existing policy now took on new emphasis and dimensions.

Industrial workers quickly began to attack their supervisors in other settings. In December 1935 workers in glass and chemicals in Moscow *oblast'* spoke up about the failure of managers and technical personnel to supply materials adequately, make timely repairs, and conduct 'correct accounting'. The problems had come to the attention of the *oblast'* administration for local industry, which remarked that it was 'necessary to end the insufficient development of work on the penetration of Stakhanovite methods'.[75]

At a meeting of Stakhanovites and executives of the ceramics industry, also held in December 1935, a moulder insisted in his own rambling way that six months before

our bosses lived, but the workers got by [*pozhivali*] . . . [now] our bosses don't look quite like that, since they are combing their hair, on the contrary, probably they are being combed . . . And they will look after us at the factory as they should. This is correct. But we don't believe it. We believe it when the director curses – well, okay, you live well, but we live badly.[76]

It does in fact appear that managers were being 'combed' by their own superiors. An official of the People's Commissariat in charge of ceramics production chastized 'Comrade Frantsev', a plant manager, at the same session for not creating the 'essential conditions' or giving workers the support they needed to improve their output. 'Shame, Comrade Frantsev', the official scolded, and called for 'wider self-criticism' as a means of eliminating the problems.[77] In Soviet parlance, 'self-criticism' implied both that one would chastize oneself and be criticized by others.

Some managers had already absorbed the message from above on how to relate to the Stakhanov movement. Another worker at the same conference outlined the ways managers in his factory had responded to his requests for help in improving output, so that he had gone from making 1,200–1,300 pieces per shift to about 2,000.[78] Such executives understood that they had better be more receptive than before to proletarians' concerns.

In February 1936 a group of Murmansk workers joined in the chorus of complaints. During a general meeting of workers from all three shifts at the city railroad depot, strong criticism of union leaders and management emerged because they had allegedly done nothing to help ordinary hands become Stakhanovites. Some workers averred that, 'Whatever you say, however many suggestions you make about removing the defects and disorders in production, no one does anything. On the contrary, later they pressure those who spoke up with criticisms. It's better to keep quiet.'[79]

This report points to several broad themes. Local officials or managers had again tried to stifle criticism, but the national trade union journal, *Voprosy profdvizheniia* (Problems of the Trade Union Movement), published the story and welcomed it. In part this was because, as the article again suggests, criticism and suggestions from workers tended to go hand in hand. Eliciting proposals from rank-and-file employees was a key element of the Stakhanovite movement. Finally, local attempts in Murmansk to silence workers had backfired: somehow they had enlisted the aid of the trade union journal and, worse yet, dissatisfaction with the pressure on critics had spread so far among the depot workers that they had turned out in a mass meeting clearly intended to intimidate management and union leadership. With the spotlight of a national publication on them, it is certain that the Murmansk officials moved quickly to attempt to satisfy their workers.

In at least two factories, workers were able to effect the firing of supervisors who failed to satisfy them in the new situation. Both cases involved heads of production shops, an important position, particularly in heavy industry. At the Chisovsk metal plant, workers ousted the head of the rolling shop for forbidding them to finish more than 50 tons of metal per shift. 'For sabotage of the [Stakhanovite] movement' the head of the rolling shop at the Chernozem metal factory lost his post 'at the insistence of a [production] conference', the report continued.[80]

These conferences, first held in 1923,[81] had fallen into quietude by the early 1930s. Now, however, they began to revive. On 17 October 1935 the party Central Committee and VTsSPS together issued a circular to all union organizations directing them to see that the 'basic content of work of the production conferences becomes the struggle for the removal of shortcomings hampering the Stakhanovite movement'. Among the problems listed were defects in the organization of production, supply of materials, and the 'inertness' of managerial personnel.[82]

Numerous reports indicate that production conferences did in fact now respond to the new thrusts of Stakhanovism. In its early phase, the sources imply, all workers in a given setting were welcome to attend the meetings. At the Vostokostal' (Eastern Steel) plant, workers made 87 per cent more proposals for changes in production in 1936 than they had in 1935. During September 1935 workers at the Skorokhod shoe factory in Leningrad made seventy-eight proposals at production conferences; in October, after the Stakhanovite movement had gained momentum and publicity, they made 212 suggestions. A further 250 followed at November meetings.[83]

Proletarians undoubtedly offered many ideas in the hope that they might be recognized as Stakhanovites simply by virtue of such contributions; nevertheless, they must have felt a greater sense of legitimacy for the political system in view of the solicitation of their views. This seems clear in an account from a railroad depot in Zagorsk, about sixty-eight kilometres north of Moscow. In the autumn of 1935 the conferences 'began not with words but with deeds'. They now allowed workers to examine collectively exactly where problems with repairs existed. ' "Until this time we had the opinion that blabbing was the occupation of the production conferences. Now we see that it isn't that way," said workers.'[84]

At the important Zavod imeni Stalina (the Factory named after Stalin) auto plant in Moscow, now the Likhachev works, the conferences also changed radically with the advent of the Stakhanovite movement. 'At once the production conferences ceased to be boring. Earlier at these conferences foremen spoke most, and [they] spoke about fulfilment of the [production] programme only drily. Now the important issues of vital practice are considered there.' Workers attended to questions of how to improve specific jobs; the discussions were concrete, probing which engineers and technicians would help workers and how. These changes improved communications at the factory between technical personnel and workers.[85] The production conferences had revived as an important means of worker participation, one which managers could not ignore.

Workers used these meetings and other means to express concerns about job conditions in view of the incentives to become Stakhanovites. An engineer speaking at the ceramics meeting of December 1935 reported that, 'The Stakhanovite demands that he comes to work and finds at the work place everything that he needs in the proper quantity.'[86]

Not satisfying such demands placed supervisors in jeopardy; in the Moscow coal basin seventeen men, ranging from directors of mines down to brigade foremen were fired, demoted, warned, or even remanded to courts in the last few months of 1935 alone for 'sabotage' of the Stakhanovite movement.[87] A dispatcher of the Moscow river port received a five-year prison sentence in late 1935 for counter-revolutionary activity after he had assigned a Stakhanovite brigade to unload a cargo that was not its speciality. The group filled only 64 per cent of the norm.[88]

Time and again, proletarians accused managers of failing to arrange conditions so that ordinary workers could become Stakhanovites. Managers supposedly did not provide proper raw materials and tools, organize production rationally, or give requisite instruction. Quite often workers linked such charges to wrecking. For instance, in the summer of 1937, with the mass arrests in full stride, the Stakhanovite Iakov Chaikovsky, a steel maker at the Comintern plant, 'sharply criticized the executives of the factory'. Earlier the factory had become a leading one, he claimed, thanks to the movement. But now the administration displayed a 'formal attitude' toward it, and the plant had regressed. It was necessary 'to bring order into production arrangements' so that 'big outputs' could be achieved again. In the same report a Stakhanovite from a Khar'kov factory accused management of allowing the movement to develop chaotically, on its own. Workers did not know from one day to the next what jobs they would be doing. All this and more was linked to 'enemies' in a series of factories.[89]

Especially in 1937, such charges could prove fatal to managers, but this did not necessarily occur. At the Red Star factory a meeting of the *aktiv* took place in May 1937. Whether or not this plant had earlier witnessed more broadly-based production conferences, at this juncture the participants consisted of Stakhanovites, engineers, and technical employees. Though participants were not identified by occupation,

Stakhanovites at least listened to a frank exchange of views on production problems. Several speakers traded charges about whose fault the difficulties were. But instead of leading to arrest, another member of the *aktiv* suggested a 'simple resolution': the antagonists should 'think over all defects, take measures and the matter will go better'.[90] Criticism did not have to mean rancour or repression.

In general, the Stakhanovite phenomenon made things more difficult for executives and engineers, as it often did for workers, with the difference that managers bore responsibility for seeing at one and the same time that production went smoothly and that workers had the chance to become Stakhanovites. That was not an easy combination to achieve. Since more responsibility rested on the shoulders of white-collar personnel than on workers, executives and engineers were more likely to be identified as the malevolent causes of shortcomings during the heated atmosphere of the 'Great Terror' and therefore to wind up in the GULag system.[91]

Certainly courts sometimes convicted workers of undermining the Stakhanovite movement. In Sverdlovsk *oblast'* thirteen workers, as well as thirty-four other people, had been convicted of this 'crime' by the end of November 1935.[92] These workers either feared that the new norms, now widely expected, would be difficult to achieve, or they resented the new higher pay and privileges of their comrades, or both.[93]

However, probably recognizing that repression was only likely to spread discontent, in March 1936 the Presidium of the Supreme Court of the USSR announced a change in policy. 'In many cases courts have incorrectly judged individual backward workers as enemies of the people for incorrect remarks', the Presidium reported. In its view such statements often reflected the workers' inability to cope with the new conditions; that is, some workers could not make the new norms. Their negative remarks do not 'indicate their opposition to the Stakhanovite movement or sabotage'. What was needed was not court action but 'mass explanatory work'.[94] In other words, workers were not to be punished for speaking against the movement; instead, managers and other officials were directed to help discontented workers master the new standards.

Criticism of Stakhanovism as a policy, which was a direct challenge to the regime, did not always result in arrest. An archival report dating from some point in late 1935 lists several workers excluded from the party or their trade union or fired for criticism of the movement, but gives no indication that they were arrested.[95] 'In our mine there was an old worker who was not afraid' to call the movement by a word derived from a vulgar term for copulation, former mining engineer recalled.[96] A woman identified as a 'pure proletarian' pronounced Stakhanovism 'nonsense' at her factory, but the only result was that managers talked to her.[97] When a young woman at one factory got a set of Lenin's works as a prize for her job performance, an old worker called out, 'That is what the whore [*sterva*] deserves'. General laughter and some confusion followed, 'but finally nothing was done about it'.[98] In contrast to the negative comments, it should be noted, some émigré workers offered a much milder, somewhat positive appraisal of Stakhanovism on their part and their fellows'.[99]

Workers continued to make serious criticisms of their supervisors and environment through the next few years. For example, in the twenty-four months following September 1937 the Central Committee of the communication workers union received 2,007 complaints from workers about 'incorrect' actions of managers. 432 were resolved in favour of the workers, 837 were rejected, and the rest were 'in process'.[100] At Leningrad factory meetings in 1937, 1938, and 1939 workers were outspoken about problems ranging from low pay through poor supply of materials to a firing after a conflict with a foreman. For example, the worker Krumgol'ts castigated the management of the Leningrad mechanical factory in May 1939 for its 'poor use of cadres' and 'disorderly attitude toward people and work'. He attacked the director, Kurushin, by name for failure to 'check decisions' in his shop. Kurushin then interrupted to say, 'They are being checked'. When Krumgol'ts rejoined with 'That's not noticeable', Kurushin remarked that, 'They are being checked every day, for your information'. This drew applause from the meeting. At the same session the worker Barzin told a long story of how he had been fired as a 'disorganizer' after a conflict with a foreman in which he had cursed the boss 'Russian style'. This description drew laughter from the audience.[101] Thus workers in the city which had supposedly suffered at least as much as any other in the 'Great Terror' were still able to criticize a director to his face and apparently to get a job back after cursing a supervisor, as in Barzin's case.

In the period just prior to the war, this picture changed somewhat. Both the Terror and the Stakhanovite movement had faded, while managerial authority had revived to a fair degree. The press spoke frequently of the need to support managers and engineers,[102] and the police ceased to arrest them so cavalierly.[103] These changes meant that a long period of turbulence in industry was over; with its passing workers' opportunities to protest, criticize, and participate in decision-making declined to some extent.

Yet this was only relative to the levels of the preceding few years. Workers continued to contest firings in the rates and conflicts commissions, the union inspectors, and the courts.[104] Complaints still came to other officials, too, for instance the 231 to the Altai *krai* soviet for the period 15 February–19 March 1940 mentioned in an article abut 'toilers' complaints'.[105]

Up to the war, factory workers frequently acted as though they possessed a mandate to criticize. One émigré recalled that his stepmother, a factory worker, 'often scolded the boss' and also complained about living conditions, but was never arrested.[106] John Scott, an American employed for years in the late 1930s as a welder in Magnitogorsk, attended a meeting at a Moscow factory in 1940 where workers were able to 'criticize the plant director, make suggestions as to how to increase production, improve quality, and lower costs'.[107]

Leningrad factory *aktiv* meetings of 1940 were relatively calm, and the charge of wrecking or sabotage was absent when participants voiced criticism. One example is a gathering at the Red Vyborzhets factory in June 1940; it quietly but frankly covered a series of economic questions. The worker Sheinin remarked that in the eight or nine years he had been there, this was the first meeting he had attended which was 'devoted exclusively to economic problems'.[108] In this sphere his right to be heard was intact.

The evidence presented here gives some indication of the range of options available to workers with grievances. Many if not most of these were well established and permanent. As far as the topics of complaint are concerned, certainly they were limited. John Scott found that if Moscow workers railed against problems within the factory itself, they fell silent when foreign policy came up.[109]

While sane, calm, and sober, no worker would have dared to say that socialism was a poor system or that Stalin was an idiot. But such bounds allowed a great deal that was deeply significant to workers, including some aspects of production norms, pay rates and classifications, safety on the job, housing, and treatment by managers. This occurred at a time when American workers in particular were struggling for basic union recognition,[110] which even when won did not provide much formal influence at the work place.

Far from basing its rule on the negative means of coercion, the Soviet regime in the late 1930s fostered a limited but positive political role for the populace. In a system whose officials at virtually all levels felt tremendous pressures to juggle figures and lie to their superiors, frank information was of great value. If it came from workers, nominally the country's rulers, so much the better. Complaints and suggestions constantly flowed upward, giving the authorities at higher levels at least the illusion that they were in touch with the people. Central officials could appear to be the defenders of the common folk. As some of the sources cited here suggest, workers sometimes believed that that was true. It cost the Stalinist leadership nothing to offer this kind of positive element in the system, and it encouraged greater productivity and commitment to the regime.

The Soviet political structure in the late 1930s was certainly authoritarian above, in the formation of broad policy guidelines. But at lower levels of society, in day-to-day affairs and the implementation of policy, it was participatory.[111] Earlier concepts of the Soviet state require rethinking: the workers who ousted managers, achieved the imprisonment of their targets and won reinstatement at factories did so through organizations which constituted part of the state apparatus and wielded state powers. No sharp distinction between state and society existed, though there were immense differences between levels of the state. Obviously such a system did not constitute democracy, but it did provide important ways of participation.

It is of course extremely difficult to say with any precision how widely workers gained a sense of the regime's legitimacy from their opportunities to criticize and participate in decision-making. One émigré recalled that life was getting better in 1940, and he linked this change to the reasons people fought for the regime in the war.[112] Admittedly young at the age of thirteen to know how adults felt, he still probably absorbed a mood from his father, who was a worker. Other evidence comes from a woman born in 1918. She also thought that 1940 was a good time: 'There was no unpleasantness, there were no arrests, nobody was sent into exile, there were no denunciations in the newspapers, everybody was working.'[113] These remarks accord well with the atmosphere at Leningrad and Moscow factory meetings in the same year. One observer noted that in 1939 the young workers of Leningrad, along with the students and the newly-created intelligentsia, were overwhelmingly loyal.[114] An émigré who had been a worker, then an engineer, believed that 'immediately before the war and during the war even the non-party element was co-operating willingly', though he tempered this statement with the opinion that older workers felt some antipathy to the regime.[115] John Scott found great optimism in Magnitogorsk at the same time.[116] Coupled with the opportunities which still characterized the system for seeking other jobs, obtaining education, and advancing in one's career,[117] workers' chances to speak out and participate in shaping the factory world must have meant a great deal to them. It is difficult to explain the level of Soviet war production, achieved under extraordinarily difficult circumstances, and the victory itself in any other way.

Only by staying on the surface of the story and limiting the use of evidence to certain kinds of sources can the system be described as one in which coercion overwhelmingly determined the course of workers' lives. Only by assuming that repression suffused daily existence have scholars been moved to see the necessity of force everywhere. Delving deeper into the picture reveals a wide range of compromises, contradictions and dynamics. Stalin may have been a vicious murderer in the Kremlin, but a few blocks away managers had to grapple with the question of how to make the plan and keep workers on the job at the same time. This and similar issues meant that ultimately relatively little was controlled by government or party decree, which often expressed pious wishes rather than commands which were then fulfilled. In grappling with the fluidity and contradictions of the situation, workers found many ways in which they could contribute their thoughts and exercise some influence over their environment. Neither martyrs nor helpless puppets, they played a significant role in both the achievements and the state-sponsored violence of the period.

Notes

1. For older treatment of workers in this period, see Manya Gordon, *Workers Before and After Lenin* (New York, 1941); Arvid Brodersen, *The Soviet Worker: Labor and Government in Soviet Society* (New York, 1966); Solomon M. Schwarz, *Labor in the Soviet Union* (New York, 1951); and Robert Conquest, *Industrial Workers in the U.S.S.R.* (New York, 1967), among other works. Newer treatments of the subject include Francesco Benvenuti, 'Stakhanovism and Stalinism, 1934–1938', CREES Discussion Papers, SIPS no. 30, University of Birmingham, 1989; Hiroaki Kuromiya, *Stalin's Industrial Revolution: Politics and Workers, 1928–1932* (Cambridge, 1988); Lewis H. Siegelbaum, *Stakhanovism and the Politics of Productivity in the USSR, 1935–1941* (New York, 1988); Donald Filtzer (who in various ways affirms the older viewpoint), *Soviet Workers and Stalinist Industrialization: The Formation of Modern Soviet Production Relations, 1928–1941* (Armonk NY, 1986); and Vladimir Andrle, *Workers in Stalin's Russia: Industrialization and Social Change in a Planned Economy* (New York, 1988). A useful work which looks at some of the same issues involving criticism and participation by workers in the 1920s is William J. Chase, *Workers, Society, and the Soviet State: Labor and Life in Moscow, 1918–1929* (Urbana IL, 1987).
2. This view of Soviet government and society draws on an old tradition of analysis regarding the tsarist state and society. See, for instance, the classic pre-revolutionary work of V. O. Kliuchevsky, *A Course in Russian History: The Seventeenth Century*, trans. Natalie Duddington (Chicago,

1968), p. 8; and Richard Pipes, *Russia under the Old Regime* (New York, 1974), p. 21. On 'totalitarianism' for the USSR in this period see, for instance, Adam B. Ulam, *Stalin: The Man and his Era* (New York, 1973); and Mikhail Heller and Aleksandr M. Nekrich, *Utopia in Power: The History of the Soviet Union from 1917 to the Present*, trans. Phyllis B. Carlos (New York, 1986). For treatments of the Terror which take this view and set the USSR into the theoretical context of totalitarianism, see Carl J. Friedrich and Zbigniew K. Brzezinski, *Totalitarian Dictatorship and Autocracy*, 2nd edn (Cambridge MA, 1965), p. 169; and Alexander Dallin and George W. Breslauer, *Political Terror in Communist Systems* (Stanford CA, 1970), p. 5. Terror and fear are considered the most essential characteristics of totalitarian systems by Friedrich and Brzezinski, *Totalitarian Dictatorship, passim* and p. 15; Hannah Arendt, *The Origins of Totalitarianism*, new edn (New York, 1966), p. 344; and Zbigniew K. Brzezinski, *The Permanent Purge: Politics in Soviet Totalitarianism* (Cambridge MA, 1956), pp. 17 and 27.

3. The epitome of this approach is probably Conquest, *Industrial Workers*.
4. ' "Kruglyi stol": aktual'nye zadachi izucheniia sovetskogo rabochego klassa', *Voprosy istorii*, no. 1 (January 1988).
5. J.K. Zawodny file, twenty-six interviews with former Soviet factory workers, Hoover Institution Archives. These interviews were conducted in the early 1950s. The Harvard 'Project on the Soviet Social System' was conducted for the United States Air Force. Interviews took place in 1950–1, largely in displaced persons camps in West Germany, although a few were held in New York. There were A schedule interviews, which were life stories, and B schedule interviews, which were sessions on specialized topics. This material will be cited here as HP, the number assigned to the interviewee, A or B, volume, and page numbers. Short biographical data from the pre-war period will also be provided, if available, using the designations given in the A series data. The interviewers translated the material into occasionally awkward English.
6. This is Siegelbaum, *Stakhanovism*. He draws on Michael Burawoy, *The Politics of Production: Factory Regimes under Capitalism and Socialism* (London, 1985).
7. Andrle, *Workers in Stalin's Russia*.
8. Ibid., pp. 29 and 61; Siegelbaum, *Stakhanovism*, pp. 10, 142, 250–4.
9. HP number 470, A, v. 23, pp. 16–17; a Russian male born about 1913.
10. HP number 380, A, v. 19, pp. 5–6; a Belorussian male born about 1923, a rank-and-file worker. Arrests of workers on this basis appear to have been rare, judging by the other sources used for this study.
11. Eugenia Ginzburg, *Journey into the Whirlwind*, trans. Paul Stevenson and Max Hayward (New York, 1967), p. 180.
12. HP number 470, A, v. 23, p. 25.
13. Raymond Bauer and Alex Inkeles, *The Soviet Citizen: Daily Life in a Totalitarian Society* (Cambridge MA, 1959), pp. 105–8.
14. See my 'Fear and belief in the USSR's "Great Terror": Response to arrest, 1935–1939', *Slavic Review*, vol. 45, no. 2 (1986). Extensive calculations of the prison and labour camp population in the late 1930s, based on

sentencing, labour force, unionization, and voting data, are in Ger P. van den Berg, 'Quantitative aspects of the Stalinist system of justice and terror in the Soviet Union', in F.J.M. Feldbrugge, ed., *The Distinctiveness of Soviet Law* (Dordrecht, 1987). On p. 139, van den Berg estimates that about 2.2 million people were in labour camps in 1940. The Soviet scholar V. Zemskov claims to have seen data from a 'civil archive' which indicates that there were 839,000 total prisoners in the prison and camp system in 1936 and 1,344,408 in 1940. Of these 12.6 per cent in the first year and 33.1 per cent in the second had been arrested for 'counter-revolutionary crimes'. At present this is as close as we have to official Soviet data on the numbers caught up in the Terror. 'Arkhipelag GULag glazami pisatel'ia i statistika', *Argumenty i fakty*, no. 45 (1989), p. 5. Such figures are far lower than the seven to fifteen million in the labour camps by 1940 given in older works and repeated in Robert Conquest, *The Great Terror: A Reassessment* (New York, 1990), p. 485. The lower numbers – which in no way reduce the horror of the arrests and the sense of moral outrage they should provoke – do however suggest that the regime did not set out to terrorize the population and that the impact of the Terror was far less than is generally thought. This is also the thrust of the impressionistic evidence and personal reports cited in my 'Fear and belief'.

15. The comment that such a system existed for workers and was the key factor in determining their behaviour was made at the IV World Congress for Soviet and East European Studies, Harrogate, England, 25 July 1990 by Francesco Benvenuti during his commentary on an earlier draft of this article. Of course, this is a restatement of the notion that a 'system of terror' gripped the USSR in the late 1930s. To some extent Andrea Graziosi, ' "Visitors from other times": Foreign workers in the prewar *piatiletki*', *Cahiers du monde russe et soviétique*, vol. 29, no. 2 (April–June 1988), repeats the view that Soviet workers' lives were overwhelmingly determined by coercion. But her reliance on testimony from foreign workers in the USSR, who often arrived and behaved as labour aristocrats, is not adequate compared to detailed testimony from ex-Soviet workers themselves.

16. Zawodny file, first interview set, respondent 2; and see respondent 11. It may well be that such general statements were prompted by the atmosphere of the early Cold War. Several respondents indicated suspicion of Zawodny, so that they may have told him things considered safe at that time.

17. I.V. Stalin, *Sochineniia*, tom 1 [XIV], 1934–1940, ed. Robert H. McNeal (Stanford, 1967), p. 238; and see similar statements on pp. 86–7, 100–1, 131, and 232.

18. Quoted in O.A. Ermansky, *Stakhanovskoe dvizhenie i stakhanovskie metody* (Moscow, 1940), p. viii. No date was given for the *Pravda* statement, but the foreword to the book was written in December 1938, so the comment came before that.

19. I have heard such remarks many times, for example at the IV World Slavics Congress and at the Symposium on the USSR's Great Purges at Michigan State University, May 1986.

20. Conquest, *Great Terror*, p. 434; Harrison Salisbury, 'Foreword', in Ruth Turkow Kaminska, *I Don't Want to Be Brave Any More* (Washington DC, 1978), p. xii.
21. Zawodny file, set II, respondent 19.
22. Ibid., set I, respondent 1.
23. Ibid., set I, respondent 8.
24. Ibid., set II, respondent 15.
25. *Tikhookeanskaia zvezda* [hereafter TZ], 21 July 1935, p. 1.
26. HP number 611, A, vol. 29, pp. 18–19. This was a male Ukrainian born about 1905 into a middle-class family.
27. Vsesoiuznaia kommunisticheskaia partiia (bol'shevikov). Smolenskii oblastnoi komitet. The Smolensk Archives. This source will be cited here as SA with a box number, reel number if appropriate, WKP (file) number, and *list* (l. or ll.). SA box 44, reel 43, WKP 386, 389. There is even a case of a member of the secret police, the NKVD, removed from his job and arrested after a complaint regarding his abuse of power: ibid., WKP 386, l. 43, 10 February 1936.
28. Ibid., ll. 314–20 and 288.
29. *Rabochaia Moskva*, 27 September 1935, p. 3, published a letter from a worker charging that she was fired because she had criticized the director of her factory for feeding his pigs from the cafeteria account and keeping the smelly animals at the plant. The local union organization would not help her.
30. Zawodny file, set I, respondent 1.
31. *Kodeks zakonov o trude*, vtoroe izdanie, s izmeneniiami na 1 oktiabria 1938 g. (Moscow, 1938), pp. 44, 155–6.
32. Soiuz rabochikh bumazhnoi promyshlennosti SSSR. Tsentral'nyi komitet, *Otchet tsentral'nogo komiteta professional'nogo soiuza rabochikh bumazhnoi promyshlennosti, 1973–1939 gg.* (Moscow, 1939), p. 44.
33. Tsentral'nyi Gosudarstvennyi Arkhiv Narodnogo Khoziaistva [hereafter TsGANKh], f. 7622, o. 1, d. 202, ll. 1–7.
34. On the supposed death of trade unions, see Conquest, *Industrial Workers*, pp. 151–6; Gordon, *Workers Before and After Lenin*, p. 98; and Jay B. Sorenson, *The Life and Death of Soviet Trade Unionism 1917–1928* (New York, 1969), p. 253.
35. L. Shkol'nikov, 'Rol' profsoiuzov v stakhanovskom dvizhenii na KhTZ', *Voprosy profdvizheniia [VP]*, no. 1 (January 1936), p. 62.
36. 'Praktika mest', *Sovetskaia iustitsiia [SIu]* no. 23 (August 1935), p. 12.
37. *TZ*, 22 July 1936, p. 3. The Justice representatives promised to investigate workers' complaints about poor ventilation, mistakes in calculating pay, holidays, and lack of help with technical study.
38. *Profaktivisty rasskazyvaiut o svoei rabote* (Moscow, 1937), p. 30.
39. On the beginnings of the Stakhanovite movement see Siegelbaum, *Stakhanovism*, pp. 66–86; and Semen Gershberg, *Stakhanov i stakhanovtsy*, izdanie vtoroe (Moscow, 1985), pp. 9–31.
40. The waitress is pictured in *Krasnoe znamia* (Tomsk), 5 February 1939, p. 2; the mail carrier's photograph is in ibid., 29 November 1938, p. 2. Tsentral'nyi Gosudarstvennyi Arkhiv Oktiabr'skoi Revoliutsii

[TsGAOR], f 5451, o. 19, d. 227, l. 28, mentions a women's hairdresser who did hair in ten minutes instead of the norm of twenty, without a single complaint.

41. The conventional interpretation of the movement may be found, for example, in one of the standard texts on Russian and Soviet history, Nicholas V. Riasanovsky, *A History of Russia*, fourth edn (New York, 1984), p. 502.

42. Norms were raised in various industries in 1932; *Rabochii klass v upravlenii gosudarstvom (1926–1937 gg.)* (Moscow, 1968), pp. 232–3. They increased in auto factories in May 1935; TsGANKh f. 7622, o. 1, ed. khr. 604.

43. Norms are discussed, for example, in Siegelbaum, *Stakhanovism*, almost *passim*; and in John Scott, *Behind the Urals: An American Worker in Russia's City of Steel* (Bloomington IN, 1973), p. 149.

44. TsGANKh f.4086, o. 2, d. 4731, ll. 2, 7; ibid., f. 7995, o. 1, d. 333, l. 198; Ermanskii, *Stakhanovskoe dvizhenie*, p. 330. Under the law, managers had the right to fire or transfer workers not making norms. But in view of the labour shortage and the pressure from above to help workers achieve norms, this was probably rare.

45. TsGANKh f. 7622, o. 1, d. 53, l. 6, a resolution of the auto-tractor industry branch conference, February 1936 stating that 'only clearly erroneous rates . . . should be reviewed'. Ibid., f. 4086, o. 2, ed. khr. 3365, l. 74, files of the Commissariat of Heavy Industry, a letter of 12 June 1936 indicating that in machine building rates are to be kept the same except in cases of technical changes; other examples could be given.

46. Ermanskii, *Stakhanovskoe dvizhenie*, pp. 17–20.

47. Tsentral'nyi Gosudarstvennyi Arkhiv Moskovskoi Oblasti [TsGAMO], f. 6852, o. 1, d. 367, l. 1, the Moscow oblast administration of local industry, division of glass and chemicals; and 'Vtoraia godovshchina', *Stakhanovets*, no. 8 (1937), p. 3.

48. V.I. Andrianov and V.V. Solov'ev, *Gavrilog-Iamskie tkachi* (Iaroslavl', 1963), p. 78.

49. B. Markus, 'Trud', *Bol'shaia Sovetskaia entsiklopediia*, the supplementary volume 'Soiuz Sovetskikh Sotsialisticheskikh Respublik' (Moscow, 1947), p. 1,117. Markus refers to 'working hours', but I have taken this as a rough approximation of number of workers.

50. *TZ*, 16 July 1936, p. 3.

51. Siegelbaum, *Stakhanovism*, p. 262. In this entire period there was strong and steady pressure on managers from above to bring workers up to fulfillment of the norms. See, among many examples, V. Chekryzhov and L. Kaminer, 'Itogi peresmotra norm vyrabotki v mashinostroenii', *Profsoiuzy SSSR*, no. 7 (July 1939), p. 51, which refers to a resolution of the VIII plenum of VtsSPS.

52. TsGANKh f. 4086, o. 2 d. 4731, l. 14. This is an undated letter to Lazar Kaganovich, Commissar of Heavy Industry, from the head of the auto-tractor division of the commissariat, Merkulov; data are given through October 1938.

53. *TZ*, 26 May 1936, p. 3.

54. Leningradskii Gosudarstvennyi Arkhiv Oktiabri'skoi Revoliutsii i Sotsialisticheskogo Stroitel'stva [LGAOR], f. 2140, o. 21, d. 265, ll. 10–11. This from the stenographic record of an *aktiv* meeting, 19 February 1940.

55. TsGANKh f. 7604, o. 8, ed. khr. 117, *passim*.
56. Ermanskii, *Stakhanovskoe dvizhenie*, p. 330. A. Minevich, 'Uporiadochit' zarabotnuiu platu v kamennougol'noi promyshlennosti', *Profsoiuzy SSSR*, no. 8–9 (August–September 1939), pp. 73–4, reports that at one Donbass mine in 1938, 35 norms were lowered even though the old ones were being filled by 150–160 per cent.
57. N. M. Shvernik, 'O rabote profsouizov po zarabotnoi plate', *Profsoiuzy SSSR*, no. 12 (August 1938), p. 17.
58. The law of 1938 is discussed, for example, in Filtzer, *Soviet Workers*, pp. 235–9. He shows that this and other laws designed to restrict workers' ability to change jobs were widely evaded.
59. *Rabochaia Moskva*, 6 April 1935, p. 2. The official was Ia. Soifer.
60. For examples of workers' active involvement in determining the new norms, see TsGANKh f. 7604, o. 8, ed. khr. 33, l. 30, for the branch conference of the linen industry in April 1936; and D. Mochalin, 'Uchastie proforganizatsii v peresmotre norm v transportnom mashinostroenii', *VP*, no. 3 (March 1936), pp. 82–3.
61. *TZ*, 15 June 1936, p. 3.
62. TsGANKh f. 7622, o. 1, d. 54, l. 208. This is from the branch conference of the auto-tractor industry, February 1936.
63. TsGAMO f. 5687, o. 1, d. 42, l. 38.
64. Ermanskii, *Stakhanovskoe dvizhenie*, p. 246; and see TsGANKh f. 4086, o. 2, ed. khr. 3365, l. 280, a communication to the division of labour of the metal industry from the Kaganovich factory, Moscow.
65. Ermanskii, *Stakhanovskoe dvizhenie*, p. 246; TsGANKh f. 7604, o. 8, ed. khr. 33, l. 154, the otdel pen'kozavodov GUPDI [?], dating from early 1936; ibid., f. 4086, o. 2, ed. khr. 3286, l. 8, from the conference of the transportation department of the Commissariat of Heavy Industry, March 1936.
66. Ibid., l. 10: one factory had recommended a 61 per cent increase in a norm, but the conference set the new one at 33 per cent. Another case involved a recommendation of a 46 per cent rise from a factory, which the conference reduced to 23 per cent.
67. See Burawoy, *Politics*, pp. 10, 183, and 287 on the constraints of working by norms in other countries.
68. *TZ*, 3 September 1937, p. 3. Some norms were also lowered in the auto-tractor industry at the beginning of 1937, when officials realized that some had been set too high in 1936: V. A. Sakharov, *Zarozhdenie i razvitie stakhanovskogo dvizheniia (na materialiakh avtotraktornoi promyshlennosti)* (Moscow, 1985), p. 59.
69. Stalin, *Sochineniia*, tom 1 [XIV], p. 62, in a speech to graduates of the Red Army Academy, 4 May 1935.
70. M. Taub, 'Kak zabotiatsia o liudakh na elektrostantsiiakh Uzbekistana', *VP*, no. 9 (September 1935), pp. 73–6.
71. Siegelbaum, *Stakhanovism*, p. 54.
72. Alec Nove, *An Economic History of the U.S.S.R.* (Harmondsworth, Middlesex, 1972), pp. 226–7.
73. *Pervoe vsesoiuznoe soveshchanie rabochikh i rabotnits-stakhanovtsev, 14–17 noiabria 1935 g. Stenograficheskii otchet* (Moscow, 1935), p. 165.

74. Ibid., p. 151.
75. TsGAMO f. 6852, o. 1, d. 290, l. 40, the Moscow oblast administration of glass and chemical plants, 17 December 1935.
76. Tsentral'nyi Gosudarstvennyi Arkhiv RSFSR [TsGA RSFSR], f. 52, o. 1 ed. khr. 14, l. 60, stenographic record, 8 December 1935.
77. Ibid., l. 18.
78. Ibid., l. 54.
79. F. Voropaev, 'Profrabotu na transporte – na uroven' stakhanovskogo dvizheniia', *VP*, no. 2 (February 1936), p. 17.
80. M. Voskresenskaia and L. Novoselov, *Proizvodstvennye soveshchaniia – shkola upravleniia (1921–1965 gg.)* (Moscow, 1965), p. 92.
81. See Chase, *Workers, Society*, pp. 264–82 on the production conferences in the 1920s. Voskresenskaia and Novoselov, *Proizvodstvennye*, p. 10, find the roots of the conferences in the production *iacheiki* (cells) of 1921 and date the first real production conference at the end of that year in Moscow.
82. Ibid., p. 91.
83. Ibid., p. 94.
84. *Profrabota po-novomu: rasskazy predfabzavkomov, tsekhorgov i gruporgov* (Moscow, 1936), p. 81.
85. R. Sabirov, 'Kak profgruppa stala sploshnoi Stakhanovskoi', *VP*, no. 1 (January 1936), pp. 66–7. See A. Egupov, 'Stakhanovskie sutki, piatidnevki i dekady na Podol'skom zavode', *VP*, no. 2 (February 1936); and L. Rovskii, 'Kak ne nado pomogat' stakhanovskomu dvizheniiu', *VP*, no. 2 (February 1936) for accounts of the revival of production conferences in Podol'sk and Khar'kov.
86. TsGA RSFSR f. 52, o. 1, ed. khr. 16, l. 173.
87. TsGANKh f. 7566, o. 1, ed. khr. 2816, ll. 4–5. Commissariat of Heavy Industry, materialy po podmoskovskomu basseinu. Stakhanovskoe dvizhenie.
88. *SIu*, no. 1 (January 1936), p. 3.
89. P. Moskatov, 'Pomoch' stakhanovtsam dal'she razvernut' stakhanovskoe dvizhenie', *VP*, no. 17 (September 1937), p. 18.
90. TsGANKh f. 4086, o. 2, d. 4265, ll. 2–5, Commissariat of Heavy Industry, otdel truda. Protokol tekhnicheskogo soveshchaniia i perepiska o provedenii aktivov na metallurgicheskikh zavodakh. 1937.
91. Arrests of engineers are recounted in, for example, G. Andreev [Gennadii A. Khomianov], *Trudnye dorogi; vospominaniia* (Munich, 1959), p. 19; and Fedor Ivanovich Gorb, 'Chernyi uragan', memoir in his file in the Bakhmeteff Archive of Russian and East European History and Culture, Columbia University [hereafter BA], pp. 16 and 48. Arrests of managers can be deduced from disturbing figures regarding executives in coal production for October 1938. Of 858, only 98 or just over 11 per cent had been in their positions for more than eight months. TsGANKh f. 7566, o. 1, d. 3537b, l. 2; Commissariat of Heavy Industry, Glavnoe upravlenie sostave rabotnikov.
92. *SIu*, no. 4 (February 1936), p. 3.
93. See Siegelbaum, *Stakhanovism*, pp. 190–204.
94. *SIu*, no. 14 (May 1936), p. 3. Already in ibid. no. 11 (April 1936), pp. 8–9,

the journal, which was the official organ of the Commissariat of Justice, denounced the practice of sending workers and technical personnel to courts for opposition to Stakhanovism, calling this a direct contradiction of Stalin's words at the Stakhanovite conference in November 1935. In fact, Stalin had said that first the 'conservative elements of industry' who were not helping the movement should be persuaded to do so. If that failed, 'more decisive measures' would be required. Stalin, *Sochineniia*, tom I [XIV], p. 98.

95. TsGAOR f. 5451, o. 19, d. 227, ll. 113, 116. This file is VTsSPS, reports from central committees of unions, 1935.

96. HP number 1497, A, v. 35, p. 18, a male Russian mining engineer born about 1909; his father was a tsarist army officer.

97. TsGA RSFSR f. 52, o. 1, ed. khr. 16, ll. 140–1, a report of 10 December 1935. An engineer at the Kuznetsk metal plant said in 1935 that the Stakhanov movement was like the northern practice of putting meat on a stick in front of a dog to make it run faster, but no action against him is recorded; TsGAOR f. 7952, o. 5, d. 66, l. 4, Gosudarstvennoe izdatel'stvo 'Istoriia fabrik i zavodov'. Kuznetskii metallurgicheskii kombinat im. Stalina. Stenogrammy besed s rabochimi o stroitel'stve i rabote zavoda, 1935.

98. HP number 65, B2, v. 3, pp. 29–30. The respondent was a construction engineer probably born sometime between 1900 and 1903; no A schedule information is available.

99. HP number 639, A, v. 30, p. 13; number 13, A, v. 2, p. 10; number 92, A, v. 7, p. 5; number 190, A, v. 14, pp. 14–15; number 65, B2, v. 3, p. 30, reported that except for the incident when the 'whore' got Lenin's works, 'you could not observe any isolation of Stakhanovites from the rest of the workers'. Most of these sources are also given in Siegelbaum, *Stakhanovism*, pp. 191–3.

100. Tsentral'nyi komitet professional'nogo soiuza rabotnikov sviazi, *Otchet tsentral'nogo komiteta professional'nogo soiuza rabotnikov sviazi. Sentiabr' 1937–sentiabr' 1939 gg.* (Moscow, 1939), pp. 69–70.

101. LGAOR, f. 1633, o. 15, d. 394, l. 37, a meeting at the Krasnyi Vyborzhets plant on 5 September 1937; f. 1253, o. 3, d. 81, ll. 50–51, a meeting of 3 June 1938 at the Leningrad metal plant; and d. 99, ll. 30–31, a meeting at the Leningrad mechanical factory on 6 May 1939. At the latter meeting the foreman Por'es reported that Stakhanovites had voiced severe criticism to him of expenditures in the plant. Workers also criticized managers by name in Magnitogorsk in June 1938; TsGANKh f. 4086, o. 2, d. 4344, ll. 4, 8, 9. This was the Commissariat of Heavy Industry, Glavnoe upravlenie metallurgicheskoi promyshlennosti, otdel kapital'nogo stroitel'stva. Preniia po dokladu nachal'nika stroitel'nogo upravleniia 'Magnitostroi' na slete stakhanovtsev.

102. See, for example, G.M. Il'in, 'Novyi pod"em sotsialisticheskogo sorevnovaniia', *Stakhanovets*, no. 11 (1938), p. 34. Il'in was director of the Hammer and Sickle factory in Moscow.

103. By 1939 NKVD investigators were 'more competent', they were 'concerned with technical and industrial sabotage' and often had the education

to look carefully into charges, and they sometimes asked civilian engineers for their opinions on cases. See, respectively, HP number 70, B, vol. 2, p. 6, a Russian shop chief in textile mills, probably born in the 1890s; S. Swianiewicz, *Forced Labour and Economic Development* (London, 1965), p. 144; also Ashot M. Arzumanian, *Taina bulata* (Erevan, 1967), pp. 109–10; and Victor Kravchenko, *I Chose Freedom: The Personal and Political Life of a Soviet Official* (New York, 1946), pp. 289–91.

104. For example, in *SIu*, no. 4 (February 1939), pp. 31–2; ibid., no. 14 (July 1939), p. 6.
105. *Altaiskaia Pravda* [Barnaul], 27 March 1940, p. 1.
106. HP number 153, A, vol. 12, pp. 31–2, a Russian male airplane mechanic born in 1927 into a worker's family.
107. Scott, *Behind the Urals*, p. 264.
108. LGAOR f. 1633, o. 15, d. 485, l. 29. Actually, as early as 3 June 1938 there was a calm discussion of the factory's situation involving Stakhanovites and other workers with the new director at the Leningrad metal factory: ibid., f. 1253, o. 3, d. 81, ll. 50–51.
109. Scott, *Behind the Urals*, p. 264.
110. See Sidney Fine, *Sit-down: The General Motors Strike of 1936–37* (New York, 1969). And see the grim letters from American workers about their conditions in this decade in *'Slaves of the Depression': Workers' Letters About Life on the Job*, ed. Gerald Markowitz and David Rosner (Ithaca NY, 1987). The first letter, p. 1, to the Secretary of Labor Frances Perkins, has the line 'I'll sign my name, but if my boss finds out – .'
111. I do not believe that this ability to participate and criticize pertained so much to peasants, but much more research is needed on that subject. In the meantime, there are a few indications that peasants had some say in day-to-day affairs on the collective and state farms and that at least in some cases they chose their own chairpersons. See Roberta T. Manning, 'Government in the Soviet countryside in the Stalinist thirties: The case of Belyi Raion in 1937', *The Carl Beck Papers in Russian and East European Studies*, no. 301 (1984); and Fedor Belov, *The History of a Soviet Collective Farm* (New York, 1955).
112. HP number 153, A, v. 12, p. 54.
113. HP number 59, A, v. 5, p. 29; a Russian female chemist born about 1918 whose family was 'superior intellectual'.
114. G. Arkitin, 'Politicheskie nastroeniia naseleniia g. Leningrada v leto 1941', BA, pp. 4–7.
115. Zawodny file, set II, respondent 16; this comment was essentially repeated in set II, respondent 13, who added that 'The workers understand the fact that we have to build and build and build'. Perhaps older workers still in the factories were more disgruntled partly because, unlike so many of their fellows, they had not been promoted out of their situation.
116. Scott, *Behind the Urals*, p. 205.
117. On education and upward social mobility, see Sheila Fitzpatrick, *Education and Social Mobility in the Soviet Union 1921–1934* (Cambridge, 1979).

Part IV

The Political Elite: From the 1930s to the 1990s

10 Portrait of a changing elite: CPSU Central Committee full members 1939–1990

Evan Mawdsley

This chapter surveys some basic features of the Soviet senior political elite over the fifty years from 1939 to 1990. The elite is defined here as those people who were elected full members of the Communist Party Central Committee at the 18th to 27th Party Congresses (those elected for the first time at the 28th Congress in July 1990 are excluded).

'The Soviet Elite Project', organized at Glasgow University by the author and Stephen White, is the basis for what follows. The project initially involved compiling machine-readable biographies of the 1,580 people who were full or candidate members of the Communist Party CC between 1917 and 1990. The present work gives only preliminary findings.[1]

Compared to the whole project, the first limitation of the present discussion is that only the period after 1939 is covered; the elite in the period 1917–1939 will be dealt with elsewhere. The positive side of this is that the present survey *does* deal with a relatively coherent historical entity, i.e. the Soviet elite after the Purges of 1937–38 (and 1990 may have marked as clear a watershed in the history of that elite). Also, the CC of 1939 was large enough to be at least roughly comparable with later versions (the earliest CCs were the size of later Politburos).

Second, the discussion is confined to the *full* members of the CC. On the positive side this does mean that it is concentrating on the most important figures. Even with the limitations of time and rank, this chapter still deals with 776 individuals (compared to a total of 1,580 full members and candidates in 1917–90). Finally, and perhaps most important, the article's scope of analysis is limited. It is hoped ultimately to make much more of career patterns and education, but that will be possible only when research findings have been fully digested. The analysis here is confined to descriptive statistics presented graphically. Nevertheless, the object is to sketch a dynamic portrait of the elite over half a century.[2]

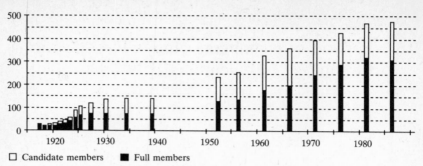

Figure 1 The Central Committee of the CPSU, 1917–1990

This chapter is about Central Committee *membership*, not about the Central Committee as a functioning political organization. Selection to the CC was a sign of political status; it defined – however imperfectly – a set of people who were politically the most important in the USSR. Also, the concern is not *individual* biography – it is prosopography, looking at the CC as a group.[3]

How can the Soviet elite be 'sliced' chronologically to study its change over time? There were in the period under review essentially nine Central Committees, elected at party congresses in 1939, 1952, 1956, 1961, 1966, 1971, 1976, 1981, and 1986.[4] For the sake of brevity much of the analysis in this article will divide the elite into six 'period-groups':[5]

Period-group	Congress	Full mems	CC elite
'39	1939 (18th)	71	71
'52	1952 (19th)	125	125
'56/61	1956, 1961 (20th, 22nd)	308	301
'66/71	1966, 1971 (23rd, 24th)	436	412
'76/81	1976, 1981 (25th, 26th)	606	567
'86	1986 (27th)	307	279

(The 'CC elite' is those full members who were not 'representative workers'; see below.)

There would have been a case for dividing the years from 1939 to 1990 into decades ('the 1940s', 'the 1950s', etc.), but – given political turning points in 1953, 1964, and 1982 – the division above seems a better starting point. The six period-groups might be further aggregated into four conventional political eras (commonly identified with individuals): period-groups 1939 and 1952 comprise the post-Purge 'Stalin' era, period-group 1956/61 the 'Khrushchev' era, period-groups 1966/71 and

1976/81 the 'Brezhnev' era, and period-group 1986 the (?early) 'Gorbachev' era.[6]

Although the CC is a uniquely clear-cut indicator of elite membership (a person was either in it or he/she was not) it has drawbacks. One point which is both important in itself and a necessary background factor is changing size. In 1939 the CC had 71 full members; in 1981 (at its largest) it had four and a half times as many, 318.

Roles

In the 'heroic' – earliest – period of the ruling Central Committee (1917–1921) its membership was actually *elected* – at congresses by the delegates. The basis for election appears to have been an individual's revolutionary and political record. By the early 1920s the process had become essentially one of co-option or selection from above, and after that time it would be fair to say that *posts* or roles rather than individuals were represented.[7] Throughout the period surveyed in this article there were a group of offices, the holders of which were awarded CC full-member status. (This relationship is part of the justification of the Soviet Elite Project.) The key ministers, the party secretaries of the most important regions, the editors of leading newspapers, and the most senior generals were nearly always selected for CC full membership; the identity of the individual post-holder was not the relevant criterion. Of course, CC membership was not an absolute sign of a post's importance. For one thing, the Central Committee steadily increased in size, and a post that did not carry with it full membership in 1939 or 1952 did so regularly in the 1970s and 1980s. Some conclusions may be drawn, however, about the changing importance of different occupational *sectors* over time, as shown in figure 2. (The basis of the categorization is the post held at the time of selection to the CC.)

Categorization of Soviet party and government posts by sector is a topic in itself. The categories used below are too general for detailed research, but they suit a broad survey like the present one.

Throughout this article the term 'CC elite' means those CC full members who were not 'representative workers'; the latter are not included in figure 2 or the other charts. 'Representative workers' (or 'token workers') were one of the growing groups within the CC and are worth examining in their own right; they were not, however, members of the elite holding top-level political, economic, or military power, and this is a study of that elite.[8] Unless the rise of the representative workers is discounted, all the other sectors seem to be declining as a proportion of the total.

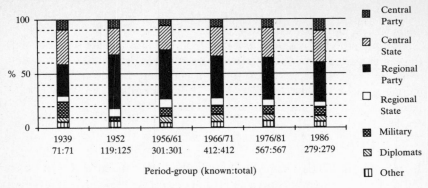

Figure 2 CC elite: known roles

The 'central party' sector includes Moscow-based CC party secretaries and other functionaries. The proportion of CC members in this category remained fairly static throughout fifty years, with a slight reduction in 1961, and a gradual rise to 11.5 per cent of the CC elite in 1986.

'Central state' takes in a larger group. Among the most important members of this group are USSR ministers. Differentiation between economic and non-economic ministries will be a fruitful line of future enquiry. Known police officials are included in the state – partly because there were so few of them, between one and four officials.[9] Trade union leaders are also treated as state officials; this corresponds to their real role through most of the Soviet period but in any event, as with policemen, they were too few to be numerically significant.[10] The weight of central state officials was fairly constant, from a fifth to a quarter of the total – more than three times the number of central party officials.

'Regional party' officials comprise the famous *obkom* first secretaries, the 'Soviet prefects'. The category also includes party secretaries of national republics. Perhaps the underlying theme of CC membership over the fifty years was 'the rise and fall of the *obkom* first secretary'. However, a few important qualifications should be made.

The proportion of regional party officials was constant after 1966, at about a third of the CC elite. The representation of regional party officials was proportionally at its highest at a time when conventional Western wisdom sees the atrophying of the party – in 1952: nearly half the full members (fifty-nine individuals) were regional party leaders. (The lowest regional party representation, conversely, was in 1939 – just after the Purges – when this category made up only a quarter.) Although Khrushchev is said to have used the regional party leaders against his Stalinist opponents in the CC Presidium (Politburo), the proportion of regional party leaders went down slightly in 1956, and would go down again in 1961 (although the absolute number of individuals went up by about a dozen between 1952 and 1961).

'Regional state' officials – mainly prime ministers and 'heads of state' of national republics – made up a smaller group of CC members, never more than 10 per cent, and gradually declined to about 5 per cent. Among the CC elite, central state officials were more strongly represented than central party officials, while regional party officials were better represented than regional state officials; this has been one of the characteristic features of the Soviet political structure.

The 'military' form the first of two specialist 'professional groups'. Military representation was fairly constant at least after 1961, at a level of 7–8 per cent. Surprisingly, military representation was at its highest immediately after the purge of the Soviet high command; in 1939 it amounted to 14.1 per cent. The need to rebuild the army, restore its status, and prepare for a war help to explain this; also, in 1939 many of the 'military' were commissars rather than professional soldiers. On the other hand it is remarkable that the military's representation was weakest at the height of the Cold War in 1952, when it amounted to only 3.2 per cent (four military men out of 125).

'Diplomats' are another specialist group. Included here are both ambassadors and Moscow-based officials of the Ministry of Foreign Affairs (but not CC secretaries concerned with international affairs). The diplomats were an interesting group as there have been numerous changes of specialization into and out of the ambassadorial ranks. From the 1960s the level of diplomatic representation was about 5 per cent, but it is remarkable that at the time of greatest international tension, before the Second World War and during the high Cold War (1939–56), this representation was at its lowest. In 1952 there was only one 'diplomat', and that was the Foreign Minister, the odious former Procurator Vyshinsky.

The final 'Other' category includes a mix of officials, including ideologists, journalists, and scientists. This group was fairly small, at about 4–5 per cent.

One question that cannot be discussed here for reasons of space is the extent to which individuals moved from sector to sector, for example, from 'regional party' *obkom* first secretary to 'central state' industrial minister, or from 'central state' minister to 'diplomat' ambassador. This is a line for future inquiry.

Looking at these fifty years of Soviet history, no one sector of the elite dominated CC membership. Although the largest single group were the regional party leaders, this group never formed an overall majority. Unusual features were the strength of the regional secretaries in 1952, the weak representation of soldiers and diplomats in the same year, and the remarkably high level of the military in 1939. The gradual influx of representative workers since 1961 should also be mentioned. But, overall, there was remarkably little change in the sectoral 'constituencies' represented in the CC elite, especially given the quadrupling of absolute numbers from 1939 to 1981.

Turnover

The stability in the elite sectors represented in the CC over these fifty years was, then, noteworthy. The stability or instability of individual membership – that is, 'turnover/holdover' – is another central question. The use of the CC as a measurement of the 'stability of cadres' is not perfect (individuals could continue unchanged as members of the CC, but move from job to job). In general, however, turnover of the CC elite is probably the most convenient indicator available for measuring the changes of the top Soviet elite.

Figure 3 shows holdover rates for the CC elite. Each column shows the proportion of full members selected in that year who had also been selected for full membership at the previous congress.

The proportion held over fluctuated. As might be expected, 1939 had the lowest-ever holdover rate, as a result of the Purges. Only 23 per cent 'survived' – often literally – from 1934 to 1939.[11] The holdover rate to 1952 was little better, although non-reelection was no longer synonymous with execution; the low holdover rate was partly due to the time span between congresses. The relatively high holdover rate in 1956 might call into question the conventional evaluation of 1953 as a watershed; the holdover rate in 1952–6, despite Stalin's death, was higher than in 1981–6.[12] The real shake-up of the elite came with the low holdover rate in 1961, as First Secretary Khrushchev consolidated his power. The process repeated itself in the next two Central Committees; there was a remarkably high holdover rate in 1966 despite the fall of Khrushchev, and then a 9 per cent drop in the holdover rate in 1971 as the Brezhnev group consolidated their power. 'Stability of cadres' was a feature of the mature Brezhnev years, and was reflected in high holdover rates in 1976 and 1981. The much lower holdover rate in 1986 is also noteworthy, especially when coupled with a high degree of post-

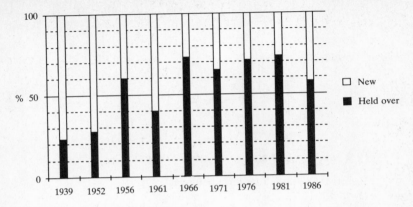

Figure 3 CC elite: holdover rates

congress turnover – especially the clearout of seventy-four full members in April 1989.[13]

The *causes* of turnover were varied. First, there was the political will of the supreme leadership groups who determined which individuals would hold which elite posts – and consequently would be CC members. Second, the length of time between congresses differed. And third, indirect 'actuarial' factors must be considered – a CC with more older members would tend to lose more in deaths. The average age of the CC elite rose – as we will see – from forty-four years in 1939 to sixty-two years in 1981.

The final points about turnover concern the whole fifty-year era. To what extent, given the turnover figures above, was there a continuity of individual membership, corresponding to the continuity of 'sectoral' representation?

Figure 4 shows that the long-term holdover rate has been low. The diagonal lines trace the decline of each cohort of selectees to the Central Committee, from 100 per cent on hand in the year of 'election' to the complete disappearance of the cohort; the chart shows the proportion of the cohort who were still full members after later congresses. The steeper the diagonals, the lower the holdover rate. The steep change from 1939 and perhaps even from 1952 might be expected, but even for the 1956 CC only half were held over to the next congress. The gentler slopes for the 1961, 1966, and 1971 CCs are symptomatic of Brezhnevite stability.

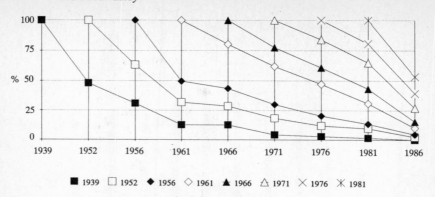

Figure 4 CC elite: long-term holdover

One element that cannot, for reasons of space, be discussed here is the relative short- and long-term holdover rate for different 'occupation' sectors. Did 'central state' CC members, for instance, have different holdover/survival rates than 'regional party' CC members or the military? This will be a subject for future analysis.

Basic features of the elite

The representation of different posts in the CC elite has already been discussed; what were the personal characteristics of the individuals in the elite?

Gender need not concern us for long, although it ought to be noted that the balance between men and women is especially affected by the inclusion of 'representative workers'. Taking the 1986 CC as an example, eight of the twelve women were 'representative workers' (or to put it another way, 1.4 per cent of elite CC members (4/279) were women, compared to 28.6 per cent of representative workers (8/28). The women who are in the CC elite were mostly in the trade union sector. But even with the dairymaids and other 'representative workers' included, it is clear that – as with all other world governments – males dominated.

Age is a more interesting element. Here again the representative workers had a significant effect in changing the average, in this case bringing it down. Thus in 1981 the average age of elite CC members was 62.4, while the average age of 'representative workers' was 51.3; looking at it another way, of all CC full members aged under 50 in the 1981 CC, 44.4 per cent were 'representative workers' (8/18).

It is hardly new to say that the Central Committee was aging throughout the period; figure 5 shows this graphically. In 1939 the

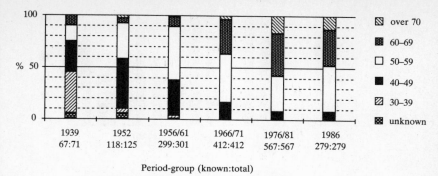

Period-group (known:total)

Figure 5 CC elite: age groups

largest group were people in their thirties. Forty years later, by the second Brezhnev decade (1976/81), there was no one aged 30–9 in the CC elite, and the largest group were people in their sixties. In 1939 the average age was 44, 42 years later in 1981 it was 62.

The essential process was not an aging of 'sitting' CC members; the long-term holdover rate was low. The age was rising because even new entrants were getting older. The aging process is even more remarkable when taken together with the other major general trend, the rise in the *absolute number* of CC members: more CC members meant that more 'junior' posts were getting CC representation, and yet despite this the average age kept going up. Figure 5 also puts the early 'rejuvenation' under Gorbachev into perspective; the CC elite may have been younger than in Brezhnev's second decade (1976/81), but it was older than in his first decade, and much older than under Khrushchev or Stalin.

It is not simply age that makes a difference, but also 'life experience'. This is a point of view of special interest to the historian, even if it is difficult to quantify the impact of life experience. Figure 6 shows the proportion in each period-group who would have been over eighteen years of age at critical points in Soviet history. Only half the 1939 CC elite had been adults in 1917. By the first Brezhnev decade less than half had been adults in 1929, when Stalin consolidated his power and industrialization and collectivization began to take off. The Purges had a longer impact, as it was only in 1986 that less than half the CC elite had been adults in 1937 (although there was an abrupt drop from nearly 60 per cent in 1976/81 to less than 20 per cent). The Second World War was a continuing memory (with about half the 1986 CC having been adults in 1945), and it is worth bearing in mind that in the era of perestroika nearly 90 per cent of the 1986 CC elite had been adults in the year of Stalin's death, and nearly all had been adults when Khrushchev fell.

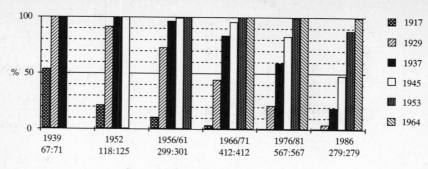

Figure 6 CC elite: life experience (aged 18+ in given year)

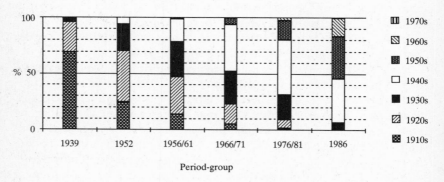

Figure 7 CC elite: decade of joining CPSU

Party experience (*stazh*) is closely linked to age and life experience.[14] Figure 7 shows the changing dates of party entry for each period-group. Later dates of joining are a natural product of passing time, but there are several important developments to note.

No one political generation could dominate the CC elite for five decades, and the information on age, life experience, and party *stazh* shows this. In 1939 by far the largest group had joined the party before 1920, and if many new members were 'men of 1938' very few had joined the party *less* than a decade earlier. In 1952 the largest part were still people who had joined the party before 1930, but by the Brezhnev years these were less than a quarter of the total.

Those who joined the party in 1930–9 came into their own in the 1960s; Leonid Brezhnev, for instance, joined the party in 1931.[15] But while the 'Brezhnev generation' may have dominated the Politburo they were soon outnumbered in the CC elite by the wartime generation of the 1940s; by the 1976/81 period they made up only about a fifth of the CC elite. In any event, the people who joined the party in the 1930s were never more than 30 per cent of the total CC elite.

The national composition of the CC elite is a more difficult question than age. Information on nationality is available for more than 80 per cent of the CC elite in the period since 1956, but for only 40 per cent in 1939 and 60 per cent in 1952.[16] But, always bearing in mind the fact that the data are imperfect, figure 8 suggests a general stability.

After the death of Stalin the 'Slavic coalition' of Great Russians, Ukrainians, and Belorussians had a gradually rising level of dominance. Great Russians always had representation higher than their weight in the population as a whole. The right-hand column of figure 8 gives for the sake of comparison the ethnic breakdown for the whole USSR population in the 1959 (the minorities of the Caucasus, Central Asia and the Baltic are merged in with the 'Other' category in this column). Great Russian representation was never higher in the CC elite than in 1986. The position of the Ukrainians has been reasonably steady – comparable to their share of the whole population – but the peak came in the Khrushchev and Brezhnev years. The Belorussians in 1939 and the Ukrainians in 1952 were badly represented. (Nationality data is incomplete for 1952 but the rather better figures for place of birth – figure 9 – also indicate a Ukrainian decline in 1952.) The decline may have been based on the peculiar effect of the Purges and the Second World War on the party elites in those regions. Central Asian represent-ation increased from 1952, although it was reduced in 1986. The 'Other' category declined remarkably after 1939, mainly due to the small num-ber of Jews in the later CCs. The representatives of the Caucasus have also steadily declined.

A similar pattern is evident in place of birth (figure 9); the right-hand column gives, for comparative purposes, the proportion of the 1959 population who lived in each region.[17] Those born in RSFSR ('European Russia' and 'Siberia') were the largest group in the CC elite, and with the fellow-Slav natives of the Ukrainian and Belorussian SSRs had a dominant position. The growth of the proportion of the CC elite born in Siberia, up to nearly 10 per cent in 1986, is noteworthy. This probably represents the changing balance of populations, with more potential parents living in Siberia by the 1930s and 1940s, but political links should not be excluded. The apparent under-represent-ation of those born in the Baltic and Central Asian republics and in the Transcaucasus and the Caucasian parts of the RSFSR (Cau/TrCau) is an important feature.

Birth 'environment' (city, village, etc.) – is a final characteristic.

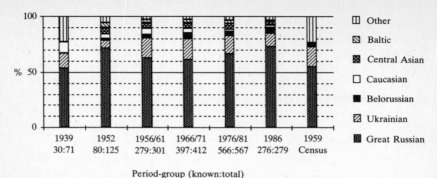

Figure 8 CC elite: known nationality

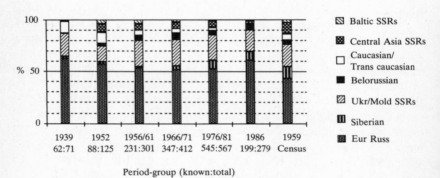

Figure 9 CC elite: known place of birth

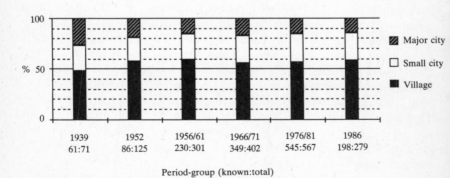

Figure 10 CC elite: known birth environment

What emerges here is a picture of stability (figure 10), surprising in a country undergoing a social and demographic revolution. Leaving out the 1939 CC, the number recorded as born in villages remained remarkably constant, at 55–60 per cent. Likewise the balance between those born in major cities (places with over 100,000 inhabitants in 1926) and those born in smaller cities stayed the same.[18]

Conclusion

Historical biography has its limitations, and the same is true of historical collective biography. It is possible to describe the personal characteristics of an individual or even of a whole elite, but how do personal characteristics affect political actions? How, for example, does a knowledge of Khrushchev's personal biography explain his behaviour? Or how does a knowledge of the background of Khrushchev's Central Committee explain the policy decisions of a decade? For each of the six CC period-groups the mean years of members' party *stazh* is known to several decimal places, but how is that linked to political decision-making? Study of the *impact* of personal or group characteristics means going from the 'certainties' of the social scientist to the impressionism of the historian.

However, some preliminary conclusions can be drawn. This half century may soon be looked back on as the 'Golden Age of the Central Committee'. In broad historical terms 1939 marked the beginning of a time of relative security for CC members and consolidation of the committee's representative function; the 28th Congress of the CPSU in 1990 may well have marked as fundamental a change in the nature of the Central Committee.

The period 1939–90 does make up a kind of historical era in terms of the membership of the CPSU CC and of the elite who were governing the USSR. The representation of the various constituencies in the CC did not change in a fundamental way – and it is important to remember that the CC was never numerically dominated by *obkom* first secretaries. The characteristics of nationality and place of origin were relatively steady.

It was a symbolic era, too, in that it spanned the political career of the longest-serving CC full member who began service in the wake of the Purges. Nikolai Pegov, the 'last of the Mohicans', served as a full member of the CC from 1939 to 1986 while holding various elite posts. Looked at from another perspective, on the eve of the 1986 congress the previous CC service of the longest-serving member went as far back as 1939, but no farther.

Although in these senses this half-century does form an historical era, it should not be given too much coherence. Robert V. Daniels has recently argued that 'one generation . . . dominated the Soviet political scene for nearly half a century', the generation of the 'youthful purge beneficiaries'.[19] This conclusion depends in part on how 'half a century' and 'dominated' are defined. However, it is important to bear in mind that even looking at the core period from 1952 to 1986 there was more than one generation at the CC level. Much can be made of the *vydvizhentsy*, the men of humble origin who received a technical education in the early 1930s and rapid promotion into party and state posts after the Purges; these have been called the 'men of 1938' or the 'Brezhnev generation'. They were an important group, and perhaps a dominant group at Politburo level. But if a broader definition of the Soviet elite is used – the regional party chiefs, the state ministers, the generals and diplomats who were represented in the CC – it is harder to see one dominant 'generation'. There was always a substantial turnover, especially seen over ten or fifteen years (although *some* of the new intake were also 'men of 1938'). But the key point is that age distribution, life experience, and party *stazh* varied considerably within each period-group, and from one period-group to another. The 'Brezhnev generation' were always a minority in a changing CC elite. The homogeneity of that elite – in terms of either sectoral represent-ation or individual characteristics – should not be taken for granted.

Notes

1. Generous support by the Economic and Social Research Council, initially as Grant R000 231491, is gratefully acknowledged.
2. A scholarly work which is close to the present article is Jerry F. Hough, *Soviet Leadership in Transition* (Washington, 1980). Hough's book is stimulating and, in anticipating perestroika, remarkably prescient. The present article differs from it in focusing on the Central Committee and in carrying the discussion to the end of the 1980s.

    Related surveys are Seweryn Bialer, *Stalin's Successors: Leadership, Stability, and Change in the Soviet Union* (Cambridge, 1980) and Robert V. Daniels, 'Political processes and generational change', in Archie Brown, ed., *Political Leadership in the Soviet Union* (London, 1989), pp. 96–126. A recent reformist survey of the nature of the current CC elite was 'TsK KPSS i perestroika', *Argumenty i fakty*, no. 5 (1990), p. 6; see also Ronald J. Hill and Jyrki Iivonen, 'Gorbachev at the Top', *Journal of Communist Studies*, vol. 5, no. 3 (1989), pp. 329–39.
3. The bulk of the pre-1981 biographies were prepared by Stephen Revell, who was the principal research officer of the Soviet Elite Project; he also developed an innovative data entry system. Steven Main prepared material

primarily for 1981 and 1986, but also on military CC members. Fiona Harrison, Peter Lentini, William MacReadie, and Ian Thatcher were involved in research and data entry at various stages.

Biographical information came from a variety of printed sources; their description would require an article in itself. Major sources include Soviet encyclopedias, especially the *Bol'shaia Sovetskaia entsiklopediia*, the Sovetskaia istoricheskaia entsiklopediia, and the *Sovetskii entsiklopedicheskii slovar'*. The *Sostav tsentral'nykh organov KPSS* (Moscow, 1982) is directly relevant to research (other editions are known to exist but have not yet been located). The new *Izvestiia TsK KPSS* has provided very full details of the 1986–90 membership. Also essential are the protocols of the party congresses, the *Deputaty Verkhovnogo Soveta* (1954–84), the *Narodnye deputaty SSSR: Spravochnik* (Moscow, 1990), and obituary material from the press.

Western reference sources have been used only where the Soviet sources were inadequate: basic works are Boris Levytsky, *The Soviet Political Elite* (Stanford, 1970), *Who Was Who in the USSR* (Metuchen, 1970), and two directories edited by Herwig Kraus: *Sostav rukovodiashchikh organov KPSS (1952–1976 gg.)* ([Munich], 1977) and *Composition of Leading Organs of the CPSU* ([Munich], 1982).

The project has benefited from information shared with William Chase, R. W. Davies, J. Arch Getty, Graeme Gill, Mark Harrison and David Lane.

4. There were no personnel changes at the 21st (1959) Party Congress. Significant changes took place at the 1941 party conference, but for simplicity's sake these are not dealt with here.

5. Period-group is an awkward term, but is used rather than 'cohort', since individuals frequently belonged to more than one period-group; A. A. Gromyko, for example, was in four. 'Cross-section' might be an alternative to 'period-group'.

6. Despite the relatively small numbers involved, the 1939 and 1952 CCs have been treated as separate period-groups. This is because of the long gap between the 1939 and 1952 congresses and the important differences between the two groups.

7. R. V. Daniels, 'Evolution of leadership selection in the Central Committee, 1917–1927', in *Russian Officialdom: The Bureaucratization of Russian Society from the Seventeenth to the Twentieth Century*, ed. Walter Pintner and Don Rowney (London, 1980), pp. 355–68.

8. They might be thought of as mainly 'crane-drivers and dairymaids' – token workers and peasants. There is a similarity to the deputies of the unreformed Supreme Soviet, although in that body the proportion of 'crane-drivers' was larger relative to the real elite. The group also includes 'representative' senior plant managers, and the line between elite and non-elite becomes blurred. In any event, the first seven CC full members in this category appeared in Khrushchev's second CC, in 1961. The numbers rose steadily, up to twenty-eight representative workers elected in 1986. In fact, with new appointments and retirements after 1986, the number in May 1990 was 37 out of 253 surviving full members, i.e. 14 per cent.

9. The proportional peak was in 1952 with three known 'policemen' (including Beria), but that was still only 2.5 per cent of membership. (There were four

206   *Evan Mawdsley*

policemen in 1981, but this was only 1.25 per cent; the absolute number dropped to two in 1986.)

10. The head of the VTsSPS has been a full member, along with a few other officials, but the share has not been more than 3 per cent in the 1939–1990 period.

11. For details see the material in *Izvestiia TsK KPSS*, 1990, no. 12, pp. 83–113. There is an analysis in Slava Lubomudrov, 'The origins and consequences of the purge of the full members of the 1934 Central Committee', PhD dissertation thesis, Indiana University, 1975.

12. A few of those who were not held over in 1956 were victims of post-Stalin trials – Beria and other policemen.

13. This is discussed in a research note based on the Soviet Elite Project: Evan Mawdsley and Stephen White, 'Renewal and dead souls: the changing Soviet Central Committee', *British Journal of Political Science*, vol. 20, no. 4 (October 1990), pp. 537–42.

14. An advantage of party *stazh* is that it is one piece of information which is known where *anything* is known about an individual. This is especially important for the 1939 and 1952 CCs, where biographical information is relatively thin. There are a number of ways in which characteristics of party membership could be studied, but space is limited. The average age of joining deserves anlaysis; it has risen. The relationship between age of joining and profession is also interesting; many of the late entrants were scientists and military men.

15. The Khrushchev decade (1956/61) had an interesting balance of people from four different decades. The gap between 1956 and 1961 (not shown in fig. 7) was especially interesting. In 1956 44 per cent of CC members had joined the party in the 1920s, and only 35 per cent in later years (including only 3 per cent in the years of the Second World War). By 1961 only 32 per cent had joined in the 1920s, 38 per cent had joined in the 1930s, and 18 per cent in the 1940s, including 16 per cent in the war years.

16. Information on national origin is now more readily available; it is known for nearly all members of the 1981 and 1986 CCs, and for earlier CC members who were deputies to the Supreme Soviet. This question has been discussed by Seweryn Bialer in 'How Russians Rule Russia', *Problems of Communism*, vol. 13, no. 5 (1964), pp. 45–52.

17. For the most recent period, data on nationality is fuller than that on place of birth. Place of birth is currently known for over 95 per cent of the 1976/81 period-group, but for only about 70 per cent of 1986.

18. The 1986 figures are probably misleading, as birthplace information is unavailable for a relatively high proportion of individuals, about a quarter. As birth environment *is* known for veteran members of that CC but not for many first-time members, it should not be surprising that the proportions for 1981 and 1986 appear similar. Given the urbanization of the 1930s it may well be that a smaller proportion of the 1986 new (and younger) members were born in villages.

19. Daniels, 'Political processes', pp. 98–9. Daniels' overall conclusion, however, is similar to that of this article: '[t]he history of Soviet politics since the death of Stalin is a story of change within a broader continuity' (p. 123).

Index

SELECTED PAPERS FROM THE FOURTH WORLD CONGRESS FOR SOVIET AND EAST
EUROPEAN STUDIES, HARROGATE, JULY 1990

Edited for the International Committee for Soviet and East European
Studies by Stephen White, University of Glasgow

Titles published by Cambridge

Market socialism or the restoration of capitalism?
edited by ANDERS ÅSLUND

Women and society in Russia and the Soviet Union
edited by LINDA EDMONDSON

The Soviet Union in the international political system
edited by ROGER KANET and DEBORAH MINER

The Soviet Union and Eastern Europe in the global economy
edited by MARIE LAVIGNE

The Soviet environment: problems, policies and politics
edited by JOHN MASSEY STEWART

New directions in Soviet history
edited by STEPHEN WHITE